D0209051

AMERICAN FEMINISM

FEMINIST CROSSCURRENTS

EDITED BY KATHLEEN BARRY

American Feminism: A Contemporary History
GINETTE CASTRO
Translated from the French by Elizabeth Loverde-Bagwell

AMERICAN FEMINISM

A Contemporary History

Ginette Castro

**Translated from the French
by Elizabeth Loverde-Bagwell**

NEW YORK UNIVERSITY PRESS

NEW YORK AND LONDON

Originally published in France as *Radioscopie du féminisme américain,* 1984, Paris, Presses de la Fondation Nationale des Sciences Politiques

Library of Congress Cataloging-in-Publication Data

Castro, Ginette.
  [Radioscopie du féminisme américain. English]
  American feminism : a contemporary history / Ginette Castro ;
translated from the French by Elizabeth Loverde-Bagwell.
    p.   cm. — (Feminist crosscurrents)
    Translation of: Radioscopie du féminisme américain.
    Includes bibliographical references.
    ISBN 0–8147–1435–8 (alk. paper)
    ISBN 0-8147-1448-X (pbk)
    1. Feminism—United States. 2. Feminism—United States—History.
I. Title. II. Series.
HQ1410.C3813 1990
305.42′0973—dc20   90–30323
                 CIP

New York University Press books are printed on acid-free paper, and their binding materials are chosen for strength and durability.

Contents

Foreword

I first became aware of *Radioscopie du féminisme américain* when I was in Paris in the fall of 1986 on a research appointment and I found my feminist friends and colleagues discussing it with considerable interest and enthusiasm. Aware of the extent to which French feminism has been misrepresented in the United States in the proliferation of works on the French movement, I was hesitant and I must admit somewhat suspicious of a work written by a French scholar on American feminism. I wondered: how would a French feminist scholar represent the American Women's movement considering the frequent misrepresentation of French feminism in the United States that misleadingly identifies French feminist theory with deconstruction or Lacanian psychology?

Furthermore, recent attempts by some American feminist scholars to write our own history have often led to excising its radicalism, the driving force which coalesced the movement and established its revolutionary *raison d'être*. The theoretical explorations of feminism which necessarily confront a male-controlled bastion of knowledge are often reduced to what I have called "ticky-tacky boxes"—radical, socialist, cultural, liberal, spiritual. . . . These labels negate the complexity of political action in the Women's movement which rarely allows any activist the purity of one position to the exclusion of and in opposition to all others. And they inappropriately segment theory into the categories which are derived from traditional (read male) social theory. For example, radicals recognize the value of liberal reform and the importance of socialist principles even if they formulate their demands from a consciousness that neither approach is sufficient to women's full emancipation. This does not mean that feminism is mired in American pluralism but rather, that the different approaches to social change are interdependent and not exclusive positions. The ticky-tacky boxes create an illusion that any woman's feminism can be summarized in a few sentences and neatly packaged into boxes that are premised upon a separation of action from theory. Having lived with this reductionism of feminism for so long, I have despaired that a valid and vital history of American feminism could be written given the ideological hegemony controlling the movement and scholarship today.

Ginette Castro has the advantage of cultural and social distance from the limitations which have framed this kind of analysis. As a European she brings a diverse and rich intellectual tradition to her study of American feminism. And I would not doubt that it is also because of Ginette Castro's own identification with feminism, that when I first read her work in French I found that she had not only surpassed the limitations of contemporary American interpretations, but had rendered a literary, political, social, and cultural study of the contemporary American feminist movement that those of us who have worked in it, helped shape it, and care about its future can recognize as our own history. In her brief but cogent Introduction, Ginette Castro rejects the "outrageous simplifications" to which the American Women's movement has been reduced and she recognizes the need to "neutralize the sensationalism attached to radical feminism, which has become perverted in Americans' perception into a sort of tribal predatory phenomenon." In this work that represents the vast landscape that constitutes the Women's movement, I was only sorry that she did not give full attention to the feminist critique of sexuality, particularly as it is represented in the movement against sexual violence and pornography.

American feminism is a dynamic movement. Key to Ginette Castro's ability to capture its vitality is the fact that she begins with *consciousness*. *Prise de conscience,* or consciousness-raising, distinguishes the contemporary Women's movement from all other organized efforts in behalf of women in the twentieth-century United States. Departing from the American tendency to reduce consciousness-raising to mere ideological modeling after left and civil rights movements, Castro locates consciousness in *its own roots,* the history of women and their experiences, their actions, protests and movements, thereby understanding American feminism as a valid movement of self-determination.

While media denunciations of bra burners and man haters have become an accepted invalidation of radical feminism in the United States, this work turns to the actions and rhetoric of radical feminists and finds in its urgency and passion profound theoretical implications which are examined in light of radical feminists' own self-criticism and in relation to other tendencies in the movement. With her objective distance from and yet subjective involvement in American feminism, Castro has been able to articulate

American feminists' "insatiable hunger for words and actions" that produced a powerful protest against the *sociological reality of gender domination*. In other words, she has been able to capture the political foundation of radical feminism that has been ignored or negated by academic socialist feminists and deconstructionists who inaccurately dismiss radical feminism as hopelessly flawed essentialism. Castro's thesis stands in refreshing opposition to the current fads that surfaced in many feminist theory articles and books of the 1980s, yet, this work is not at all an exclusive study of radical feminism. Castro understands well the different tendencies, their oppositions and their possibilities of finding unity among themselves. It is thus her ability to capture the fullness of the feminist landscape in its various shapes and forms that conveys the meaning it has held for its diverse participants, making this an important European study to introduce to American audiences.

The other advantage of a European study of American feminism is that it is able to identify where and how feminist protest, even in its revolutionary moments, unwittingly reflects national values and ideals. Necessarily, American feminists are embedded in their own cultural and national situation even when they are in protest against it. It is therefore useful to be alerted to the unexpected ways that feminism reflects national characteristics. Most critical reflection about the Women's movement to date has been aimed primarily at the ideology of liberalism and its particularly American individualist character. Although such a critique has been necessary, it has become boringly repetitive.

This book is not only a descriptive literary, cultural, and political history of contemporary U.S. feminism. Its analysis is also cogent because the work is based on its own definitive theoretical approaches, a new interpretation of androgyny. I must admit that for the last twenty years I have been among the American feminists who have vociferously rejected theories of androgyny as some kind of sociological bisexuality that is overly concerned that men might be alienated if women champion their own cause. But in her discussion of androgyny, Castro captures the deeper intentions and fuller significance of that theory by identifying how it invalidates the "otherness" to which women have been relegated. Rather than being only a conciliatory social idea, androgyny theory is a social critique of "sexion" and the sexual polarization of gender identity that underlie radical models of equality. Surprising to me was the way that Castro demonstrated androgyny theory at work in the early works of Mary Daly and Phyllis Chesler who each respectively challenged political and psychological determinisms by putting religion and psychoanalysis on trial for their gender dichotomization. In the sense that Castro uses it, androgyny theory becomes the logic of sex equality which, when achieved, will reformulate gender relations and reshape the society. Woman-centered realities would be shaped from fundamentally different presumptions if they did not have to be formulated from a denunciation of otherness—the situation that sexual inequality has produced.

Warning against the fragmentation that results from the absence of philosophical synthesis, Castro points to the elements of coherence within the U.S. Women's movement from which that synthesis could emerge. Already since the French publication of this work, we have seen evidence of the possible "panfeminism" she proposes in the feminist fight for abortion rights and the massive demonstrations organized by NOW and NARAL. Bringing this work into translation through the Feminist Crosscurrents series contributes to reestablishing equilibrium and honesty of representation in the history of the contemporary American Women's movement. As such it offers Americans insights for reflection on our past and encouragement for considering new possibilities for our future.

KATHLEEN BARRY
Pensylvania State University

Introduction

Feminism is a cyclical phenomenon. Each cycle bears its own fruit, and thus it was that the first wave of American feminism culminated in 1920 when American women achieved the right to vote. However, women's participation in elections did not change the election results in America any more than it did in other countries. Not, at least, until 1980 when the campaign preceding Ronald Reagan's election revealed the existence of a distinct women's vote. No doubt this phenomenon was to be accounted for somewhat by the sexism of the man who was to be president for the next eight years; but it also owed much to the long and difficult labor that had brought forth the new feminist movement. This movement was born at full term after a slow gestation period, the offspring of a silent revolution in the world of women that had occurred through succeeding crises, finally being hurled into the world by the convulsions of the 1960s.

The second wave of American feminism has both shaken and strengthened the myth of the American woman, symbol of the free and powerful womanhood of the New World, endowed from birth with inalienable rights, facing the frontier with indomitable spirit. In the matter of rights, it took American women three-quarters of a century (from 1848 to 1920) to obtain the right to place a ballot in a ballot box; no doubt it will take them just as long, if not longer, to see equality of the sexes enacted by law by the formal adoption of an Equal Rights Amendment to the Constitution. It is widely perceived that the Equal Rights Amendment is an avatar of the new feminist movement; feminism itself is often thought to be a recent phenomenon, a ripple among the waves of the 1960s. In fact, the ERA is seventy years old, and was first presented to Congress in 1923. The first battle for it was fought and finally lost in the years following World War II. The long interval separating the initial presentation of the ERA in the 1920s and the second battle for it by the new feminist movement in the 1970s, as well as the defeats suffered both times by the women of the United States, can be explained by the dilemma of "combat by proxy," which American women share with other women in the world, and from which they are not likely to escape unless they create a third way, distinct from the traditional bipartite system.

Fortunately, American feminism is not focused only on a battle for the ERA. During the past fifty years, its militants and sympathizers have followed the tried and true path of all political minority groups, which are organized in rebellion and engaged in a patient quest for identity. The first phase was individual and collective consciousness-raising; the second involved exploration of women's historical legacy. Feminist theorists next devoted themselves to developing an ideological framework; this inevitably led to action. It also inspired the creation of literary and artistic works that constitute the point of departure for an entire special culture, which is beyond the limits of this present study. The various ideological points of view did not all arise at the same time, but have developed in parellel with each other, and each one presents its own evolutionary curve.

The work that has been accomplished by American feminists is immense, both in theoretical analysis and in practical action, reinforcing the myth of the strong, capable American woman. In describing these events, I have followed two apparently contradictory paths. The first will attempt to show that the issues of feminism cannot be reduced to outrageous oversimplifications, providing facile excuses for traditionalists to hide behind. I will stress the importance of theoretical, ideological writings to demonstrate the diversity of expression, which can be interpreted as a compensatory reaction to women's previous silence and restraint, a sort of insatiable hunger for words and actions, on which American feminism is built. The second path will seek to reveal an underlying unity. Starting from the premise that feminism is the refusal to define all women, and therefore all human beings, solely in terms of sex, we shall nevertheless sometimes speak of ambivalence and heresy. However, the thesis of this book is that the possibility of ideological synthesis exists, and that this synthesis, already being developed within feminist culture and action, is the only way to guarantee that American feminism will survive in all its originality and richness.

The time has come to reinterpret American feminism, and especially, to neutralize the sensationalism attached to radical feminism, which has become perverted in Americans' perception into a sort of tribal predatory phenomenon. The time has come to put into proper perspective all the rhetoric that belonged to a period when feminist theorists were still at the stage of raising the cry of alarm. Those early fulminations proclaiming hate for all men and likening love to the response of a rape victim must be seen in context, as a protest against a sociological reality that routes all human beings on their lifepath on the basis of sex, rather than as a denunciation of all individual men as hopelessly irredeemable. In short, the time has come for reconciliation. A pattern for agreement is offered by the feminist "androgyny" theory, which is based on the premise that both women and men are, above all, human beings, and which asserts the equality of the sexes in mutual reciprocity, seeing each sex at this stage in our evolution as the necessary complement of the other. This concept seems to provide a model, first, for reconciliation between feminists, then between feminist and non-feminist women, and, ultimately, between the sexes.

The thesis for reconciliation proposed here expresses the hope that American feminists will manage to overcome their ideological differences in the course of the "long march" in which they are engaged. It also aims, through the inspiration of the American example—the most convincing achievement ever accomplished by the Women's movement anywhere in the world—to reconcile more people (women and men) with the philosophy of feminism, which many have rejected without bothering to understand it.

Indeed, many women, including those struggling for women's rights, deny being feminists—"I'm not a feminist but . . ."—without really understanding what feminism is, no doubt associating it with widely heard clichés or with so many other "isms" that do violence to their own sense of individuality. Even more numerous are the men who tune out or laugh at the notion of feminism, without realizing how much their rejection or derision is a desperate act of flight, betraying their fear of discovering that their own identity cannot be defined except in terms of sexism.

Finally, there are those who declare imperiously that feminism is already a thing of the past. What paternalism! This view does not allow feminists, and women in general, the freedom to decide the outcome of their own commitment. And what hurry to bury feminism! No doubt feminism is seen as an obstacle to some other "isms," just when the revolution in life-style and personal identity to which feminism has given birth is at last beginning to stand on its own feet. After two decades of the new wave of American feminism, Gloria Steinem, in *Outrageous Acts and Everyday Rebellions*, deplored that "polarized, prefeminist styles [were] still turn[ing] up" in the Women's movement. The purpose of this book is to contribute toward advancing it further in its evolution.

PART I

Consciousness-Raising and the Return to the Past

ONE

Power Struggles: A Play in Four Acts

The awakening of consciousness that climaxed in a new wave of American feminism began at the close of World War II, and not, as is often mistakenly believed, in the 1960s. It developed through a drama of power conflicts in several acts; men claiming to be of good will managed to entice American women into playing this drama for three decades. In reviewing the various episodes of conflict that these women confronted, a feminist today cannot help but be struck by the subtle alliance among men, between the "villains" — those who (claiming the best intentions, of course) openly declared themselves hostile to the promotion of women—and the "false friends"— those who represented themselves as the champions of women. Even today, some would call the latter group male feminists, without noticing the contradiction implied in their attitudes and in the very terms they used.

ACT I: EVEN THEN THEY WERE TALKING ABOUT THE EQUAL RIGHTS AMENDMENT

At the end of World War II, American women represented 36.1 percent of the national labor force, and, according to economists, they controlled two-thirds of the country's wealth. Naturally, women's holding such power aroused concern. Besides, it was thought, shouldn't women bow graciously before the returning GIs, crowned with glory? In 1945, the old slogan, "A woman's place is in the home" came back into circulation; in less than a year, four million women lost their jobs. In 1947, according to statistics published by the Women's Bureau,[1] American women represented only 27.6 percent of the national labor force. Rosie the Riveter had had her day, and American women were confined in their role as a reserve labor force, to be called on in case of emergency and laid off as soon as the crisis was over.

However, according to a survey carried out by Elmo Roper for *Fortune* magazine, two women in three would have liked to keep their jobs. Many working women expressed their bitterness in the pages of *Independent Woman,* a monthly publication of the National Federation of Business and Professional Women's Clubs (BPW). Their indignant feelings of frustration and their desire to support themselves by working were the first signs of feminism that had been shown by American women in many decades.

In 1945, of all the participants in the earlier feminist movement which, after three-quarters of a century of struggle, had obtained the right of American women to vote, only one organization survived. This was the National Woman's party (NWP), a now rather tame organization headquartered in ladylike style in the Alva Belmont House, near the Capitol Building in Washington. The NWP had barely thirty thousand members who, like the women of the BPW, were mostly recruited from among a professional elite class.

Since 1920, the NWP had tenaciously persevered in presenting to every session of Congress the draft of an amendment to inscribe equality of the sexes in the Constitution of the United States. World War II had furnished further proof of the need for such a constitutional amendment; when, in fact, women doctors who had joined the army demanded the same salary as their male colleagues, claiming equal protection under the law as guaranteed by the Fourteenth Amendment to the Constitution, they received the interpretation from the comptroller general which amounted to saying that, in its accepted constitutional meaning, the term *person* did not include women! Admittedly, a law was adopted recognizing equality of the sexes, but it was a temporary measure, intended only for the duration of the war.

This masculine-biased interpretation of the law and the refusal to recognize the equality of the sexes could have incited the feminists of the 1940s to make the same sweeping value judgments and female-chauvinist assertions that typified some publications early in the second wave of feminism. However, at no time did the postwar activist groups undertake the kind of patient, painstaking investigation done later by militant women of this second wave, in which they considered all the implications of the confrontation between the sexes. The postwar activists denounced the government's interpretation of the term *person,* presenting it as *prima facie* evidence of an enormous injustice that deprived women of economic privileges, but they never went further than that. They never entered upon the grand philosophical debate about the equality of the sexes, nor did they consider the political identity of women as a group. Equal salaries or equal rights, the awakening of consciousness was still limited to the economic terrain, a prisoner of the imperatives of the time.

In addition, the battle was still being waged primarily on the legislative front. The NWP, although remaining within accepted channels, had a naively heady feeling of having been called by destiny to be the avant-garde, responsible for the fate of American women. In the eyes of the NWP activists, this could not be anyone's battle but theirs. They got excited, they presented arguments, but they did not really fight. They were far from the revolutionary feminism of the original NWP. Of course it is true that with the Equal Rights Amendment, the NWP and the BPW were aiming at a more ambitious goal than the equality of salaries being sought by the Women's Bureau, but in the end, all three organizations saw themselves as being allied with the same respectable reformist spirit of feminism.

Careful never to appear to be inspired by selfish motives, and concerned with giving their group a respectable image at a difficult time in national life, the women of the NWP led their struggle with the only weapons they thought were available to them: their monthly magazine *Equal Rights,* and genteel lobbying activities in which they invited the gentlemen of Congress to come and be entertained on the green lawns of Alva Belmont House. From 1945 to 1954, *Equal Rights* stoically published all the twists and turns in this first battle for the ERA. The events bear a strange resemblance to those of the second battle, and the ruses invented by the members of Congress have no equal except the underhanded maneuvers engaged in more recently by members of the state legislatures to block ratification of the same amendment.

In the late 1940s, opponents of the ERA claimed they wanted to "protect" women (somebody is always trying to protect women from what doesn't threaten them) from an amendment that would abolish protective labor legislation passed in another era to shield women workers from the exploitation of bosses. In reality, the ban on night work or carrying certain loads "protected" women from the privileges of overtime, bonuses, and job promotion. If not, why, then, allow night work for the cleaning women who do heavy manual labor in the huge high-rise office towers in New York, but forbid it for women proofreaders in publishing firms or newspaper offices, doing work that is otherwise quite safe?

The senators opposed to the ERA outdid themselves in finding a whole gamut of last-minute maneuvers that their colleagues defending the ERA contrived never to foresee. Thus, in 1946, the first vote ever held in the Senate on the Equal Rights Amendment was called very suddenly without any prior notice, following a modification of the legislative calendar. The ERA was easily defeated for lack of any supporters present to argue for it. At the second vote, in 1950, it was actually adopted by the Senate, but with an added clause, the Hayden Rider, which did no more nor less than to annul the ERA completely, since it called for the maintenance in force of all so-called protective legislation. This lamentable farce was played again three years later with a variation: this time, the senators voted first on the added clause before voting on the amendment itself, thereby having a perfectly safe way to pronounce themselves overwhelmingly in favor of equal rights. The humiliation inflicted on the women of the NWP was all the greater as they had already done a good deal of groveling, having believed with naive optimism in the good faith of their allies in government.

In many ways, their situation was comparable to that of the nineteenth-century feminists who, having fought side by side with men as abolitionists, were abandoned after the Civil War by their former allies on the question of the vote for women. Both episodes illustrate the dilemma of "combat by proxy." Women will continue to face this obstacle on the political chess-board as long as they do not form a united feminist party to fight their own battle, and instead, keep putting their faith in the promises of elected men (and women) who owe their offices to party loyalty and will always put political interests before the justice of women's rights. As long as women continue to act circumspectly and humor the men in power, or join them only to imitate them, instead of carrying out the patient work of spreading feminist ideas among the great mass of women, they will be eternally swindled.

Cut off from women workers worried about keeping their jobs or subject to the directions of their union, cut off from the young women of the silent generation, scornful of housewives, the NWP activists had smugly believed that they could win the ERA battle. The National Women's party had nothing of a party but the name. Having earned respect in their professional capacities, the members had transformed it into a simple women's club whose main virtue was to keep the eternal flame of memory burning; they did so until 1954 when their magazine *Equal Rights* ceased publication. Two years later, the BPW rechristened *Independent Woman* as *Business Woman;* now blushing under the feminist label, the BPW turned its attention instead toward good, feminine civic work. The NWP, however, faithful to its principles, continued to submit the Equal Rights Amendment to Congress. It was not until the 1970s that both the House of Representatives and the Senate deigned to vote in favor of the text granting equality to the sexes.

ACT II: THE HOUSEWIFE'S SYNDROME

Meanwhile, it was the housewife who was showing more and more marked symptoms of the "feminist illness" and suddenly became, to her misfortune, the center of attention of the post-Freudian psychologists. We say "to her misfortune," since the remedy prescribed by the therapists proved to be worse than the illness, while the problem was taking on the dimensions of a national catastrophe.

The "epidemic," widely called the Housewife's Syndrome, affected primarily middle-class women who had given up pursuit of higher education or a career in favor of devoting themselves to the role of wife and mother. Their case was notably analyzed by Ferdinand Lundberg and Marynia Farnham in *Modern Woman: The Lost Sex*.[2] Their book was to feminism what the witch-hunt of Joseph McCarthy was to communism: it bombarded the reader with a whole armory of unsubstantiated assertions. Migraines, hypertension, pain, gastric upset, constipation, sexual troubles: such, they said, was the unhappy lot of the dissatisfied American housewife—for every dissatisfied housewife was, by definition, neurotic. Whether her syndrome was accompanied by frigidity or aggressive sexuality, she was always the castrating wife, and since, said the post-Freudians, in the general disarray of her emotional and sexual life as a wife, she took out all her emotional needs on her son, it was a short step to cast her also as an abusive mother. The hour had come for a sort of witch-hunt against "momism," to be tracked down in all its manifestations: from the "suffering" mom to the "overprotective" or "dominating" mom, American mothers were said to be making homosexuals out of all-American boys.

In a medical-journal style presentation of the etiology of the syndrome, Doctors Lundberg and Farnham took the reader back in time to the trauma caused by Copernicus. Man, no longer the center of the cosmos, compensating for the loss by launching himself in a race for power, imposed his virile mark on the universe thanks to the divine phallus with which he was endowed: Reason. So great was the admiration of some women for this powerful animal that they wanted to capture it, having become enthralled by "penis envy," which gave rise to the illness of feminism. "Feminism [. . .] was at its core a deep illness," they wrote in 1947, and "the more educated the woman is, the greater chance there is of sexual disorder."[3] The doctors said the extreme case of this illness was that of Mary Wollstonecraft.[4] To her personal neurosis, which gave birth to an ideology, there was grafted a collective neurosis called feminism, which women fell into in trying to compensate for the wound inflicted on their biological identity by Malthusianism, that is, the voluntary restriction of procreation. This wound was an inevitable consequence of the Industrial Revolution, itself also a consequence of the Copernican trauma.

Thus, for Lundberg and Farnham, feminism was an impossibility, since it had only one goal: the masculinization of the female. Women must therefore be protected from feminism, that is, from sexual freedom and higher education (since women are always to be protected from what does not threaten them). Sexual freedom, the authors said, can only be the privilege of the male, who alone plays an active role in the sexual act, in which the female has a solely receptive role and in which her pleasure, inseparable from the possibility of impregnation, is necessarily centered in the vagina. Women must also be protected from higher education, since education for them was a passport to frigidity, another symptom of neurosis. In support of their thesis, Lundberg and Farnham cited the preliminary findings of the Kinsey survey of American sexual habits, which tended to show that the rate of orgasms among intellectual women was lower than that among black nonintellectual women. We will restrain ourselves from comment except to recall that Kinsey was to draw diametrically opposite conclusions from the same statistics.

It is clear that Lundberg and Farnham approached the issues of education and the problems of the housewife from a sexual perspective. For these worthy emulators of Freud, sexuality explained everything; anatomy controlled destiny, and the essential function of a woman was to be a submissive wife and fecund mother. This ineluctable purpose was, moreover, not denied by educators of that time. They, too, were concerned with the problem of women's education. They, too, of course, wanted to protect women! In their exercises of self-criticism during that era, educators accepted the post-Freudian reproaches as being well founded. They said they had misunderstood the differences in mental capacity between the sexes, and they had done violence to feminine aspirations in subjecting females to a typically masculine plan of education. Everyone now strove to underline the mismatch between the education given to women and the life-style that they were destined to lead, without ever questioning the value of this life-style. For example, for Lynn White, president of Mills College, a specifically feminine education was needed, stressing the humanities and domestic science.

The second remedy prescribed by the psychologists of the period was the restructuring of the household, with the primary emphasis on rehabilitating women, which meant, in post-Freudian terms, giving renewed value to motherhood. Freud's emulators suggested this could be done by increasing social benefits and tax allowances for families, by abandoning painless childbirth, which was said to deprive women of the joys of giving birth, and finally, by encouraging a return to breast-feeding of babies by their own mothers, to eliminate the intermediary of bottles or wet nurses. Emphasis was laid on the nurturing function, and American women were urged to return to their hearthfires. The superiority of the male chef was denounced as a myth, and the gourmet cooking ability of the mistress of the household was attested to by a Cordon Bleu diploma proudly displayed on the kitchen wall.

The diagnosis and treatment offered by Lundberg and Farnham can only be greeted by feminists today with howls of laughter—except that they must turn sober again, seeing a disturbing trend to a revival of this imagery. *Modern Woman: The Lost Sex* sees the housewife's problems as originating in individuals—women, of course—and not in the institution of marriage. At no time, in fact, was the system of matrimony questioned, doubtless because it had been so long accepted. For the authors, then, it was obvious that the institution of marriage should be perpetuated, with the same role division, and all that was needed to adjust matters was to recreate the conditions that had existed in the good old days. There was nostalgia for some lost golden age, which seemed all the more appealing as the world was emerging from the nightmare of war. Those who profited most from this operation were unquestionably the companies selling beauty products or household appliances and the magazines featuring saccharine feminine literature. The market expanded to satisfy the demand created by the new mystique of wedded bliss. For American women, the return to the myth of the fecund mother and nurturer only aggravated their problem.

The feminist response came from isolated individual women, such as Della D. Cyrus or Mary McCarthy, who reacted on their own in books or in the press. As early as 1948, in *Adam's Rib*,[5] a work sparkling with humor, Ruth Herschberger dared to stake out a place for herself in the same territory as the Freudians—sexuality—in order to counter their sexual theories and dispute their right to be the arbitrators of normality. The discontent of American women was indeed linked to their frigidity, she granted, but this was the result of the Freudians' dual *diktat* in this matter: that is, the transfer of erotic climax from the clitoris to the vagina, and the attribution to the male of a monopoly in sexual activity.

Without entirely denying the existence of vaginal orgasm, Ruth Herschberger opened the way to the theories of radical feminists on clitoral orgasm. In 1948, however, *Adam's Rib* went largely unnoticed; the book was a generation ahead of its time.

Other noteworthy contributions were made by the "functionalist feminists" of the 1950s, such as Mirra Komarovsky (*Women in the Modern World: Their Education and Their Dilemma*), and Alva Myrdal and Viola Klein (*Women's Two Roles: Home and Work*). In an early burst of sympathy for the housewife, and in the name of feminism, all rejected the equation "dissatisfied housewife = neurotic woman" and the idea of a specifically feminine education. Nonetheless, in the name of functionalism, they advised women to tailor their ambitions to the role of motherhood by choosing so-called women's professions or by pursuing two-phase careers. Concerned about women's psychological well-being, the functionalist feminists wanted to avoid provoking new tensions in women; hence, they posted a lot of warnings along the road: "proceed with caution." First, they felt, it was necessary to prove that it was possible to combine home and work responsibilities; therefore, they advised relatively easy professions that would guarantee success in this undertaking. This initial success enabled women to achieve a new plateau, signaled by the publication of an incisive analytical work of major influence: *The Feminine Mystique*, by Betty Friedan.[6]

Betty Friedan's now-classic book takes its place in the continuum of feminism. It is false to say that it represents either a complete break with the past or a totally new approach. It takes over the discussion from the functionalist feminists, condemning, certainly, their timorous options, but retaining their feminist contributions, adding unquestionably to them through the new awareness of the 1960s.

The first task the author undertook was demystification: to reveal to the housewife the overrated value of the feminine mystique of which she had been a victim throughout its reign in the postwar years, during which she had sacrificed everything to the new religion of femininity and the Wife-

Mother goddess, reinterpreted and transformed by the mass media into a sexual object. Identifying the source of the mystique, the author pointed yet again to the great master Sigmund Freud, a prisoner of his own culture, whose archaic and very subjective theories his disciples were attempting to apply to the twentieth-century American woman. The priests of this mystique, in league with the post-Freudian psychologists, were the educators, who gave priority to the marriage bed over the mind and spirit and who were more concerned about their students' ability to achieve orgasm than about their intellectual ability.

The author then traced the path of the Housewife's Syndrome. In a general obsession with sexuality, characteristic of a sick society, the American woman had sought her identity in an unbridled sexual quest, demanding of the orgasm more than it could deliver. While, in the postwar polemic, Ruth Herschberger had limited herself to responding to the accusation of frigidity being flung at American women, Betty Friedan went farther and perceived, beyond it, the mystique of sexuality; she accused the Freudians of seeking to imprison American women in the sexual mystique by presenting the orgasm to them as an end in itself.

Doomed to defeat, the search for an identity in sexuality was necessarily accompanied by a related search, defined by psychiatrists as a transferal phenomenon, in which the woman sought identity through the possession of objects, or even of beloved persons. In the market of mass consumption, adroitly manipulated by the experts in human emotions, the housewife identified sensually with the material goods she bought, drawing from them the illusion of an identity, because they symbolized her success as the fulfilled wife and mother. As a wife, the prisoner of the feminine mystique hitched her wagon to the rising star of her husband, driving him with an ambition that could only lead to new frustrations. As a mother, she merged herself with the personality of her child so much that when the child was grown, and she could no longer pursue the neurotic flight of a life by proxy, she ended up with a feeling of worthlessness and a sense of her own self-destruction.

The author spared no detail and desperately dramatized her narrative; for one of the essential aims of the book was to achieve a catharsis for all those women who recognized themselves in its pages, and who here confronted for the first time all the anguish that they had previously buried. Here, there was no question of denying that the pathological symptoms of discontent existed, in the manner of the functional feminists. On the contrary, the unnameable must be named, and the shock would not destroy the individual woman because now she would know that the problem was no longer hers alone, but was shared, thanks to the collectivizing operation carried out by the author. The picture was certainly as black as the one drawn by Lundberg and Farnham, but whereas they had talked of the guilt of individuals, Betty Friedan incriminated an entire alienating system. *The Feminine Mystique* seems to have been conceived as a powerful antidote to the bible of the cult of femininity, *Modern Woman: The Lost Sex*. It was powerful, in that the themes are often formulated with the same degree of outrage. It can be seen as an antidote, since the Freudian premises and conclusion have undergone permutation, and Betty Friedan's chapter titles seem to have been chosen in direct counterpoint to those of Lundberg and Farnham. For the latter, the Women's Rights movement simply illustrated "the feminist complex," in psychiatric terms; for Friedan, it has become "the passionate journey." For them, the modern woman was "the lost sex"; for her, she is "the forfeited self." Finally, the "restructuring of the household" that they proposed had, according to Friedan, imprisoned women in "a comfortable concentration camp," condemning them to progressive dehumanization through the gradual loss of their personal identity.

In choosing the "feminine mystique" model of womanhood, American women had transferred their own ego-identity to an image that condemned them to immaturity. They had refused all mental growth, and the Housewife's Syndrome was the price paid for their denial and repression of their own personality, a sort of rejection phenomenon in which their individuality was rebelling against a borrowed identity. The Housewife's Syndrome was thus reinterpreted as an identity crisis, and the dissatisfied housewife was no longer an anomaly, a discarded reject bearing the cause of her neurosis within her own soul, but the victim of an alienating system, who was showing a healthy reaction to this system. The anomaly, from that point on, was the *happy* housewife.

I wonder if a few problems are not somehow better than this smiling, empty passivity. If they are happy, these young women who live the feminine mystique, then is this the end of the road?[7]

Precisely by resituating the housewife's dissatisfaction in the context of the drive toward women's rights that had begun in the nineteenth century, Betty Friedan, with good reason, presented it as a symptom of the "feminist realization." And by turning the Women's Rights movement into a search for identity, she gave meaning and purpose to the new wave of feminism that was just getting started.

Not that Betty Friedan launched an appeal for an organized movement. That was to come later. But she called on women to be less pusillanimous. In 1963, the key to the problem seemed to her to be work without functionalist limitations or exclusions so that women could have an identity through work, what she later called the fourth dimension. As for femininity and the ability to achieve orgasm, these could only be the better for it.

Reacting against the feminist mystique did not necessarily mean denying certain options of feminity. Nor did it mean one sex aggressively asserting itself against the other. It meant the desire to stop being unhealthily locked into the syndrome, and to find self-fulfillment by integrating *all* the roles in the course of a single lifetime. Betty Friedan did not tell precisely how to go about combining such demanding tasks. This is certainly the main weakness of the book. Its strength lies in the author's faith in women's potential, and in the depth of her analysis. *The Feminist Mystique* restored the American housewife to the dignity of her right to be a full human being, and gave a new dimension to her dissatisfaction, making it a problem for society as a whole and no longer a neurosis specific to one sex.

Since 1963, no other important work has been published on "the American housewife" as an identifiable sociological type. It appears obvious that her day of glory has passed and that she, in her own way, has brought a contribution to American feminism. In this sense, it can be said that American feminism has, and perhaps has always had, a broader basis than might be thought if one judges only by the highly visible, vocal minority.

ACT III: FROM OFFICIAL "PROTOFEMINISM" TO A NEW WAVE OF ORGANIZED FEMINISM

The exhortations that Betty Friedan addressed to American women in 1963, calling for their engagement in massive numbers in every field of work and at every level of activity across the nation, were soon to be taken up by new official bodies charged with studying the status of women in the United States. As early as 1961, President Kennedy had created a Presidential Commission on the Status of Women, whose report, entitled *American Women,* was the prelude to a new and sustained awareness of women's issues. However, once again the game had been rigged in advance, to the degree that, deliberately or not, behind the facade of promoting feminism, there were hidden nonfeminist or antifeminist motivations: the political concerns of a president courting women's votes, the desire to catch up with the Soviet Union (which had made good use of its female labor resources), and particularly, the desire to halt the Equal Rights Amendment. In other words, the federal government was launching an egalitarian movement, but for nonegalitarian reasons.

Thus, the stage was set for a third episode of conflict. Sooner or later, differences were bound to arise between the official agencies and the women involved in the Commissions on the Status of Women, which began more or less spontaneously to be formed at the state level under local authorities. Among these women, there were quite a number of holdovers from the postwar feminist organizations, who had had a lot of experience being duped by officialdom.

There is no question that the balance sheet reported in *American Women* focused attention on the insufficient use of female labor resources at the higher levels of private employment and public service. Likewise, the authors of the report denounced the restriction of women to a marginal group, victimized by a double standard in hiring and salary policies. Nevertheless, they rejected the notion of deliberate sexual discrimination and set aside, for the moment, any need for an Equal Rights Amendment. Clearly, the appeal for action launched by *American Women* called for the promotion of women through an all-out talent search, and for the end to sexual polarization through an extensive educational campaign intended to stimulate the ambition of young girls and to overcome the prejudices of their fathers and employers. Admittedly, a year after the adoption of the law requiring equal salaries for equal work, Congress had added a clause to the 1964 Civil Rights Act, the famous Title VII, which forbade all discrimination based on sex in the matter of employment in the private sector. Nonetheless, three of the five members of the newly created Equal Employment Opportunity Commission (EEOC), which was charged with administering Title VII, refused to take seriously the complaints filed charging sexual discrimination, claiming that this notion had been inscribed accidentally in the law[8] and did not actually cover any reality.

In the face of this attitude, disappointment and tension continued to grow within the Commissions on the Status of Women, and the breaking point was reached in 1966, when the EEOC reaffirmed its refusal to recognize the illegality of help-wanted advertisements specifying sex. After the organizers of the Third Conference of Commissions on the Status of

Women had rejected the very principle of the notion of sexual discrimination, a small number of delegates decided to found an autonomous movement that would militantly fight for the rights of American women. Thus was born the National Organization for Women (NOW), the first independent association for decades within the American Women's Rights movement that dared to claim the epithet *feminist* in its statement of purpose, and the first new feminist organization intending to combat sexual discrimination in all areas: social, political, economic, and psychological. The process started by the federal government five years previously had escaped from its official boundaries. Proposing to use all the resources of women's potential while being unwilling to recognize any systematic sexual discrimination, the official bodies had placed themselves from the outset in an untenable position. It only took a few clear-thinking and determined women to expose and denounce this hypocrisy. By the founding of NOW, American feminists took the first step toward releasing themselves from the trap of "combat by proxy."

Immediately after its creation, NOW launched a spectacular campaign against the EEOC, demanding that the Commission take measures against sexism in employment advertisements and address the contradictions between Title VII and the so-called protective legislation on the books in several states. From all over the country, members of NOW went to Washington to picket before the offices of the EEOC, while the indefatigable organization simultaneously took the Commission to court. The impact was such that in 1969, new regulations on sexual discrimination were published, announcing that "protective" laws could no longer be considered appropriate to modern technology and to the increasing role of women in contemporary society. These laws were recognized as incompatible with Title VII, and were superseded by it.

The final obstacle to the Equal Rights Amendment was thus eliminated, and one by one, the official agencies charged with issues related to the status of women took positions in favor of the ERA. The most spectacular conversion was unquestionably that of the Women's Bureau, on its fiftieth anniversary. Seven years after the signing of the law requiring equal pay for equal work, the second goal in the postwar feminist struggle, adoption of the ERA, appeared to be nearly won. The 1969 *Handbook on Women Workers* published by the Women's Bureau had just legitimized the fight for the ERA on the basis of irrefutable facts. Although the book could be considered as the ultimate summation of all previous official reports, it differed from them radically by systematically comparing the positions of women and men in the United States, providing clear statistical evidence of the inequities suffered by American women. The proof of these inequities was in itself a call to action, and the *Handbook* was to remain, for many years, the bible of the modern feminist movement.

ACT IV: THE AWAKENING OF CONSCIOUSNESS

The fourth episode of conflict was the 1960s experience of women students who were militant in the radical protest movement. They had become sensitized to issues of social and political equality through their commitment to the fight for black civil rights and the protest movement against the Vietnam War, through such organizations as the Students' Nonviolent Coordinating Committee (SNCC) or the Students for a Democratic Society (SDS). But they very soon realized that a gap existed between the egalitarian rhetoric of their "brothers" in the struggle and the discriminatory actions of these men toward women. For the "brothers," there was glory and speechmaking; for the "sisters," there was obscurity and the dirty work. It is interesting to note that black and white male radicals had similar reactions to the demands made by their female fellow militants. The men of both SNCC and SDS, independently of each other and without discussion, fell back on the same insults, presenting a united front of sexism in which *machismo* transcended ethnic differences. After the insults, both groups hurled the same accusations at their female companions, saying they were guilty of diverting the revolutionary struggle to the profit of selfish and futile goals. At the National Conference for a New Politics, in 1967, the male militants of the New Left refused to recognize any political value in women's issues, and substituted a pacifist motion for the feminist civil rights motion prepared by the women of SNCC and the SDS. In the 1960s, the male radical, with a reputation as a fighter for justice, was acting out the same drama of power in the setting of the protest movement that the senators and congressmen had performed on the legislative stage twenty years earlier, after the Second World War.

From then on, militant women understood that if they wanted to address women's issues, they would have to do so outside of the existing radical movement. Naomi Weisstein, Jo Freeman, Shulamith Firestone and a handful of others began meeting regularly in Chicago. As they believed male radicals had excluded themselves from feminism, they moved logically to ostracism of men, and to a rupture with the political Left. This latter decision provoked a major schism in feminism, which I describe as separating the *feminist radicals* from the *radical feminists*. The feminist radicals—those whose primary loyalty remained with the Left—departed; the radical feminists—those who gave priority to feminism—went on to found NOW. By doing so, the radical feminists took the second step likely to wrest women from the impasse of combat by proxy, by liberating feminism from the alienating and patronizing sponsorship of the socialist or socialist-oriented Left. In June 1968, in their pamphlet *Toward a Female Liberation Movement*, Beverly Jones and Judith Brown denounced male chauvinism, giving the struggle between the sexes priority over the struggle between the classes, and reiterating that in order to fight the battles of others, one must first free oneself. The Women's Liberation movement was born.

It remained for the militants of this movement to prove their political skill. Their first test came when they decided to attempt a feminist exploitation of a conventional political event. While women's pacifist groups demonstrated against the Vietnam War, the radical feminists enacted the symbolic burial of traditional femininity in a torchlight procession at Arlington Cemetery, grafting their shock action onto the orthodox parade. In a tract written by Kathie Atmaniek Sarachild, they called on women to stop defining themselves in terms of their relationships with men; in this case, as weeping widows and bereaved mothers whose reactions to war deaths were minimized by the patriarchal society as a strictly personal emotional problem. It was essential for women to rediscover and define their own identity and to act in unison. Thus was born the slogan Sisterhood Is Powerful. The burial of traditional femininity was the prototype for a series of shock actions that were carried out to arouse public awareness, and not from motives of exhibitionism, as has often been claimed.

The movement grew, and in November 1968, two hundred radical feminists, who had traveled from thirty-seven states and Canada, gathered in Chicago to hold the First National Convention of the Women's Liberation Movement. Two themes were debated: one, sexuality, with a paper delivered by Anne Koedt, "The Myth of the Vaginal Orgasm"; the other, a new vision of the Women's movement, sketched out in a report by Kathie Sarachild, "Program for Feminist Consciousness-Raising." The two documents gave concrete form to the debate that had been led by the feminist intelligentsia for the preceding two years. Although Anne Koedt's essay is not much more revolutionary in its facts than *Adam's Rib*, it nevertheless arrived at much more radical conclusions. Denying vaginal orgasm, said to be institutionalized by the male as a self-defense mechanism to ensure his own sexual pleasure in heterosexuality and to subject the female to the bondage of the reproductive function, the essay dissociated female erotic pleasure from reproduction, thus opening the way for women's sexual freedom. While the militants of the earlier Women's Rights movement had only talked about sexual discrimination, those of the Women's Liberation movement dared to speak of sexual oppression.

As to the "Program for Feminist Consciousness-Raising," it aimed to awaken a sense of class consciousness in women. The theory of consciousness-raising was carried further by Pam Allen in her work *Free Space*, where she described the experience of the San Francisco women's group, which took the name Sudsoffloppen.[9] Their method, which was also typical of other groups, involved gathering about fifteen women who would meet regularly for a period of about six months, during which time they would traverse four succeeding phases. In the first, or opening phase, each woman recounted her own life experiences and expressed her feelings; this phase was based on giving political value to feelings, mutual trust, frankness, and respect for each other's words. This was followed by a phase known as sharing, a sort of collage of the various experiences of the members, intended to reveal the collective aspect of the problem and to move from the personal to the political. At this point, during the third phase, analysis was brought into play, to define the causes and forms of oppression so as to arrive at an objective view of the condition of women in society. The last phase was thoroughly abstract, devoted to the development of feminist theory.

What did consciousness-raising bring to those who took part in it? First of all, it brought liberation through the word: women were no longer to let themselves be destroyed by the "unsaid." In this regard, some women tended to divert consciousness-raising from its ultimate objective and to turn it into personal therapy, getting bogged down in their subjective problems and never moving on to the political stage. The issue as to whether in fact class consciousness developed was not so simple. The first plateau had been reached by the collectivization of problems, in that women had experienced the sharing phase sparked by Betty Friedan in *The Feminine Mystique* and had developed a sense of "sisterhood." Yet some of the emotional testimonials written during this period read more like intimate confessions. Regarding class identity, the consciousness-raising process served to arouse a perception that women collectively were being oppressed and alienated by the cultural notion of femininity and life by proxy.

Through the phenomenon of their collective alienation, those who had had their consciousness raised saw themselves as the victims of a fundamental form of oppression: sexism. It goes without saying that, at the time when feminists created the epithet, they were consciously evoking associations with the word *racism:* for them, the process of oppression was identical, whether the oppressed were blacks or women. In this view, just as racism implies revulsion for black skin and is postulated on a theory of the inferiority of blacks, sexism implies scorn for the female sex and is based on the theory of the inferiority of women. Just as white racists do violence to the individuality of each black person, imposing upon him or her a process of acculturation and transforming the individual into an "Uncle Tom" who is subject to the will of the white master even to the point of adopting his values and stereotypes, so sexist men do violence to the individuality of each woman, submitting her to a process of exaggerated feminization and transforming her into an "Aunt Tom" who is subject to the male master even to the point of trying to imitate his feminine ideal.

Following the example of blacks who took pride in their blackness and showed off their racial characteristics, women in feminist discussion groups learned to take pride in their sex. An example was the women's collective in Boston whose consciousness-raising led to their becoming completely identified with their bodies, as witness their works, *Women and Their Bodies, Women and Our Bodies,* and finally, *Our Bodies, Ourselves.* They analyzed what a French feminist, Françoise d'Eaubonne, has called *féminitude,* that is, womanliness as distinct from femininity; furthermore, they seem to have been fascinated by it. (It remains to be seen whether consciousness-raising groups will resist the temptation of *féminitude* to get every single woman to explore her true life story.)

In fact, it is difficult to minimize the problems experienced by women attempting to live out the revolutionary theory propounded by the radical feminist thinkers. The first problem is the gap between women's new identity and the constraints imposed on them by a society that remains sexist. The second problem is that oppression of women cuts across the lines of all economic classes, while women's relationships with their male "oppressors" are sealed by blood kinship or emotional ties, and lived in mutual complicity.

This relationship of complicity explains how women could allow themselves to be deceived in the drama of power conflicts, so strong is their illusion of sharing or at least influencing power. Such was the case in the United States of the professional or intellectual feminist elite whose thinking led to the new wave of feminism. The catalysts of the new feminism came from three male power groups: there was the fierce antifeminism of the post-Freudian psychologists; then, the timorous protofeminism of federal officials and government agencies; and finally, the male chauvinism of the men in the radical protest movement.

Consciousness-raising has continued because of the perpetual nature of the issues involved, and analysis of these issues has gradually become much more profound. The first of these is the *socioeconomic oppression* of women, perceived at first as an injustice solely from an economic viewpoint, subsequently as psychological alienation through the socioeconomic determinism of motherhood, and finally as sexual discrimination exercised against the entire socioeconomic class of women.

The second issue that has retained the attention of feminist thinkers is *sexuality*. The need for a feminist position on sexuality arose very early because of the importance given to it by the post-Freudians and the antifeminism of their theories. Two orientations toward sexuality developed. One focused on denouncing the repression of women's sexual needs, claiming sexual oppression through disregard for the clitoris. The renewed value given to the clitoris led feminists to demand liberation in terms of sexual behavior and to affirm the clitoral orgasm as enabling women (like men) to experience sexuality independently of its reproductive function, making reproduction a matter of free choice. The other orientation toward sexuality emphasized the way women had been alienated from themselves by the feminine mystique, which was viewed as psychological manipulation on a grand scale. This analysis was particularly strong in the egalitarian wing of the Women's movement, which perceived sexuality, if linked to the chances of maternity, as an obstacle to job promotion for women.

The third issue addressed by feminist theorists has been the *cultural oppression* of women. It first received the attention of individuals; for example, Betty Friedan did this when she demonstrated the cultural and social death entailed by the traditional role of the housewife and presented the Housewife's Syndrome as an identity crisis and healthy search for individuality. Later, the issue of cultural oppression was taken up by the feminists of the Women's Liberation movement who sought to provide women with the practical means to conduct their quest for personal identity. While Betty Friedan and the earlier Women's Rights movement had proposed that the remedy was a mass movement by women into the working world, the theorists of the later Women's Liberation movement laid down a precondition that women must first liberate themselves through the process of consciousness-raising, with the intention of developing an ideology and an action program appropriate to a political movement.

New feminism, launched in 1966 as the Women's Rights movement with the founding of NOW, and pursued from 1967 as the Women's Liberation movement, operated on fertile ground: the psychological malaise of American women. This explains the movement's initial resounding success, as evidenced by the national strike carried out by American women on 26 August 1970. On that day, thousands of women refused to perform household duties, sometimes sexual duties, and participated in the largest women's demonstrations seen since the days of the suffragists. With this highly political act, the new feminist movement came of age.

TWO

The Glory and the Oppression

Historians have a selective memory. Moreover, it is sexually selective. In history, therefore, women have been the victims of a conspiracy of silence: feminists of all schools of thought have pressed forward to demonstrate the truth of this argument. In 1946, in *Women as Force in History*,[1] Mary Beard reproached American historians for having deliberately ignored women's contribution to the building of the American nation throughout its history. For Elizabeth Gould Davis, author of the very controversial *The First Sex*, it was a question of nothing less than *gynikomnemonikothanasia*,[2] or the systematic effacing of women from the record, all the way from the mother goddesses of antiquity to the female Pope Joan, whose untimely giving birth to a baby during a religious procession traumatized the church fathers.

Investigating the motivations of this conspiracy of silence, American feminists distinguished not only the all-too-familiar scorn for woman and the fear of setting a subversive historical precedent, but also feelings of discomfort, since, according to radical feminists, women's history is one of long oppression that would be embarrassing to reveal in a country with a reputation for liberty and equality. Moreover, women's history does not always look the same when seen through the eyes of different feminist groups. To some of them, their sex has had many moments of glory; to others, the story is mostly one of oppression. However they see it, all feminists have agreed that the history of women must be written—Herstory, some called it—and that this could only be done by uncovering the record of women's past in such a way as to give a death blow to history as patriarchal rhetoric.

THE GLORY

It was feminist historians of the egalitarian school who took up the task of testifying to the glory side of women's history. Until the 1970s, the glory they uncovered was limited mostly to the nineteenth century and relatively

26

recent historic times, but the publication of *The First Sex* took it back all the way to the prehistoric era. Whatever period was examined, the goal was the same: to fill the gaps in the record left by the sexually selective work of conventional historians, and to prove that women, too, had made history. The content of history was changed, but not the concept, as these feminists, like previous historians, continued to place the emphasis on major events or the outstanding figures that had created them. In this emulative work, women historians simply practiced revisionism on the prior historical rhetoric by instilling a dialectic of excellence, which highlighted women's contributions by a reversal of the patriarchal relationship of force.

This is the case in some feminist histories dealing with the birth of civilization. Mary Beard and Elizabeth Gould Davis represent woman as the original civilizing agent, the first being who was able to express the longings of her spirit, and whose feeling of motherly love was, according to Elizabeth Gould Davis, the only example of loving human feeling for thousands of years. This is a dangerous thesis, since in giving women a monopoly on love, it presupposes the existence of a specific, innate feminine nature, thus going against one of the fundamental tenets of feminist philosophy. The description offered by Davis of the prehistoric cave paintings of Altamira is bathed literally in the same feminine subjectivity to which she attributes the birth of the first artwork. The feelings of the Cro-Magnon woman are said to be the central axis around which the large fresco is organized: woman's compassion for the hunted animal, shown by the delicate feminine lines of the drawing, but woman's hostility toward the hunters, shown with bestial masks and caricatured in stick figures. There we have an example of feminism of the primary type, essentially seeking revenge, since it reproduces, turned to women's advantage, the same old patriarchal relationship of "otherness." That is, the sexual relationship is not conceived simply as the balance of forces of two individual personalities, but as the annihilation and dehumanization of one sex—man, in this case —by the other, dominant sex.

With a new view of women's contribution to history came a new view of their participation in events, especially war. There again, it was not a case of questioning the intrinsic value of war, but of taking a position in a dialectic between the sexes: early feminist authors responded to the old (in their view, sexist) argument that women are not fit for military combat by exalting the exploits of the Celtic warrior queens, Tomyris and Boadicea, or of the Irish women who, from the thirteenth century B.C., took part in the sport of war games until they were banned from doing so in the seventh century A.D. by the bishop-saint Adamnan.

The viewpoint of these American feminists analyzing women's glorious past, universalist though it has tried to be, is nevertheless deeply anchored in their national history. In a country with a nationalist tradition, it has seemed appropriate to prove that the female citizens, like their male counterparts, have done their part to build the nation. Two particular episodes have undergone feminist "historical revisionism" and entered into the "dialectic of excellence": the American Revolution and the abolitionist struggle. The point has been, in effect, to defeat the presumed fathers of the nation on their own ground, that is, democracy. In doing so, the rules of the game of the dialectic of excellence have consisted of highlighting the radicalism of women colonial revolutionaries or abolitionists.

The first playwright of the revolutionary period, and the first historian of the American Revolution, Mercy Otis Warren, is thus presented as the Egeria of the colonies' struggle for independence, in a dialectic whose principal targets are John Adams and the Federalist clan. In a short biographical essay written by Kathryn Taylor, Mercy appears as the champion of democratic freedoms, the guardian of natural liberties, and the artisan of the Bill of Rights, while the male John Adams, by participating in what Taylor sees as the antidemocratic maneuver of the secret drafting of the Constitution, is transformed into the hired bodyguard of private property owners and mercantile interests.

Two leading figures of the abolitionist movement, around whom the feminists developed a similar dialectic, were the Grimké sisters, two young white women from the slave-owning South. A biography of them by Gerda Lerner[3] not only stresses the rarity of their contribution, doubly exceptional by virtue of sex and geography, but also presents it as a model of uncompromising radicalism that dared to attack the deepest roots of the evil of racial prejudice. Here again, the male is shown as a reactionary hypocrite, whether it is the Quaker brethren who censured the two sisters for having violated the racial code of their religious community, or the male abolitionists who abandoned their fellow militants Angelina and Sarah Grimké when they identified themselves with the slaves and began to plead the cause of women along with that of blacks.

Another contribution of American women to their nation's democracy and history, the struggle for women's rights from 1848 to 1920, was taken over until the 1970s by feminist historians and biographers as their special subject. The exaltation of the same militant figures, the insistent recurrence of the same vicissitudes, and the similarity in the order of the narrative cast events in the form of a saga, recounting the glorious past of a very old feminist movement. From Anne Hutchinson who, in 1637, dared to defend the rights of her sex in the puritanical theocracy of Massachusetts, to Alice Paul who, in the early twentieth century, introduced militant revolutionary tactics in the struggle for the right to vote, heroines linked arms in the epic story of feminism. Generally described in periphrastic rhetoric in the manner of mythical heroes, women rebels and militants were seen in terms of simple psychological attributes: defined by their commitment to a common cause, which generated both physical vigor and moral greatness, they were given a superhuman dimension. In their own lifetime they became legendary, for in the eyes of the American people, experiencing their first century of independence, these women incarnated the virtues of the race: inexhaustible capacity for hard work, courage and endurance, and faith in the perfectibility of American society. Across the pages of history, the feminist epic unfolds on the same scale as that of the conquest of the vast continent. It was no easier for women than for men: in pursuing their rights, American women had to achieve a second territorial conquest. Inch by inch, in effect, the reader sees the first feminist generation stake out the terrain.

Slowly, the heroines travel the road toward their feminist destiny. Their commitment to the cause of women was not a given assumption, a priori. It developed gradually, within abolitionist organizations, growing out of their direct experience of sexual discrimination. In 1838, the Grimké sisters, touring New England Quaker meetings on behalf of abolition, were refused by the brethren the right to speak in public. Two years later, American women delegates to the Universal Antislavery Congress in London, who had made the long sea voyage across the Atlantic to attend, were not allowed by the male organizers to take their seats. Fired up by these experiences, women in 1848 were emboldened to hold the first women's rights convention in Seneca Falls, New York, and passed the famous Declaration of Sentiments and Resolutions.

Just as the Declaration of Independence is the sacred text of the American nation, the Seneca Falls Declaration of Sentiments and Resolutions, which deliberately echoed the 1776 text, is the charter of American feminism. The analogy may have found inspiration in a celebrated example from the French Revolution, when in 1790, a woman, Olympe de Gouges, responded to the inadequacies of the Declaration of the Rights of Man by proposing a Declaration of the Rights of Woman. Nevertheless, the fact is that this analogy between one of the sacred texts of American nationalism and a feminist text exists in the minds of modern feminist historians, just as it existed in the minds of the Seneca Falls initiators and other nineteenth-century feminists, and this phenomenon is unique in the annals of world feminism. There, we must see a desire to link the American struggle for women's rights with the country's grand will toward egalitarianism. This action is not without a certain irony: the feminists are denouncing an omission by plagiarizing the political texts, but in doing so, by antithesis, they are also rendering tribute to the ideas of the Founding Fathers. Thus, nationalism and feminism go together in the writings of feminist historians in a subtle blend, but unfortunately, the first ingredient sometimes seems to dominate the second.

From vicissitude to vicissitude, fictional votes or state-by-state campaigns for the right to vote, we are led down the epic road to the climactic exploit. This was the concentration of feminist forces in Washington for the suffrage march of 5,000 women up Pennsylvania Avenue on the eve of President Wilson's first inaguration in 1913, followed again, when women militants demonstrated outside the gates of the White House in January 1917. The dénouement came after nearly three-quarters of a century of struggle when women's right to vote was finally inscribed in the American Constitution by the "Susan B. Anthony Amendment," voted by Congress in 1919 and ratified in 1920 after a last battle waged at the state level.

The saga of feminist heroism is not just a factual narrative. From one work to another—and here again, in the manner of epics, the same episodes are repeated—the story is told as an epic tale, whose cantos are the major feminist texts published in the press of their day or pronounced at public meetings. Among the most frequently quoted models of bravura, *The Letters on the Equality of the Sexes and the Condition of Women*, by Sarah Grimké, already contain the germ of Simone de Beauvoir's idea that one is not *born* a woman but *becomes* one. "The Solitude of the Self," by Elizabeth Cady Stanton, denounces the sexual division of roles and claims equal worth for the minds of both sexes. Finally, the moving harangue "And Ain't I a Woman," spoken in 1851 at the Akron feminist convention by Sojourner Truth, a black woman who had escaped from slavery, pulverizes the stereotype of the fragile, helpless woman and takes on symbolic value as a refutation of the false quarrel between two causes often presented as mutually conflicting: the racial cause and the cause of women.

It is said that the epic form flourishes during the infancy of a people and that it responds to the need of each people to nourish its development with fine, inspiring stories. The feminist epic narrative is intended to fulfill the same function for women. Inspiring feminist stories were the first works of women's history, a naive form born out of the feminist imagination, which embroidered on tradition and mingled elements of fantasy with reality. This saga not only satisfied the young American feminist movement's passion for uplifting fiction, but also created a link between the past and the present. It helped American feminism become conscious of its collective spirit and its continuity across time and space.

As the continuation of a militant tradition, the feminist epic tended to inspire a dynamic of imitation. However, not everything in the past is worthy of imitation, as Eleanor Flexner wrote in 1959 in *Century of Struggle*,[4] a work that made feminist historiography take a long step toward maturity. Recalling history was now seen as a way of learning lessons from the past so as to generate a different historic future. Thus, the first break with the past occurred when modern militant forces rejected the previous feminist stance of focusing the battle on a single issue, which, in their view, had been the mistake made in prior generations by the American Woman Suffrage Association and other early feminists demanding the right to vote. This disavowal of the past attitude was in itself an invitation to radicalism, implying the need to address all the problems concerning women, so as to give women practical survival skills as well as to develop a feminist ideology. The ideological vacuum, which in hindsight was seen as the price paid for obtaining the right to vote, explained why, in 1920, the old feminism had stopped short.

The generally conceded exception was Elizabeth Cady Stanton, who, by continuing to address all possible issues, had managed to establish a basis for feminist thought. Particularly pursuing the line of thought of the criticism of biblical sources (started by Sarah Grimké, who had dared to question the divine origin of the Scriptures), Elizabeth Cady Stanton published *The Woman's Bible*, which proposed a feminist reading of the Old and New Testaments. She thus opened the breach that was later enlarged by feminist theologians in a bold, sweeping denunciation of the patriarchal Judeo-Christian tradition. The crowning work in this field is Mary Daly's

Beyond God the Father.[5] Here, feminism overcomes Americanism, breaking with the traditional supersanctification of the Bible by a nation seeking to legitimize its divine right. In demystifying a book that has sometimes been interpreted as a justification for sexual discrimination and slavery, the feminism of Sarah Grimké and Elizabeth Cady Stanton remains faithful to the great American tradition of equality for all and exorcises one of the contradictions of Americanism.

Another break with the past by feminist "historians of glory" involves the economic or ethnic cleavages that have affected the Women's movement. An important task has been to convince women that feminism is not the privilege of a certain race or class but that it concerns all women. Toward this end, the black woman and the woman worker have been integrated into the feminist pantheon. The former has been cleansed of the racial accusation of submissiveness and restored to her moral dignity; the courageous feats of Harriet Tubman and countless anonymous black women slaves on the underground railroad are seen anew as valiant acts in a brave resistance movement, and the black woman is seen as a heroine in both causes— racial justice and women's rights. In the same way, the woman factory worker has been restored to her just worth: the women workers of Lowell, Massachusetts, who organized themselves as early as 1840 into a movement to obtain fair wages and a ten-hour day, are seen as a credit both to the labor union movement and to feminism. If feminism is to take up common cause with women workers—Eleanor Flexner and Alma Lutz present Susan B. Anthony as the inspiring example of this alliance—then women workers will have to be persuaded that feminism transcends the labor union struggle. (In the 1860s, this hard lesson was painfully learned too late by Augusta Lewis, founder of the Women's Typographical Union.) To be successful, feminists have argued, women will have to unite in an autonomous feminist form of labor unionism. An early prototype for this idea was the Women's Trade Union League, active in the early twentieth century, within which educated society women trained women factory workers in organizing techniques to help them prepare for the labor struggle and for union leadership.

While still continuing this same undertaking of glorious rehabilitation, Elizabeth Gould Davis, in her book *The First Sex*, introduced a new element, differing from other "historians of glory" of the Women's movement in the sense that her work rests on the ingenious adaptation of a particular theory of history to manifestly feminist ends. The book's thesis is the rediscovery of a great lost civilization that is said to have preceded our era in the obscure dawn of prehistory, whose existence is asserted by the author in a vast perspective of history viewed as swings of the pendulum, in which opposing tendencies alternate. This cyclical conception of history, which recalls that of Oswald Spengler, breaks with the evolutionary theories of Darwin and Huxley. The feminist motivations of this rupture are obvious. To accept evolution, which, by definition, is mutation for the better, would be to recognize the worth of a patriarchal system as a civilizing force toward progress, and to grant the stamp of approval to Judeo-Christian culture, while instead, we are told, the Judeo-Christian culture, by its intolerance and barbarism, has turned civilization backward by fifteen centuries. Davis's rejection of evolution is accompanied, furthermore, by a reversal of the Spenglerian theory of history. Whereas Spengler blamed periods of decline on degeneration resulting from effeminacy, Davis, on the contrary, credits the great periods of ascent on feminizing influences, in particular, the ancient civilization of Anatolia, the cradle of humankind's first settled habitations, which she sees as the land of matriarchy.

For this obscure librarian from Florida, myth is historically true. The feminist motivation on which such an assertion rests is apparent from the first chapter, where the author reminds us of the theme of human development common to all the world's mythologies, from the creation of the universe by a great mother-goddess giving birth to a son by pure parthenogenesis, to the takeover of power by this son who becomes, successively, lover, consort, and finally a god. It is clear that for the author, the story told in myth is the true factual history of humanity, not a symbolic interpretation of evolution. For her, the word *matriarchy* does not represent merely a psychological fact expressed by the cult of the mother-goddess, as in the theory of Neumann in *The Great Mother*, but a true historical past, referring to the actual existence originally of a matriarchal society. Thus the author affirms a basis in historical fact for two myths: that of the mother-goddess, whose latest avatar is said to be the Virgin Mary, and that of the great gynocracies.

The historical reconstruction proposed by *The First Sex* is divided into five major periods. The first was the golden age, or the era of the lost civilization. It is supposed to have come to an end because of a great natural cataclysm, and to have been followed by a second phase, a period of chaos and savagery, at the end of which the women revolted about 5,000 B.C., probably under the leadership of the warrior queen Basilea, who, according to the Greek historian Diodorus Siculus, was the first ruler of Atlantis. Amazonism brought humanity into the third phase of its history, that of a primitive matriarchy, in which the basic unit of society was the group formed by a woman and her children, both boys and girls, while men lived a life of marauders. The fourth phase saw the blossoming of the great civilizations of Sumer, Egypt, and Crete, emanating from the original settled civilization in Anatolia. Unfortunately, in the last phase, beginning in the third millennium B.C., matriarchal agricultural communities were overthrown by masculine carnivorous hordes consisting of the fathers, who were joined regularly by some of the sons. It could be that women, by practicing sexual selection and preferring carnivorous males who were more highly sexed than their vegetarian companions, were the instrument of their own downfall.

Elizabeth Gould Davis's historical reconstruction depends a great deal on drawing morals from the tale, and is filled with numerous, glaring extrapolations. However, the argument is so skillfully and ingeniously woven that the woman reader cannot help but be swayed. Patiently revealing the common archeological foundation and using myth as a historical link with Anatolia, Davis weaves the matriarchal tapestry and imposes an entire feminine landscape on the Near East and Europe: Sumer, with the royal tombs of its queens; Egypt, with its female Sphinx, its breast-shaped pyramids, and the symbol of the vulva on the Pillars of Sesostris; Southern Italy, where the Temple of Hera was decorated with the same sexual symbols as those of Catal Huyuk, a famous Anatolian neolithic site in Turkey; and finally, the British Isles and the labia on the stones of Stonehenge.

With Catal Huyuk and the exploitation of recent archeological discoveries of a site whose foundations could go back to the ninth millenium B.C., we come to the keystone of the author's argument. Extrapolating from the conclusions of Atkins and Mellaert on the historical truth of the mother-goddess cult, Elizabeth Gould Davis asserts the historical truth of the matriarchal society as a political fact and sees the religious cult phenomenon as a sort of self-veneration by women. The great matriarchs are reinstated in their dignity: Potnia, Anat, Eve, Metis, Athena, and especially Tiamat; the book of Genesis is said to be a plagiarism of the myth of the venerated matriarch Tiamat, masculinized into the god Jehovah. The taboos of incest and of menstrual blood are themselves reinterpreted as matriarchal taboos, invented by the first matriarchs to protect themselves from the bestial sexuality of their sons.

The beneficent atmosphere of matriarchal society is the other point evoked by the book. At first sight, it appears as a vegetarian Arcadia where people were nourished by the fruits of the earth, honey, and goat's milk. This world is presented as a classless society, seeming to belong to the egalitarian tradition of utopias. However, several shadows appear over this idyllic picture as contradictions in the text. To begin with, there is the very term *matriarchy*, understood not in its etymological sense of the oligarchic power of mothers, but taken to mean the domination of one class over another, since the author uses it interchangeably with *gynocracy*. It is a question of the power of the biological and social class of women—the first sex—over men, in a society where the patriarchal relationship of "otherness" has simply been reversed. In their diplomatic missions, men are said to have been turned into transvestites, rigged out with false breasts and women's clothing. In daily life in matriarchal society, they are objects of scorn, as shown by the names they are given—Thief, Stench, Filth—and their corpses are thrown into common trenches at Catal Huyuk, while women have the honor of a tomb. The dirty work is left to men, as witness the example that has come down to us in Greek mythology of Hercules cleaning the Aegean stables. The complacency that Davis feels in this brutally contemptuous repainting of a virile myth betrays the author's vindictive feminism and destroys the initial impression of pastoral serenity.

Rather than a model plan for society, the structure elaborated by Elizabeth Gould Davis appears to be a feminist counterattack stigmatizing the patriarchal present and seeking compensation in the past. Letting herself give in to a revenge-seeking form of feminism, the author builds her case on the humiliation of men. In this way, the feminist philosophy, in its broadest definition, is doubly betrayed: first, in the absolute priority that Davis gives to sexual gender in determining individual human existence, thereby repeating the sexist error; second, in the assertion of a specifically feminine nature, said to be morally superior. This twofold treason seems doomed to be inevitable as long as organizational frameworks for society are conceived in terms of matriarchy and patriarchy, that is, of sexual power.

Although it is difficult to grant the book any immediate practical value, it must be recognized that it has a cultural interest, that of exposing the sexual substrata of our culture. Davis reduces patriarchal interpretations to the lucubrations of male chauvinism, but she proposes ingenious counter-lucubrations that are rooted in the purest female chauvinism. The work definitely takes part in the great adventurous sport of shooting down patriarchal writings on history and myth, demonstrating that truth is relative.

Although it is too soon to pass judgment on the question of the historical veracity of matriarchy, *The First Sex* has undeniably played a heuristic role by fascinating women into doing research into their past, if not their lost "golden age" of civilization.

THE OPPRESSION

Of the two antithetical interpretations of women's history that we are offered, glory and oppression, the one that prefers to place history under the sign of oppression is the more authentically feminist, since this view lies at the root of the entire Women's Liberation movement. Indeed, this interpretation is what sustains all the major original texts, from Olympe de Gouges's tract (1790) and Mary Wollstonecraft's *Vindication of the Rights of Woman* (1792) to the 1848 Seneca Falls Declaration of Sentiments and Resolutions. In 1949, Simone de Beauvoir renewed this tradition with *The Second Sex,* but wider acceptance of the thesis that women have always been the second sex had to wait until 1970 and the full blossoming of radical feminism. Although radical feminists recognize that writing about great women in history can be useful and comforting, they have nevertheless denounced the distortion inherent in singling out the exceptions. They have criticized the "historians of glory" for favoring anecdotal accounts of the few over the collective history of womankind as a whole (which still remains to be written), and for giving credit to the individualist thesis that any woman, through her own willpower and talent, has the ability to control her own destiny. While the "historians of glory" think mainly in terms of feelings, particularly of self-respect, the "historians of oppression" think mainly in terms of politics. In placing women's history under the sign of oppression, they do not, however, wish to elicit pity for their sex. Their goal has been to initiate women into applying the analytical method to their collective historical experience, leading them to exercise critical judgment on the present. In so doing, feminist historians have engaged in an act of liberation.

The most interesting contribution in this domain is that of Shulamith Firestone in *The Dialectic of Sex.*[6] As the book's title suggests, the author offers us a feminist adaptation of the theory of historical materialism as it was classically defined by Marx and Engels. Her analysis is placed in a dialectical perspective, since it studies the reciprocal play of opposing forces in the war between the sexes. It also accords with the Marxist theory of materialism, in that it seeks material factors as the real causes of historic and cultural transformations, especially those presiding at the birth of the class system. But whereas Marxist materialism seeks the "first cause" of class differences in economics, for Shulamith Firestone, the crucial factor is sexual, specifically, the difference between the reproductive functions of the two sexes, which caused the first division of labor. Firestone proposes a scheme of history divided into three phases, all meshing to form our current reality: the dialectic of sex, based on the biological division, which has never ceased to cause psychosexual distortions in human beings; the dialectic of class, based on the division of labor; and finally, the dialectic of culture, opposing the aesthetic (female) mode to the technical (male) mode.

Thus, the dialectic of sex is confirmed in its priority and all-inclusive reach, that is, as having antedated and transcended all others since primitive times. These being affirmed as absolutes in historical development, the author shows women's progress through history as a cumulative accretion of oppression. Gradually, women as a defined class fell under the domination of a quadruple subjection imposed by a male ruling caste: sexism, racism, capitalism, and technocracy. Here, definitively, are the four fronts on which feminism must operate, and here is where the author demonstrates the real importance of what is at stake for society. Proclaiming the all-inclusive reach and priority of the dialectic of sex in society is tantamount to proclaiming the priority of the feminist revolution, giving priority to feminism over socialism and proclaiming its autonomy from the socialist revolution. Moreover, the author thereby affirms the historical and contemporary truth of women's collective status as an oppressed class. This double affirmation can only be perceived as a unifying message addressed to black and militant socialist women, reminding them that feminism, far from being in contradiction with the racial struggle and the class struggle, rather embraces them both. Shulamith Firestone thus resituates feminism within an evolutionary perspective, within a dialectic of heredity versus environment, and within the logic of a constant march toward progress, which now is to be turned to the advantage of women. This affirmation also attributes a dual nature to the collective of women: first, as a sexual class, that is, as a political artifact, it has the nature of historical fact, occurring in time and engaged in the historical process; but also, as a living dynamic, operating in the present and the future, the collective of women has the nature of world-creator and history-maker, that is, the ability to give sense to the world and the power to change it by freeing it.

It goes without saying that Shulamith Firestone's theory excludes the possibility of a prehistoric matriarchy such as defined by Johann Bachofen and Friedrich Engels, or exalted by Elizabeth Gould Davis. For Firestone, matriarchy exists only in psychology. It is the mentality of primitive man who, having experienced his physical force but still ignorant of his fecundating power, yields a fraction of his own existence to woman, since she alone seems to him to participate in the mystery of life. In this view, matriarchy was never a factual creation of women, but only a perspective, a way to lighten the oppression of society, in which the veneration of the female principle was already the bearer of the seeds of alienation, since it was born of the will of man.

Once this general philosophy of history had been defined, radical feminist historians began applying it to specific historical events. Their main concern seemed to be to demonstrate that oppression is relative and to reveal it as a political fact perpetuated by means of an ideology. In this case, the ideology is sexual politics, which Kate Millett[7] defines as the relationship of force in which one group in society, defined by its sex, exercises general power over another group, also defined by its sex.

The framework within which Kate Millett and Shulamith Firestone place themselves is that of the decline of the patriarchal system, which began in the nineteenth-century wave of feminism, when the first shots in the sexual revolution were fired at sexual dualism. In 1970, Millett and Firestone believed in the effectiveness of revolutionary action and in the imminence of total change. Their optimism was based on a revised Marxist vision of historical evolution, adapted to a feminist perspective. Just as Marx had predicted an ultimate crisis leading to the downfall of capitalism, Millett and Firestone have faith in a final grand climax where technological progress in biology will have made such a great leap forward regarding reproduction that subjection in the old way to reproductive forces will become outmoded. They make a significant choice in interpreting the two major events they see as belonging to the final crisis: the first revolutionary phase—first-wave feminism—is given less emphasis than the reactionary counterrevolution that has followed it. Whereas the "historians of glory" centered their studies on individual outstanding women, focusing on their militant exploits and their errors, the radical feminists see feminism as an engagement in a class struggle for power, and focus their attention on the mentality of the oppressor, using the age-old war tactic, "know your enemy so as to fight him better." This shift of emphasis marks one of the essential differences between the "historians of glory" and the "historians of oppression."

The two examples chosen by Kate Millett to illustrate sexual counterrevolution are Nazi Germany and Soviet Russia; this choice implies that sexual politics override all other issues, in every political system, from fascism to socialism. It is left up to the reader to work out the essential mechanism from the facts presented to her. In both examples, the primary mechanism is the family, used as an instrument of socialization in the service of a totalitarian ideology. Hitler's government asked women to devote themselves to motherhood for nationalist ends; in the same way, the Soviet authorities, branding the sexual revolution as degenerate and seeing it as a destabilizing threat to the socialist revolution, sacrificed the former for the latter and defined the family as the bulwark of communism.

From this perspective on history, the family emerges as a structure to oppress women, the keystone in the arch of sexual politics, whose solid strength the women in the first-wave feminist movement had made the mistake of underestimating. Following the first revolutionary phase, indeed, only a simple operation of psychology was needed to restore the patriarchy and the family to their original power. It was for this purpose that Freudianism was used. Although born of the same fertile ground as feminism, that is, a desire for sexual liberation, Freudianism was distorted in order to stem the tide of feminism. In a vast commercial and political operation, camouflaged under a scientific label, psychoanalysts prostituted themselves to sell psychoanalysis to the patriarchal powers in order to serve the policies of sexual polarization and relegate women to domesticity. They transformed Freudian biological determinism into political destiny: any personal ambition in women was labeled as penis envy, any sexual initiative as castration, and the claimed passivity of the feminine constitution was used to keep women in their place, while the theory of feminine masochism convinced them this was where they would find pleasure and fulfillment.

In exposing the commercial or political utility of psychoanalysis toward the goals of the sexual counterrevolution, American radical feminists sought to desanctify the panacea of psychoanalysis dispensed as penance by the priest-psychoanalyst to so many women found guilty of having transgressed against normality. The feminists wanted thereby to initiate women into the secrets of psychological warfare; for that, indeed, was how they saw the post-Freudian exploitation of psychoanalysis. Their reading of Freudianism and post-Freudianism, placed in a historical perspective, underlined how much the clinical practice of psychoanalysis had profited from the patriarchal system.

The other major example of the use of dialectical materialism for purely feminist ends is Susan Brownmiller's book, *Against Our Will: Men, Women and Rape.*[8] It offers us a retrospective look at rape, with wartime rape and domestic rape viewed as the same phenomenon, since the author asserts the existence of a single unifying ideology of rape, constant and universal in human history. For women, according to Brownmiller, rape has always been an integral part of their oppression and is the quintessence of the relationship between the two sexes. Her study, then, amounts to yet another demonstration of the mechanism of male sexual politics.

Two fundamental propositions are offered: rape is contingent on circumstances, and rape is political. To assert the contingency of rape, as demonstrated by homosexual rape in men's prisons where the victim is not predestined as such by sexual body type, is to release women from the false claim of biological determinism. To assert its political character is to perceive it as a demonstration of power; the recurrence and the mere possibility of it are a dissuasive force operating in the service of the patriarchal system. It is interesting to observe, with the author, the frequency with which rape occurs inside a patriarchal institution—the police or the army—which, to some extent, validates it. Wartime rape is thus an officialized expression of the masculine collective, perceiving woman as the enemy by reason of the sexual group to which she belongs and seeking to annihilate the whole group by violating her in her sex. This is evidenced by the destruction of the vaginal space, the ultimate gratuitous act of violence, by the forcing of a stick or a bottle into the vagina in a sort of collective exorcism of the vaginal phobia. Susan Brownmiller's evocation of history also demonstrates that the dialectic of rape is a relationship of force, not only in terms of males' superiority over females (in the theorem "$M > F$," male is greater than female), but also in terms of confrontations between two males or two groups of males over one or more female bodies, which have become merely objects of property. In this aspect, American society, caught in the racial trap, has never ceased to present an enlightening spectacle of the play of sexual relations, from the rape of the black slave woman by her white master, to the revolutionary rape of white women by blacks that was once part of the militant program of Eldridge Cleaver.

However, as Susan Brownmiller underlines, there can be no such thing as a revolutionary theory of rape, because that would give rape a political alibi and justify the very social and psychological alibis that feminists and civil rights activists denounce. There is no possible justification whatsoever for rape, says Brownmiller. Whether it is individual or collective, rape is not an act of insurrection. Those who claim it is, black and radical men, are closing ranks with the old alliance of males, for rape arises simply out of a debauched phallocratism (rule of the phallus) and out of the old hatred of one sex for the other, which is its property. To convince the diehards, Susan Brownmiller devotes herself to a whole exercise of bringing rape into the open, seeking to resituate rape in the criminal context of organized violence and to destroy the myths upon which the phallocratic ideology has flourished. She particularly attacks the myth of the "heroic rapist," who has transformed an act of cowardice into a demonstration of virile prowess, resulting from an overfull sac of semen, for the greater satisfaction of the male ego.

For it is here that the problem of sexism lies, in this conscious form of degrading the female sex with the intention of inflating the male ego and providing it with proof of its natural superiority. As long as this hollow ideology of virility is perpetuated, rape is perpetuated. This is the theory proposed by *Against Our Will,* which is both a work of analysis and a call to battle. As analysis, it places rape in the historical dialectic of sex and denounces the terrorist ideology to which it belongs. As a call to battle, it aims to release women from vaginal determinism and appeals to them to act, in the areas of the law and in self-defense. In doing so, it is a work of pure radical feminism.

Whatever the seeming divergences between the feminist "historians of glory" and the matriarchy utopia, on one hand, and the radical feminist "historians of oppression," on the other, they are not irreconcilable, and they meet on several essential principles.

Both perceive the past in terms of a relationship of sexual dialectics. It matters little whether the balance of powers is seen as favorable to the woman in the dialectic of glory or favorable to the man in the dialectic of oppression, so long as the two points of view are expressed regarding different historical events and persons and can complement each other. The essential point is that both perceive the relationship of sexual dialectics as the determining factor, and the feminist battle as transcending racial and class struggles.

It is also possible to reconcile the divergent positions on matriarchy— that of Elizabeth Gould Davis, who sees gynocracy as a historical fact, or that of the radical feminists, who see veneration of the female principle as a worldview that somewhat lightens an oppressive system—if we place ourselves in an evolutionary perspective. Both concepts consider that women's lot in human society has gradually worsened owing to political exploitation of man's physical force and increasingly rigorous institutionalization of a patriarchal system. The fact that, from both viewpoints, evolution is seen as going in a negative direction, indicates a consensus rejecting the deterministic theory of oppression and affirming the arbitrary contingency of current patriarchal societies. The two matriarchal theories implicitly contain the same appeal to feminist rebellion.

We also find in both cases the same equation, "ideology = mythology." Admittedly, the analyses of Firestone, Millett, and Brownmiller are clearly a much more political view of feminism since they expose the actual workings of the sexist machinery. But the "historians of glory" as well as the "historians of oppression" perceive the same substratum of sexual coercion which, by establishing physical advantages as an absolute value, has relegated all women collectively to an inferior status. Both viewpoints reject the claim that this status is natural, and see it as a man-made artifact.

Openly asserting that a phallocratic ideology exists already goes a long way toward depriving it of its mystical power. It is also an affirmation of the need for a countermythology and a counterideology. The feminist saga inscribed in the national iconography by the "historians of glory," as well as the iconoclastic prowess of Elizabeth Gould Davis, partake of countermythology. But the importance given by the "historians of oppression" to Elizabeth Cady Stanton's pioneering philosophical work, the praises sung of early radicalism and first-wave feminism, and the adaptations of Marxist theory made by contemporary radical feminists, all point to a will to develop a counterideology, and to make a genuinely new contribution to the principle of the natural inalienable rights of all human beings.

PART II

Ideological Currents and Tensions

THREE

Egalitarian Feminism

Egalitarian feminism, or liberal feminism, is the ideology of the large feminist organizations. Being mainly geared toward action, they have spent relatively little effort on theory, in comparison with the rich contribution made by radical feminists. Another reason for this bias toward action is that egalitarian feminism had already been codified long before the emergence of the new wave of feminism. It is, in fact, anchored in the oldest American feminist tradition, going back to the voice of Anne Hutchinson in colonial times, evoking the sexual equality practiced in radical Protestant religious sects in Europe, and the 1848 Seneca Falls Declaration, redolent with the philosophy of the French Age of Enlightenment that inspired both the American and French Revolutions.

THE THEOLOGICAL ARGUMENT; OR, THE NEGATION OF THE DIVINE PLAN

For the majority of liberal feminists, the equality of the sexes no longer needs to be demonstrated. A last attempt was nevertheless made in the 1960s by Mary Daly, who, not finding any institution in the United States willing to receive her, had to go to Europe to prepare her doctorate in theology. On the eve of the Second Vatican Council (1962–65), hearing the same old arguments reiterated about the inferiority of woman, she became convinced that there was still a need to prove the equality of the sexes. In choosing to make the theological argument, she offers the view once again of religion as a socialization agent *par excellence*, which has served to convince women that their inferiority is inscribed in the Divine Plan and which, because of the immutability of this Plan, continues to operate to keep women down.

The debate is not new; it has been raised before by women within the framework of egalitarian feminism, who themselves believed in the Church and in the Revelation. It was initiated as early as the Middle Ages by

45

Christine de Pisan in *La cité des dames*. Like this French pioneer before her, Mary Daly asserted that woman is equal to man from her origin, for God created her as a perfect being in His own image. Just as Christine de Pisan saw woman as man's companion and not his serf, Mary Daly gives an egalitarian reinterpretation of the Creation myth, as told in the second chapter of Genesis. An error occurred, she tells us, in the translation of the ancient text: the word that was translated as *servant* or *helpmate* expressed not an ancillary relationship but a complementary one. Ultimately, then, the final version as told in the first chapter of Genesis would not be a denial but a confirmation of her theory. According to the feminist theologian, this version lays emphasis on an original sexual duality. "The image of God is in the human person, whether man or woman." [1]

The same argument of the anthropomorphism of God is used to refute the interpretation by which the Church Fathers have asserted the inferiority of women in referring to the masculinity of Jesus and in exercising a gross distortion of the profound significance of Christ. In the expression, "God was made Man," the last word has a universal, generic sense: God took human form.

THE PREREQUISITES FOR FULL EQUALITY: COMPLETE PARTICIPATION IN WORKING LIFE AND WOMEN'S AVAILABILITY

With the equality of the sexes having been demonstrated one last time, the concept of equality is imposed as self-evident, without further need of explanation. This is the irreducible point of departure for most liberal feminists. A representative statement of the liberal feminist perspective is expressed by Betty Friedan in *It Changed My Life*,[2] defining the ideology of NOW. Equality is perceived as meaning just that—full equality, in every way. Above all, it means the integrality of rights: the surest means of cutting short any possible quibbles over fine points. Egalitarian feminists do not get entangled, for example, in questions over the content of work that have been raised by those claiming "equal pay for equal work." They intend to take advantage of all the benefits that they are entitled to by rights. Thus, the women who wrote the NOW *Statement of Purpose* hoped to achieve "true equality for all women in America . . . a fully equal partnership of the sexes, . . . in truly equal partnership with men."[3]

But what is meant by "true equality,'" perceived as the integrality of rights for women? According to Betty Friedan in *The Feminine Mystique*, creativity and full participation in working life are the essential path leading to self-fulfillment and transcendence. Following Friedan's prescription, the NOW *Statement of Purpose* and the NOW *Bill of Rights* assert above all women's full right to work, that is, the right to all types of work and to all the benefits connected with these types of work. To refuse women the right to work, or to grant them a counterfeit or parsimonious version of it, is quite simply to amputate an essential organ from them. The two NOW texts are also based on the realistic perception that, in a patriarchal society, the assertion of such a right is nothing more than a pious wish for many women if it is not accompanied by a demand for what we shall call the right to be available: the physical and mental availability that women will enjoy when freed from inopportune pregnancies and full-time child care responsibilities. Hence the demand for child care centers and for the right to contraception and abortion. With this last demand, the NOW *Bill of Rights* distanced itself considerably from the pusillanimous feminism of the postwar years, and such an initiative did not fail to arouse keen controversy.

From 1969, for Betty Friedan, the right to abortion and contraception appeared as "a civil right of women," "an inalienable right." The notion of inalienability is taken here in all its senses; it implies for women the power of self-determination, that is, control of their reproductive capacity. Refusing them this right, according to Friedan, constitutes permanent rape and maintains them in their status of sexual objects. The question of contraception and abortion thus goes beyond the framework of political opportunity; it poses the essential problem of women's dignity and identity. What is more, for the author of *It Changed My Life*, the self-determination of women in this area is the necessary prerequisite for love and the sexual revolution: for love, because it will mean an end to the fear of pregnancy that inhibits women in their sexual activity and inspires them to secret resentment against their partner; for the sexual revolution, because an end to the dehumanization of women into sexual objects and their emergence as strong, independent people will free men from a monopoly on force, liberating them from identification with the alienating image of virility.

Inalienable and indivisible rights, faith in work, the *Statement of Purpose* and *Bill of Rights*—here we reencounter the spirit and the letter of the American egalitarian tradition. This tradition is referred to constantly by liberal feminists in order to underline the defects in the words of the Constitution when they proclaim the necessity for an Equal Rights

Amendment. Such an amendment has become the symbol of full equality, and it is expected to lift the heavy burden of ambiguity weighing on the word *person* in the Constitution.

> The Constitution . . . represents what is tantamount to legislation without representation. . . . Women have never legally been declared persons in this country by the Supreme Court or by the Constitution.[4]

Here we reencounter the feminist rhetoric of the postwar era such as it was expressed in *Equal Rights.* In evoking the famous phrase coined by James Otis, the statement also echoes the rhetoric of the Patriots; this repetition, already used to good effect by liberal historians, aims to catch American citizens in the trap of their contradictions and to anchor feminism in the national historical tradition.

REFORMISM

This will toward Americanism is a proof of the postulate that inspires egalitarian feminist ideology: that the present system, although established by men, and by white men at that, is nevertheless imitable and perfectible. If we go back to the NOW *Statement of Purpose* cited above, it is obvious that the author of the text (Betty Friedan, as it happens) had some hesitation as to the egalitarian phrase: although the term *partnership* suggests the interaction hoped for by the androgynous approach, the second phrase, *partnership with men,* reveals that men and the system created by them remain the norm.

Egalitarian feminist ideology vacillates constantly between the *credo*—a declaration of ultimate faith in the system—and the *j'accuse*—an accusation and a rejection of an imperfect, discriminatory reality. This ideology is therefore resolutely reformist and definitely wishes to adapt itself to the regime of a liberal democracy. Thus in 1972 Shirley Chisholm and Bella Abzug,[5] two old hands at the game of American politics, were prescribing the full participation of women in American political life, within the traditional bipartisan framework, while the League of Women Voters offered American women a whole panoply of aids to success in political action.[6] Thus, Mary Daly, at that time still defining herself as a Catholic feminist, rejected a complete break with the Catholic church as a "neurotic reaction." The desperate efforts that she went to in her first book are typical of the behavior of the liberal feminist trying to adapt herself to existing institutions: patriarchal though they may be, they can still be saved. Hence the importance given here to her work attempting to rescue the Catholic church—an exploit in itself—in *The Church and the Second Sex.*

The reformism of the egalitarian feminist movement is characterized by a marked preference for optimism, consisting of an overestimate of the gains achieved and a great faith in evolution. In the overestimate of the gains achieved, elements of the system are judged by what they lack, perceived as so many gaps to be filled, and thus seen as potential factors for change. In this way, Mary Daly highlighted the *Pastoral Constitution of the Church in the Modern World* proclaimed by Pope John XXIII, stressing what he did *not* say: there was *no explicit condemnation* of artifical means of contraception, and the familiar jargon on the subordination of women was missing. At that time, Mary Daly saw the absence of such rhetoric as a positive sign leaving the door open for wider consideration, and not as a cautious strategy that, in reality, amounted to a verdict of refusal for a rehearing. Her conclusion to her study of the innovations brought in by Pope John XXIII is a masterpiece of laudation, a hymn of praise seeking to amend the ways of an institution which, she later decided, is manifestly incurable!

Liberal feminists' overestimate of the gains achieved rests on the conviction that established institutions have a great capacity for evolution. The existing relations between the sexes, institutions in themselves, are thus resituated in a historical perspective. Mary Daly's first book presents them to us as having been necessary at a time when civilization was being developed and stable structures were needed. Thus, Saint Paul's severity toward women was required by the fragility of the early Christian church, which was accused of being effeminate and immoral. Likewise, Christ, choosing only men to be his Apostles, was thinking in terms of the cultural context of the time.

The thesis sustained by the author was thus that the writings of the Scriptures and the declarations of the church fathers have been historically necessary and reflect a sociological situation. Such an assertion is typical of the generosity of liberalism in the sense that it gives man an initial alibi, that of the pressure of circumstances. Nevertheless, it contains its just proportion of feminism, since it underlines a double impropriety which, according to the author's generalization, is characteristic of all patriarchal institutions: both the anachronism of the institution, which does not correspond to present-day sociological reality, and the imposture of those who have maintained it in this state in the name of a supposed law of nature ordaining the inferiority of women and the inevitability of sexual roles.

CONCRETE ACTUALIZATION IN THE HERE AND NOW: SEXUAL DISCRIMINATION

Before coming out with a program of reforms, egalitarian feminist ideology anchored itself in facts. Egalitarian feminist theorists reject all symbolism, whether it dresses in the style of apocalyptic rhetoric and an Afro wig, as with the radicals, or decks itself out in the false eyelashes of the feminine mystique.

The factual field on which egalitarian feminists concentrate their critical analysis, because of the priority they give to the right to work, is the condition of women in employment. Research studies by liberal feminists are oriented toward specific sectors; for example, the university, for Marijean Suelzle[7] and Jessie Bernard.[8] Broader studies have also been undertaken, of which the best documented is certainly *Born Female,* by Caroline Bird. The following two excerpts come from different contexts; one cannot help being struck by the recurrence of the perennial theme:

> This is a frankly feminist book. It counts the social, moral and personal costs of keeping women down on the job and finds them high: We are destroying talent. . . . We are wasting talent. . . . We are hiding talent.[9]

> The problem is that the sexual relationship is soured and dehumanized by the workaday relationships of men and women in society. Its converse is the equally obsolete image of virility—MACHISMO—which enjoins men to dominance.[10]

Like the works of Marijean Suelzle and Jessie Bernard, the first excerpt, published in 1970, belongs in the context of official statements following the publication of the reports by various commissions on the status of women, and the heyday of the economic concept of *womanpower.* The second excerpt, also from 1970, was written in the context of a critique of some feminists' concentration on bedroom politics, and was republished in 1976, when egalitarian feminism was coming back in force after somewhat diminishing. Together they reveal the central place that the work theme has always occupied in the egalitarian approach, this being the only element of the sociological context to be mentioned. It is perhaps an exaggeration to say, as does the radical feminist Colette Price,[11] that the liberal feminists are confusing cause and effect when they reason that women are oppressed because the system of employment is unfair to them. But any impartial observer must recognize that Betty Friedan is not far from a similar conclusion; studying the origins of the misunderstanding between the sexes, she sees one of the key factors as being the system of employment as it is conceived in the patriarchal society.

The word that keeps recurring in the works quoted or in the depositions before the New York Commission on Human Rights is *discrimination*, along with its variants, *invisible bar*, or *sex line*. In retrospect, after the bold language used by the radical feminists, who substituted such terms as *oppression*, *obliteration*, or even *massacre*, the word *discrimination* sounds like a euphemism. But it is revealing of a period, from 1967 to 1969, when the vast majority of feminists did not use any other term. In the context of the time, the word was very strong and innovative compared with the conclusions of the EEOC and of *American Women*, the 1963 report of the President's Commission on the Status of Women. It is precisely because feminists dared to use the powerful word *discrimination* that they were able to denounce the paternalistic and patriarchal attitudes of employers that the term represents, and in so doing, they completed the work done by the official investigations.

The most thorough study of employers' attitudes is offered to us by Caroline Bird, who examined the subtle stratagems of unadmitted sexual discrimination. She devotes herself to revealing the existence of a whole system of rationalization of sex roles. The best example is the presentation by Talcott Parsons of the sexual division of labor as belonging to every culture, through an infallible polarization that assigns to men the "instrumental-adaptative" role, and leaves the "expressive-integrative" role to women. This is understood to mean that men, in their instrumental role, act on the physical environment, and as adapters, they define the strategy for the family, the firm, or the group. Women, in their expressive role, concern themselves with emotions, and as integrators, they look after the cohesion of the group. In other words, men operate, women cooperate. Feminists argue that the expert jargon is brought in solely to lend a semblance of scientific verity to the habitual prejudices about women's predisposition for certain kinds of supportive work roles. It is cerebrations of this type that ensure the acceptance and perpetuation of the three rules, according to Caroline Bird, that govern employers' politics on the sexual frontier: women should work inside, behind the scenes; men should earn the money; machines, prestige, and the top of the pyramid should be a privileged domain reserved for men.

The most recent avatar of paternalism and underhanded sexual discrimination is "new masculinism." The old masculinists, like Freud, assigned only one place to women: the home. The "new masculinists"—David Riesman, Margaret Mead, and Mary Bunting—do not assign a place to women. They are in favor of women working! But Caroline Bird takes pains to expose their equivocation, asserting that their sudden conversion to favoring women working is not based on a recognition of women's value. The "new masculinists," in fact, do not want women to work for their own glory, nor do they want women's work to entail the least change in the lives of men. For this reason, they have invented the "U-shaped career," or the woman's career in three phases: an active phase immediately following university studies; a less active or inactive phase during the years of motherhood; and finally, a return phase of reentering and readapting to the working world. All things considered, the real reason that pushed the "new masculinists" of the 1960s to preach the gospel of women at work was simply a lack of sufficient labor force, felt particularly keenly in offices, which have become bastions for the concentration of working women.

The illustration *par excellence* of the patriarchal attitude can be found among the fathers of the Judeo-Christian church and their successors. The most revealing problem is that of the ordination of women as priests in the Catholic church. Mary Daly, from the outset, has found no theological objection whatsoever to prevent the ordination of women. The arguments raised by the Church, which are based on the writings of Saint Paul and the masculinity of Jesus and the Apostles, are easily refuted. Those who, in spite of everything, admit that they find the idea of women priests inconceivable, are betraying a profound prejudice which consists of identifying women, but not men, solely with their sexual function. Quoting from Professor Stendhal, Mary Daly recalls that the last-ditch stand of partisans of the status quo in the Church has always been the reference to the subordination of women at the Creation. It is here, as the author justly points out, that we see the far-reaching importance of the battle: what is at stake is not only equality between men and women in the *Church* of the future, but equality between men and women in the *society* of the future. The underlying reasoning is clear: to refuse the ordination of women by alleging their subordination at Creation is to affirm what may be called inferiority by divine right, and thus to close the door forever on women's eventual "emancipation." As a good Catholic feminist, Mary Daly, at that stage of her commitment, never used the word *liberation,* which would imply a verified finding of oppression.

THE EXORCISM OF MYTHS

Sexual discrimination is nourished by a whole set of preconceived ideas. The essential task laid out for themselves by egalitarian feminists has been to isolate these assertions under the heading of *myths* in order to be better able to destroy them. The term has, in addition, become part of the official language, as witness a document from the Women's Bureau set forth in two columns, opposing "myths" and "realities." [12]

The central myth, which gives birth to all the others, is the "eternal feminine" concept. The most coherent analysis of this, again, is found in *The Church and the Second Sex.* In it, Mary Daly studied the eternal feminine myth as a functional entity, operating to neutralize individual abilities and relegating women to an enclosed world, the better to promote sexual discrimination. Considering the attributes of the eternal woman, the author saw her as a mysterious personage placed on a pedestal. Any cult is alienating for the figure who is worshipped by it, and the dehumanized cult-object abandons itself to being adored, resulting in the paralysis of its will for freedom and self-fulfillment. The symbol of the eternal woman has become a standard of measurement for all women, and this is how generations of individual women's personalities have been made captive in confining feminine roles underlying the symbol, that is, virgin, wife, and mother.

Far from being a fact of nature, the eternal feminine myth is derived from a whole set of "theological distortions," which constitute the "symbol syndrome," according to our theologian. Under the strictures of the Divine Plan, Mary, the ideal wife of a celibate clergy projecting its fantasies, has become the model held up to all women, while the interpersonal relationship between Mary and Jesus has been transformed into a symbolic prefiguring of a generic relationship between women and men, fixed forever in terms of a hierarchy. But, Mary Daly's first book reminds us, symbols and myths grow old and die. Because of changes that have occurred in women's aspirations, the time has come for the eternal feminine myth to die, and, with it, all the myths that gravitate around the eternal woman and that serve to control the place and the role of the second sex in employment.

A whole discourse exists on the subject of women and work, and it is against this discourse that egalitarian feminists have directed most of their attacks. In 1970, Elizabeth Koontz, then director of the Women's Bureau, skillfully demolished three myths about women and work: "woman's place is in the home"; "an increase in the number of women working outside the home has led to a rise in juvenile delinquency"; and finally, "working women have a history of absenteeism." The first two allegations were refuted by the conclusions of specific investigations undertaken by the Women's Bureau, establishing that, in the matter of parental responsibilities, the quality of time spent with children matters more than the quantity. As to women's absenteeism, the Bureau's studies revealed that women were absent from work only three-tenths of a percent (o.3 percent) more often than men, and that the reasons for these absences were linked to the role assigned to women.

Three other myths dealing with women's job performance and sexual discrimination in universities were demonstrated as false by Marijean Suelzle, a militant member of NOW: "women do not succeed as well as men"; "women are less motivated than men"; "innate intellectual differences exist between the sexes." Certainly, the sociologist admits, women earn many more master's degrees than doctorates; however, the reason for this is not their innate failure, but rather is found in their choice of careers. Likewise, the assertion that women are less motivated is a distortion of reality; statistics from the University of Chicago, for example, reveal a very high level of motivation among women students. The underlying reason that impels them to abandon a career is the fear of social rejection for not conforming to the norm of femininity. As to innate intellectual differences, Marijean Suelzle refers to the work of the psychologist Eleanor Maccoby, demonstrating that cultural conditioning, more than genetic factors, intervene to explain the differences in behavior and performance between the sexes.

The ultimate myth denounced by egalitarian feminists is the one that consists of denying that any problem exists, alleging that women are already in a position of power. Gloria Steinem offers us a witty sketch of this view, in the pages of *Ms.*

We are perceived as *already powerful*. . . . There is still the conviction that women exercise some great behind-the-scenes power. . . . We are said to be domineering or castrating, . . . to be matriarchs. All the stereotypes come to mind: there is the pampered housewife, sitting at home in wall-to-wall comfort while her unfortunate husband works long hours to keep her that way. There are the lazy women getting a free ride on alimony. . . . There are those grand figures of American mythology, the rich widows who are supposed to control most of the stock, and travel Europe on the life insurance of some overworked spouse.[13]

The destruction of the myth is accomplished through figures, and first of all, those concerning support payments. Steinem as a journalist was one of the first to look at the facts. She considered them from two aspects; the first question was how widespread the phenomenon was. At the time of the study, support payments were granted by the courts on a temporary basis in 10 percent of divorces, and on a permanent basis, in only 2 percent of cases. The second was to what extent such support payments were actually made over the course of time: 38 percent of fathers fully met their court-ordered payments, 20 percent paid partially, and 42 percent did not honor the judgment at all. Ten years after the divorce, court-ordered support payments were still being made in only 13 percent of cases. As to driving around in Cadillacs paid for by welfare checks, this would be quite a feat, since the average public allowance per dependent child at the time of the study did not exceed the meagre sum of thirty-five dollars a month.

Regarding stock ownership, women do indeed represent a large percentage of stockholders (49.9 percent at that time), but the feminist journalist analyzed the statistics more closely. Steinem showed that the numbers of shares held by women are usually insignificant, so that the 49.9 percent of stockholders who were women together owned only 38 percent of all shares. Finally, in the matter of life insurance pensions, she found it was true that the majority of beneficiaries were women, representing two-thirds. However, the benefits were usually low, and all the more insufficient when they had to cover the support of children. Although Gloria Steinem's demonstration here commits a rather serious fault in its paucity of figures and in its use of evasive expressions of probability and frequency, the final balance is convincing enough to destroy the myth of feminine high finance:

How true is the stereotype of pampered and powerful women of large incomes? One good overall measure is this: if you look at all the people in this country who have incomes of $10,000 a year or more [at 1973 values] from whatever source. . . , you find that less than 9 percent of them are women. And that includes all the divorcees and rich widows.[14]

The basic premise of egalitarian feminist ideology is thus intended to awaken a critical spirit in women about a concrete, present reality, to provoke them to question assertions that they have accepted without protest up to now. Women have internalized the myths; now it is important to exorcise the evil. Mary Daly defines this as a self-fulfilling prophecy carried out through a process where the dominant class projects its own self-hatred on the inferior class, whose members, by internalization, integrate it into their own personalities. A sort of vicious circle is established in which the myths support the facts and the facts confirm the myths. In this game, the woman is always the loser. If she fails in her attempts at promotion, what do you expect, she is a woman! If she succeeds, she is accused of masculinity!

It is not a question of blaming women, but of making them conscious of the mutilation they have suffered in their creativity. The opprobrium is reserved only for the token women, the "Aunt Toms," as Betty Friedan calls them in *It Changed My Life;* the mistake made by these women, according to Caroline Bird and Marijean Suelzle, is to attribute women's lack of success to women themselves and not to prejudices inherent in the system. If there is one group who particularly flog the hypocrisy of the "Aunt Toms," it is no doubt the egalitarian feminists who, ironically, are themselves seen by the radical feminists as the token women of the new feminist movement! Caroline Bird, among others, is pleased to quote Gunnar Myrdal: "There are anti-Semitic Jews, there are anti-Negro Negroes, and anti-women women." [15]

Suffering from self-hatred by introjection of the feminine stereotype, the "Aunt Toms" try to resolve the problem by distinguishing themselves from other women and closing themselves off in selective associations.

The egalitarian feminists propose a different approach. Again, it is to Mary Daly that we owe the best statement. The responsibility for exorcism of myths is incumbent, says she, on those who have an awareness of the problem as well as the necessary creative energy and independence. To these women is entrusted the mission of changing the feminine image by promoting their own image. Token women again, say the radical feminists. No, because, in contrast to the "Aunt Toms," these women will look on the side of women and not of men. They will have feminist generosity toward other women, perceiving their own success as the prototype of women's successes to come, seeing themselves not as emulating men but as an example to be emulated by women, who will then free themselves of the sexual prejudices that are the neurosis of an entire culture.

At the end of the 1960s, two names were regularly mentioned by the egalitarian feminists: Simone de Beauvoir, and Indira Gandhi (whose image had not yet been tarnished). In choosing two such different personalities, seeing one as outside the system and the other within it, egalitarian feminists meant to propose two possible versions of feminine power and to show that they transcended not only sexual polarities but also political cleavages, with a single goal in view: to provide a convincing demonstration, quantitatively and qualitatively, of the creativity of women. The intended audience for this demonstration was not only women, who had to be released from the noxious psychology of sexual roles, but also the public, since the presupposition of the liberal approach is that the public is willing to let itself be convinced.

The usual objection is that the solution proposed by the egalitarian feminists can only be addressed to a minority of women, those who have what it takes to raise themselves up to the highest ranks of the social hierarchy. To make such an objection amounts to ignoring the fact, implicitly taken into account by egalitarian feminists, that men who rise to the highest ranks are not necessarily exceptional. From the egalitarian perspective of sexual nondiscrimination, the same rule must be applied to women; it must no longer be demanded of a woman that she should be twice as gifted as a man in order to obtain the desired promotion. It must only be accepted that just as many women with average talents as men with average talents should achieve the summit. Such, it seems, is the vision of justice that inspires the egalitarian feminist approach to the problem of women and work.

THE EGALITARIAN FEMINIST REVOLUTION

"Our revolution is unique,"[16] declared Betty Friedan, president of NOW, in 1968. Although the emphasis on uniqueness implies the rejection, on the one hand, of a separatist ideology copied from that of black power, and on the other hand, of a Marxist solution, the statement does proclaim a revolution. It is proclaimed in the name of all women, in spite of the leftist viewpoint, expressed by a male student at Cornell College where Betty Friedan was speaking, disputing women's right to do so independently of socialism. It is proclaimed in personal terms: "I am a revolutionary."[17]

In the same spirit, Gloria Steinem, comparing her ideas with those of the Australian radical feminist Elizabeth Reid, held that the measures demanded by liberal egalitarian feminists—equal salaries, child care centers, refuges for battered women, legal abortion—are revolutionary, for two reasons: they free women from their status of a cheap labor force, and they free women for the revolution. Here again, to understand this claim of egalitarian feminists, it is necessary to distinguish it from the narrow definitions which, unmindful of the sexual caste system, perceive revolution as the overthrow only of economic classes. Wherever one places it on the political chessboard, it must be recognized that full, integral sexual equality would entail the most radical reorganization that American society has ever known. Radical reorganization, indeed, for it implies a restructuring of all institutions, through a revolution in sexual roles, of which the first imperative, as Betty Friedan stated in 1969 and recalled in 1976, is this: "We must challenge the idea that it is *women's primary* role to rear children." [18]

This rule having been laid down, the egalitarian feminist utopia organizes itself around four major institutions restructured to enable full participation by women in the active life of the country: education, the family, work, and the home.

In the egalitarian society, according to the NOW *Statement of Purpose*, education will be the key to women's participation in the national economy, the main criterion by which to judge their degree of usefulness to society. In 1976, Betty Friedan considerably broadened the role of the educational system, transforming it into the cornerstone of the egalitarian society, since this society will result from an educational revolution, consisting of opening a great debate on sexual roles and educating men and society so that men accept equal responsibility with women for raising children. The educational revolution thus defined ought to begin in the universities, with every academic community having a child care center and school for the children of faculty members and students.

In view of the redistribution of parental and domestic responsibilities, it is clear that, in the egalitarian feminist society, there should no longer be any such role as "housewife," as defined in the traditional postulate in which the man alone supports the family's needs and the woman allows herself to be kept. As women regain their dignity, this logic flows naturally, as we are reminded by Caroline Bird. In a well-known analogy, she likens the old faulty and simplistic reasoning to a contract of prostitution. The militant women of NOW also take a stand against this false postulate:

We believe that a true partnership between the sexes demands a different concept of marriage, an equitable sharing of the responsibilities of home and children and of the economic burdens of their support. We believe that proper recognition should be given to the economic and social value of homemaking and child care. To these ends, we will seek to open a reexamination of laws and mores governing marriage and divorce. [19]

In the future egalitarian society, the housewife or househusband will receive pay for her or his domestic work. Gloria Steinem recalls the ethic applied by liberal feminists: "*All* human labor deserves to be rewarded." [20]

This aspect of liberal feminism is certainly one of the points most disputed by the radical feminists, who see there yet another effective institutionalization of the relegation of women to domestic tasks. If, indeed, the remuneration for domestic work were to stagnate at the bottom of the salary scale, would there be many househusbands? But there again, a rejoinder can be made that the question does not take account of new mental attitudes, which will have been acquired through the educational revolution. The debate therefore remains open.

Egalitarian feminists also tested their ingenuity to remain faithful to their ethics and, at the same time, avoid the trap of a formal systematization that would rigidify sexual polarities even before the desired evolution of attitudes could take place. As Simone de Beauvoir put it, they put domestic work "in the past tense." Thus, according to Caroline Bird's suggestion, in case of divorce, a lump-sum separation payment would replace the degrading support allowance; it would be a case of retroactive recognition for past domestic work. We reencounter the same idea with Betty Friedan: she proposes, besides, the payment of state social services or retirement benefits to women who have remained at home for ten or twenty years.

In the future egalitarian society, the right to work, for those who no longer choose the domestic role, will be guaranteed by the recognition of a right to be available. As early as 1966, the NOW *Statement of Purpose* posed the issue of the creation of child care centers as the necessary guarantee of truly equal opportunity and freedom of choice for women. The question of child care centers thus makes its entry into feminism in relation to women's right to work; some say that this is going in "by the back door." Feminism had to wait for the theorists of the androgynous approach for the issue of child care centers to be raised in terms also of the children's education. In the society of the future, women's availability will also be assured by the control of reproduction, with women themselves exercising management over their own bodies, making motherhood a joyful and responsible act.

This is the notion of choice that is introduced into women's lives. In her article, "Can Women Have It All?" [21] Letty Cottin Pogrebin feels it necessary to state that the women's movement has not called upon women to demand everything, to demand the right to try "to juggle all three balls" of career, marriage, and motherhood. It has simply called on them to exercise options. Thus, we have come a long way from the time when Betty Friedan, in *The Feminine Mystique,* prescribed the integration of the three roles in the course of a woman's life. Evaluating the road traveled at a time when solitude has become much less frightening to women, feminists can speak in terms of alternatives. Have we then returned to the days of the neo-Freudians, to the unavoidable choice between a career and femininity? Certainly not, since at that time it was not a question of choice, but of blackmail. From now on, according to liberal feminists, women will no longer be subjected to an ultimatum; with full knowledge of the circumstances in the case—*their* case—they will be able to choose all the options or just one, it being accepted as a matter of course that if they choose all the options, this must be made possible by a redistribution of parental and domestic responsibilities.

Finally, revision of the laws and customs surrounding the family does not really threaten the family as an institution. In the eyes of egalitarian feminists, who nevertheless leave the door open to individual solutions, it assures the family, on the contrary, a new lease on life. If Mary Daly, for example, vituperates against the eternal feminine myth, it is because the identification of the woman with the roles of wife and mother is particularly dangerous for her marriage. As Betty Friedan asserted:

> Everything we are doing in the women's movement, not only the specific reforms of marriage and divorce, but everything we are doing in the women's movement for equality, should make it possible for our daughters and our sons to have different and better marriages and families.[22]

It is possible to glimpse between the lines a hint of *The Second Stage,* the postfeminist book in which Betty Friedan, twenty years after having denounced the *FEMININE mystique,* attacks the *FEMINIST mystique* and presents the family as the new frontier of feminism.

In 1976, another new frontier of feminism was perceived, in terms of the influences of the sexual revolution on city planning. In the city of the future, there will be an end to urban design plans that incorporate the polarization of sexual roles in the division between city and suburbs. The structure of the community and the habitat will be reconsidered to reintegrate women into city life, and the concretization of the feminine mystique in the isolation of suburban homes and the masculine mystique in the urban office and factory will disappear.

Caroline Bird paints a broad picture of work in the city of the future:

> We are heading into an androgynous world in which the most important thing about a person will no longer be his or her sex. . . .
> In this brave new world, . . . sex would be a personal characteristic of only slightly more consequence than the color of one's hair, eyes — or skin.
> Sex is here to stay, but its future is in private life, not in the office. [23]

One could wish that the author had gone further in her investigation of the androgynous future; androgyny here only covers the end of sexual discrimination in employment, when the working world will have been enriched by ten million persons freed from domestic tasks. The national work force will then have attained full employment. Furthermore, as women come out of their homes, new jobs will be created in child care, laundry, restaurants, and other services. The egalitarian feminist here foresees the creation of community agencies employing true salaried professionals, both men and women. Finally, technology would open all professions to women, as physical strength would no longer always be necessary. This would mean the end of segregation in employment and the end of the relegation of women to the role of a reserve labor force. It is difficult to verify the accuracy of the economic analysis on which this forecast is based, but all feminist attempts of this kind ought to be considered as efforts to find an honest solution, a breeding ground of ideas among which some, certainly, in practice, will prove to be ingenious.

DISSONANCES

The synthesis presented above summarizes the average position of the main current of liberal feminist thought. This study would not be a faithful reflection of reality if it remained silent about the divisions that eventually threatened the cohesion of NOW.

The first point of contention arose over the inclusion of the Equal Rights Amendment in the NOW Proclamation of 1967. Women union members of the United Auto Workers (UAW) opposed this inclusion, not because they personally were against the ERA, but because their union was. Here we are touching on the delicate problem of double allegiances that is particularly familiar to feminist radicals. In this case, it was a question of choosing between the union option for the "protective" laws, supposedly benefiting the least-favored women, and the feminist option for full equality of rights. Women union members in the automobile industry proved their political maturity in avoiding a break with both NOW and the UAW. Although they suspended all activity with the feminist organization as soon as the ERA was included in its program, they nevertheless did not resign from it. Furthermore, having respected union discipline, they were able to act within the UAW and gradually to lead the national office of their union to give its official support to the Equal Rights Amendment. The cause of women's rights therefore emerged strengthened from this episode, with this group of militant women having been able to establish a convergence, alas still rare, between feminism and unionism.

The problem of abortion and contraception was the second cause of conflict within NOW. The inclusion of the right to contraception and abortion in the program of NOW shocked the conservative wing, whose members seceded and founded the Women's Equity Action League (WEAL). Devoting itself to economic and legal problems relating to education, WEAL has always loyally joined its efforts with those of NOW in the struggle for employment and the Equal Rights Amendment. On the points of common agreement, therefore, there was convergence here as well, and the cause of women's rights was not hindered. Much more disturbing were conflicts between liberal and radical feminists, as we will discuss further on.

BETTY FRIEDAN JUDGES THE WOMEN'S MOVEMENT

Addressing the internal discord that rent the Women's movement beginning on 26 August 1970, the day of a national strike by women and a peak moment in new feminism, Betty Friedan saw the divergences as symptoms of the vulnerability of a movement in full flower, which had become, precisely for this reason, the favorite target of hostile forces. This vulnerability is anchored in the very history of women: they have lacked power, therefore they are inexperienced with power. This vulnerability affected the Women's movement in two ways.

Above all, it became easy prey for its adversaries. Made to feel guilty, not daring to admit the hunger for power awakened in them by long starvation, militant women attacked all women who appeared to enjoy the authority that the movement needed so much to have. Hence the accusations of elitism. Betty Friedan responded to these accusations by recalling that in a society not under threat, it is easier for authentic militants to have influence from a position of power than from the fringes of society; marginality proves nothing except inferiority in the eyes of the public and of women themselves. The perverted expression of a desperate desire for power was naturally exploited by the enemies of the Women's movement, the agents of the FBI and the CIA who, according to revelations made during hearings organized by Senator Church and the Rockefeller Commission, infiltrated the ranks of feminists. If we can believe Betty Friedan, the tool used to discredit the movement was lesbianism. Lesbians in the pay of the FBI began working to undermine the movement, laying the accent on a problem that was not a problem for the lesbians of NOW, but that nevertheless shocked many militant women and thus divided feminism. The march of 12 December 1970 was turned away from its initial purpose—a demand that the City of New York provide for infant and child care services —and was transformed into a parade of lavender armbands. Likewise, the movement witnessed Kate Millett, under extensive pressure from some anonymous entity, feeling forced to make a public declaration of her bisexuality.

The hostility Betty Friedan expresses in this regard is less concerned with lesbianism as such than with a suspected campaign of lesbians to proselytize within the Women's movement. This hostility seems to be a response to strategic and philosophical motivations. As to strategy, these events occurred at a point in history when the Women's movement was beginning to worry certain interest groups because of the extraordinary mobilization of women achieved in the strike of 26 August 1970. It was important for the movement that new or potential recruits should not be alienated, and therefore, that credence should not be lent to the traditional cliché equating feminism with lesbianism, which so many men have used to mask their fear of feminism and to seek to intimidate its adherents. As to philosophy, Betty Friedan thus was obeying a conviction that the choice of lesbianism was not a political solution but constituted a new obstacle.

Within the movement, the lack of experience in holding power led certain militants not to understand the difference between militant power and personal power. Only first names were mentioned—Gloria, Bella— but they suffice to identify those whom Friedan calls the power brokers and the manipulators of the Women's movement. A dual problem seems to be raised here. First, a distinction has to be made between viewing these women, on the one hand, as the stars of the feminist movement, using the movement for personal goals, and on the other hand, seeing them as gifted militants, ahead of their time in their awareness, who had ideas and dared to express them. The second problem then appears (and it is a problem posed by any avant-garde movement playing a driving role for social change, a responsibility which falls particularly on radical groups): as long as the Women's movement refused to delegate power to some of its militant members as spokeswomen responsible for representing the whole movement, prominent feminists could present their personal points of view as those of the movement and say whatever they liked. Paradoxically, in refusing to choose responsible spokeswomen in order to avoid creating a star system, the Women's movement encouraged an unofficial star system.

Born out of powerlessness and lack of experience in holding power, internal dissensions thus are part of the pathology of oppression. Such is the diagnosis offered by the black lawyer Florynce Kennedy[24] regarding the hostility of many black women to the Women's movement. Such is also the analysis applied by Betty Friedan, not only to internal struggles, but also to the expressions of self-pity that characterize the process of awakening consciousness and radical analysis, which she sees as just so much "contemplating the navel." In Friedan's view, to speak in favor, as Ti-Grace Atkinson did, of a woman called Valerie Solanas who attempted to kill Andy Warhol and who recommended the gradual elimination of all males, or to speak, like Kate Millett, of the politics of sex, is to confuse the feminist revolution, which is necessary to change oppressive conditions, with the pathology that is a consequence of these conditions.

The author of It Changed My Life states that she rejects "sexual politics," using this feminist expression in an extremely curious way. However, here she is not referring to masculine-biased politics or disagreeing with feminist denunciations of such politics; instead, she means feminist politics that amount to female chauvinism. The expression, as used by Friedan, additionally covers a second implication, "bedroom politics," that is, the priority given by some radical feminists to sexuality, either in the choice of orientation (lesbianism), in the demand for the right to sexual pleasure (clitoral orgasm and the superior position during intercourse), or finally, in rejecting it as anathema (asexuality). Expressing approval for Simone de Beauvoir's comment that the reason many women feel debased when they are in the inferior position during sexual intercourse is that they resent occupying an inferior position in society, Friedan concludes: "So it is not sex that reduces women; it is society. . . . When we change society, we can choose our sexuality."[25]

The need felt by Betty Friedan to restructure priorities comes from the confusion on which she bases her analysis of radical feminist theory; this theory, contrary to what Friedan states, does not say that the sexual act is naturally oppressing, but that it has been institutionalized by men into a symbol of male power.

Friedan's denunciation of "bedroom politics" also refers to her rejection of the "focus on the kinds of sexual orgasm." She affirms the necessity to associate sex with love, preferably in heterosexuality. In asserting the need for this synthesis, that is, in interaction between the two sexes, Betty Friedan is already coming close to the so-called androgynous approach.

Limited though it might be, a similar tendency can be detected in Caroline Bird. We shall see that even egalitarian feminists, the staff of Ms. in particular, have not only borrowed from androgynous feminism but also have brought original contributions to it. Such a trend can only enrich egalitarian feminist thought, encouraging it to leave the confines of the privileged domain of employment. It can also grant a broader appeal to an approach which, all things considered, is the most American of all the new feminist ideologies.

The partiality for the work theme has nevertheless had positive consequences. It especially explains the effective action of egalitarian feminism and its remarkable cohesion; we have seen, in fact, that the dissonances of the early years have been successfully resolved through the realization of a consensus on the areas of possible agreement.

Resolutely situating itself within the existing system, egalitarian feminism naturally finds its task made easier from a practical point of view. It is the form of feminism that, among the male public and government agencies, is the least embarrassing and the most accepted. The best proof of this is the popular majority which, according to surveys,[26] favors the adoption of the Equal Rights Amendment; or again, the success of the march on 9 July 1978, when 100,000 demonstrators gathered in Washington in support of the ERA; or yet again, the presence of three presidents' wives[27] at the 1977 National Women's Conference in Houston, unquestionably dominated by egalitarian feminists.

FOUR

Radicalism

When the radical label is applied to feminism, it covers at least three principal tendencies: *radical feminism, political lesbianism,* and *feminist socialist radicalism.*

Radical feminism is by far the most important of the three. This ideology has inspired a whole variety of small militant groups which set themselves apart from the National Organization for Women by their absence of strong structure and by their exclusion of men. Although greatly diverse, they have at times been so widespread that they constituted an important infrastructure and an effective communication network. The most well known of these groups were the New York Radical Women, Cell 16, and the Feminists—all founders of the radical feminist segment of the new feminist movement; the New York Radical Feminists (not to be confused with the New York Radical Women), who, until 1978, published the *NYRF Newsletter;* and the Redstockings, whose contribution to feminist theory was the "pro-woman line." Finally we must mention WITCH, a guerrilla action group, who gave their acronym a variety of interpretations to suit the action of the moment.[1]

The second tendency represented by the radical label is *political lesbianism.* Here it applies only to those lesbians who considered their sexual option to be a conscious political choice, as opposed to the lesbian members of NOW, who, following the tradition of the Daughters of Bilitis,[2] had never really stated their problem in feminist terms. The lesbian contribution to radical feminism was essentially the work of two groups, both products of the new feminism, the Radicalesbians and the Furies. The lesbian issue is treated separately here because of the dilemma it has posed for feminists, and also because of our concern for faithfully depicting militant reality, since lesbian groups have maintained their existence independently of other feminist groups since 1970–72. During that period, a great debate on lesbianism divided the Women's Liberation movement, placing heterosexuals in opposition to what some saw as virulent proselytizing by lesbians.

Finally, the third tendency to be examined in this chapter is *feminist socialist radicalism*. It is characterized by a double allegiance to the political left and to feminism. Spokeswomen for this tendency include minority women and members of the Young Socialist Alliance (YSA), a spinoff from the old Socialist Workers party (SWP). (The SWP was born in 1925 when the Trotskyites first seceded from the Communist party.) The Young Socialist Alliance emerged in the 1960s as the leading leftist group after the elimination of the Students for a Democratic Society (SDS). From 1969, the YSA concerned itself with the revolutionary potential represented by the possible radicalization of the Women's Liberation movement. Its militants infiltrated feminist groups. Their ideology was codified in a work published in 1973, *Feminism and Socialism,* under the direction of Linda Jenness.

RADICAL FEMINISM

Radicalism

For radical feminist theorists, sexism is at the very root of patriarchal institutions. Whereas the liberal or egalitarian feminist perception of society sees merely failures in a system that is fundamentally perfectible, the radical feminist views the system itself as the incarnation of sexism, with everything being organized around intersexual relations established on the basis of power. The radical feminist theorists therefore set out to demonstrate the institutional nature of every relationship, to study the institutions thus revealed—sex, social class, family, marriage, prostitution, love, culture—and to expose the ways in which these are all interconnected. This premise explains the organic way in which their arguments are structured, and the impression of great coherence in the theories of those who carry this reasoning to its ultimate development, Ti-Grace Atkinson being the classic example. This also explains their marked taste for definitions that enable them to delimit and describe concepts.

"What's Personal Is Political"

There is no question that the richest contribution to feminist theoretical analysis comes to us from radical feminism. We saw in chapter 2 how, from

1970, some feminist authors took the dialectical materialist approach to history and adapted it to feminist terms. Kate Millett and Shulamith Firestone, in ambitious, groundbreaking books, were the first to attempt to define a revolutionary feminist theory. This concern for theory is characteristic, at this point, of all the militant feminists. Ti-Grace Atkinson, for example, perceived the development of a feminist theoretical framework as the indispensable prerequisite if the Women's movement were ever to become a political movement. Likewise, the Redstockings congratulated themselves on their initial choice of working first toward developing a general feminist political theory, and scorned the priorities of both egalitarian feminists and socialist feminists, which they summed up respectively in two gemlike phrases: "Jobs first, and all else will follow" . . . "Socialism first, and all else will follow."[3]

Political is obviously the key word here. In the context of relations between the sexes, everything is political: this is the fundamental postulate of radical feminist theory. The New York Radical Women and the Redstockings assert the political value of feelings, thus rendering the domain of individual women's lives open to ideological analysis and shattering the solitude to which women have always been condemned by society's judgment of their experience as "merely" personal. Taking up the same theme, Charlotte Bunch states two interrelated propositions: "There is no private domain of a person's life that is not political, and there is no political issue that is not ultimately personal."[4]

This synthesis operated by the radical feminists was perceived as a welcome innovation in the history of militantism. A new political style was born, establishing a connection between the personal domain, which had always been a feminine prerogative, and the outside world, making this outside world rediscover the domain of feelings, of which it had been deprived. For Shulamith Firestone, it was this dichotomy between the emotions and the intellect that had caused the downfall of the general radical protest movement of the 1960s. According to her, the orthodox radicals had got lost in ineffective abstraction or smug, sexist self-righteousness, while the hippies had gone astray in apolitical sentimentality. The feminist movement, for Firestone, thus was to be the salvation of the entire radical movement.

"Men Are the Enemy"

The first necessity of any organized protest movement is to identify the oppressor. As early as 1968, Beverly Jones and Judith Brown had insisted on this priority and defined it as male chauvinism. Following their lead, the radical feminists deliberated about who was responsible for the oppression of women and came up with the answer: men are the enemy.

We identify the agents of our oppression as men. . . . All other forms of exploitation and oppression (racism, capitalism, imperialism, etc.) are extensions of male supremacy. . . . *All men* receive economic, sexual and psychological benefits from male supremacy. *All men* have oppressed women.[5]

Here we reencounter the argument of anteriority, or "first cause" that had been used by Shulamith Firestone. In addition, the stress is laid on the integrality of the oppressor group as a whole, thereby labeling it as a *class* which includes each individual man personally known by every woman in a private relationship.

The word *class*, furthermore, appears formally in the second paragraph of the *Redstockings Manifesto,* somewhat mitigating the force of the clause identifying men the enemy. This bias appears in virtually all the writings of the radical feminists. Thus, Robin Morgan, preening herself over her declaration of hate for all men, legitimizes this hate as an "honorable political act" in a context of class dialectics: "The oppressed have a right to class hatred against the *class* that is oppressing them. . . . I *hate* that class."[6]

At this point in our review, it is possible to draw a first conclusion: in general, the radical feminist proposition "men are the enemy" is aimed not at the genetic individual man but rather at men collectively as an oppressor class. It is only this *class*, as an agent of oppression, which must be changed.

Here is where the "pro-woman" variant appears, consisting of exonerating women from blame. On this particular point, the Redstockings were protesting against the idea that men are supposedly helpless victims of their conditioning, while women, having internalized their oppression, are themselves held accountable for their own subjugation, to the degree that they are willing to accept it.

Women's submission is not the result of brainwashing, stupidity or mental illness but of continual, daily pressure from men. We do not need to change ourselves, but to change men.[7]

This "pro-woman" position is disconcerting, and can only create a dilemma within the mind of any logical feminist who interprets feminist philosophy as a refusal to see all personality narrowly defined in terms of sex. This "pro-woman" position leads to a forced choice between two illogical hypotheses. In the first, neither men nor women are victims of their conditioning, and if women do not need to change, it must be that men are by nature imperfect or inferior and women are by nature perfect or superior. In the second, both men and women are products of their culture, and in that case, it would appear that women's perfection or superiority must result from their conditioning, a reasoning which, paradoxically, would justify the current system of an assigned feminine sexual role, thereby legitimizing oppression and consecrating the status quo. But if the Redstockings draw anything from this reasoning, it would seem to be a concept that submissive behavior is externally induced. While recognizing the soundness of their interpretation that many women's acceptance of the feminine role is a survival solution, one cannot help being astonished to see a denial of any psychological effects of oppression. This denial indeed implies the existence of an inalterable, biologically inherited feminine superiority, and it smacks of female chauvinism, a heresy in feminism.

Much more coherent is the position of Ti-Grace Atkinson. Identifying the oppressor, she says, means seeking to know not only *who* is responsible for the oppression, but also *why* it exists, and *in what* it consists. Therefore, we must examine "the pathology of oppression." The use of this expression by both the radical feminists and the egalitarian feminists becomes a sort of "litmus test" for distinguishing these two groups from each other according to the way they perceive the issue of assigning blame. For the egalitarians, or liberal feminists, the pathology of oppression concerns only the oppressed woman, with the problem of culpability being effectively evaded, since blame is vaguely attributed to society or some institution. For those members of the radical feminist camp who do not subscribe to the "pro-woman" line, there are two aspects of this pathology: one affects the male who oppresses, the other the female who submits.

According to Ti-Grace Atkinson, the pathology of oppression arises out of a particular characteristic of human nature: "constructive imagination." Any individual person can only have a partial perception of the self, resulting in a sense of insecurity. Furthermore, she says, the person seizes upon the enormous gap between what the body can do and what the mind can imagine. The powers of the body and mind are in conflict within one organism. This second factor adds frustration to the first factor of insecurity. The individual finds solace for this insecurity and frustration in exercising oppression over others.

This process absorbs the free will of the victim and destroys the evidence that the aggressor and the victim are the Same. The principle of "metaphysical cannibalism" seemed to meet both needs of Man: to gain potency (power) and to vent frustration (hostility).[8]

This "metaphysical cannibalism," says Atkinson, has been exercised by men (and she does not mean *men* in the generic sense of *mankind*) against those human beings who bear the burden of the reproductive function. Men define these human beings solely in terms of their function, or as "females." Thus, the original rape was political: it consisted of dispossessing half the human race of its humanity.

From this it results that the pathology of the oppressor finds a correlation in the pathology of the oppressed. This postulate is thus set up in contradiction to the "pro-woman" line. Women play the role they have internalized —the "female-woman" role. If the role of the oppressor was to solve his dilemma by destroying the humanity of others, the role of the oppressed is to solve hers by destroying herself, physically or mentally.

The feminist dilemma is that it is as women—or "females"—that women are persecuted. . . . These individuals who are today defined as women must eradicate their own definition. Women must, in a certain sense, commit suicide.[9]

Ti-Grace Atkinson here merges the two terms, *women* and *females*, in a single oppressive reality, meaning by this fusion that the oppression of women is essentially due to their belonging to the female sex, in its capacity as the sex that performs gestation. Here we have a new view of the formation process of the bio-social self, in which the quest for identity necessitates self-annihilation or "suicide."

As victims of complementary systems of the same pathology, both men and women, in this view, must free themselves from predefined sexual roles. It is clear that the "metaphysical cannibalism" diagnosed by Ti-Grace Atkinson affects the whole human race; this tendency exists in the bud in women, too. In the course of development of civilization, men have simply been able to take unfair advantage of the reproductive capacity of women and turn it into a handicap. Therefore, "metaphysical cannibalism" is learned behavior, a form of mental derangement, and is not genetically determined. Ti-Grace consequently rejects the idea of eliminating all men.

I believe that the sex roles—both male and female—must be destroyed, not the individuals who happen to possess either a penis or a vagina, or both, or neither.[10]

Through the triple rejection of the traditional criteria of sexuality, bisexuality, and asexuality, the author summarily dismisses all sexist reasoning, avoiding any contradiction that might exist between denouncing the Freudian slogan Anatomy Is Destiny and talking about a supposed genetic inferiority of the male.

Robin Morgan expresses a similar point of view, all the while proclaiming her hate for men. The series of justifications that she gives for her aversion is merely a catalog of various "typically male" aggressions—"that's how men are!"—against the Women's movement, whether this "male style" behavior is represented by homosexual men, socialist men, the hippie culture, or the false sexual revolution. It is important not to let ourselves be blinded by the radical rhetoric; the hate for men proclaimed by Robin Morgan is not at all a homicidal hate. It is aimed only at a type of behavior, and can very well respond to the challenge issued by that other radical feminist, Dana Densmore, spokeswoman for the group Cell 16: "Who is saying men are the enemy?"[11]

This leads us, at this point in our study, to a second tentative conclusion: for the radical feminists, in general, the proposition "men are the enemy" is aimed at man not as a biological animal but as the incarnation and perpetuation of a behavior that has become the glue binding together a sexual class.

The exception to the rule would appear to be Valerie Solanas, expressing her views in the *SCUM Manifesto*. It is indeed man, the biological animal, that she attacks: this genetically inferior animal, resulting from a "biological accident," is said to be an "incomplete female . . . an emotional cripple," mired in his animal nature. This pitiable creature is afflicted by "pussy envy" (a parody on "penis envy"); psychically passive, he projects his hateful passivity on women, and through the act of coitus, tries to prove that, on the contrary, his nature is active. Trying to prove the unprovable, since an active nature is possessed only by females, he is condemned to an "eternal fuck," an act of sublimation by which he defends himself from his desire to be female.

Since a man's life is a desperate search to "complete himself," that is, to become female, he attempts to do this:

by claiming as his own all female characteristics—emotional strength and independence, forcefulness, dynamism, decisiveness, coolness, objectivity, assertiveness, courage, integrity, vitality, intensity, depth of character, grooviness, etc.— and projecting on women all male traits: vanity, frivolity, triviality, weakness, etc.[12]

As to the assertion that women fulfill themselves through motherhood, this is supposed by Solanas to be purely a projection of male fantasy, betraying a tenacious envy of the birth-giving function.

It goes without saying that the creativity of an inferior biological animal can only be disappointing. Hence, men are condemned for all the evils of the patriarchal society: war, money, marriage, prostitution, mental illness (linked with the patient's experience of his or her father), sexuality reduced to a solitary experience, hate and violence. Such are the broad outlines of the picture of the patriarchal society painted from the SCUM perspective. Published in 1968 in French by Maurice Girodias, who saw there an excellent commercial opportunity after Valerie Solanas had shot at Andy Warhol, the *SCUM Manifesto* was much talked about in France as well as in the United States, and was greeted as the expression of a characteristically feminine paranoia. It is high time to bring back the *SCUM Manifesto* to its true proportions. The author tried to do this in 1977 by writing an introduction to a new edition of the original text, freed from the accretions of Maurice Girodias.

If we examine the text more closely, we see that its analysis of the patriarchal reality is a parody. The author chooses to express herself through the channel of an outrageous conscious parody intended as exorcism. It is the well-known device of resorting to madness in order to expose the truth. The content itself is unquestionably a parody of the Freudian theory of femininity, where the word *woman* is replaced by *man,* and where, in a reversal of the psychological spectrum, the word *femininity* has been replaced by *masculinity.* All the clichés of Freudian psychoanalytical theory are here: the biological accident, the incomplete sex, "penis envy" which has become "pussy envy," and so forth. This reversal of the psychological spectrum plays with the Freudian explanation of projection-internalization, and this waggish exploit loses the reader in a maze of sexual labels, whether the behavior they describe is supposed to be innate—the masculinity of males, as reviewed and corrected by Valerie Solanas—or acquired—the femininity of women, which, in contrast to what French feminists call *féminitude* (womanliness), is none other than the projection of the masculinity of men! Here we have a case of absurdity being used as a literary device to expose an absurdity, that is, the absurd theory which has been used to give "scientific" legitimacy to patriarchy. To "misogyny" disguised under a pseudo-scientific mask, Solanas responds with "misandry" disguised under the same mask. What about her proposal that men should quite simply be eliminated, as a way of clearing the dead weight of misogyny and masculinity? This is the inevitable conclusion of the feminist pamphlet, in the same way that Jonathan Swift's proposal that Irish children (as useless mouths) should be fed to the swine was the logical conclusion of his bitter satirical pamphlet protesting famine in Ireland. Neither of the two proposals is meant to be taken seriously, and each belongs to the realm of political fiction, or even science fiction, written in a desperate effort to arouse public consciousness.

An Analysis of the Patriarchal Reality

The Institution of Sexual Intercourse. We have seen the important place given to the issue of sexuality in radical feminist consciousness raising, with "The Myth of the Vaginal Orgasm." Sex and sexuality remain the main themes of radical feminist theory, for they are seen as the point of departure and the kingpin of the system they denounce. Responding to egalitarian feminists who were disturbed by the granting of so much importance to sex in the debate, Ti-Grace Atkinson pointed out with some justice that if society defines women by this as their prime characteristic—if women are equated with sex—then the relationship between feminism and sex is obvious.

This concern for bringing sex into the discussion seems to have had several purposes. Above all, it was important to break the law of silence surrounding this subject, which remained taboo for women until the 1960s. From this sundering of the silence there would arise a redefinition by women of their own sexuality. This explosion would give birth to a new firm notion of feminine self-determination, and would end the paradoxical situation in which women accepted a definition of their sexuality imposed by men, or more precisely, by one man, Sigmund Freud. This redefinition by women of their sexuality would have a double implication: it would affirm women's claim to the dual rights of sexual pleasure and personal freedom; by the same token, it would negate the dual myths of the frigidity and the inferiority of the female sex. For Mary Jane Sherfey, there is demonstrated proof that women are sexually insatiable; if there is such a thing as feminine frigidity, it comes from a lack of prolonged and frequent coitus. Women, says this feminist psychiatrist, were not made for monogamy, even less so than men. She believes that in the beginning, there was unbridled female sexuality, and postulates: "The rise of modern civilization, while resulting from many causes, was contingent on the suppression of the inordinate cyclic sexual drive of women." [13]

Hence the ban on clitoral orgasm, hence the focus on the reproductive function, hence monogamy; in other words, this suppression was at the very origin of the patriarchal system.

In modern-day patriarchal society, sexuality is perceived by Ti-Grace Atkinson and the radical feminists as organized around sexual intercourse, a political institution which still has the function of guaranteeing the survival of the species. When this institution is threatened by women's claims to sexual freedom, the patriarchy supports it by the myth of the vaginal orgasm. The institutionalization of sexual intercourse is antifeminist, since it does not take into account the reality of women's eroticism, the true erogenous zone for women being the clitoris and not the vagina. The Freudian theory of feminine sexuality, which stipulates that women's sexual maturity occurs through the transfer of sexual pleasure from the clitoris to the vagina, is perceived as the negation of feminine sexuality, in the same way as in the known historical practice of the clitoridectomy, the surgical operation in which the Freudian metaphor is literally carried out. In addition, this form of the relation between the sexes has inexorably driven women into the roles of wife and mother. Therefore, as we are told by Susan Lyndon, [14] there does indeed exist such a thing as the "politics of orgasm" in the service of sexual politics.

The proposals of radical feminists have often been distorted, lumped together and interpreted as a pure and simple rejection of sexuality. In reality, the feminist rejection expressed here concerns solely the institutionalization of sexual intercourse, as focused on reproduction and the denial of woman's right to orgasm.

Class. From the institutionalization of sexual intercourse, whose social purpose is the survival of the species, there arises the system of sexual classes. We have seen the importance of this theme of sexual classes among the feminist writers who devote themselves to consciousness-raising or who reexamine the past under the sign of oppression. Following the lead of Shulamith Firestone, the radical feminists assert the primordial and universal existence of an all-inclusive system of sexual classes. According to them, sexual class precedes all other systems of oppression, since racial minority groups are just historical accidents and the struggle of the proletariat is merely an economic development; sexual class cuts across all other classes.

The political theory of Ti-Grace Atkinson has the merit of being anchored specifically in the concept of women as a sexual class, and of proposing one of the rare definitions of this concept. Women, she says, are first of all a political class, and this fact is the very reason for the existence of feminism. So what does she mean by "political class"? "Individuals grouped together by other individuals as a function of the grouping individuals, depriving the grouped individuals of their human status." [15]

The feminine political class, she specifies, is not the same as the female biological class defined by its reproductive capacity, but rather the sociological class of women, whose reproductive capacity, intended by nature to be a contingent function, has been transformed under the decree of "metaphysical cannibalism" into a social function, that is, an imperative duty to society, with political sanctions. In this way, women are victims of a process of dehumanization and objectification; defined solely in terms of their function, they are no longer classified as humans but as functional objects. Radical feminists make a distinction between the reproductive *capacity* and the reproductive *function,* seeming to base it in the fact that nature, as the French feminist Evelyne Sullerot points out, provides for alternating periods of fertility and infertility, obliging us to recognize that "nature has programmed women's sexual pleasure independently from the reproductive purpose." [16]

The notion of function occupies an important place in radical feminist thought, for if the function of a woman as sociological object is procreation, then procreation is perceived as the essential impediment, not only to woman's availability for work, as with the egalitarian feminists, but to her very freedom and dignity as a human being. It is the unnecessary handicap by which men, even apart from any hypothesis of patriarchal revolution, have been able to keep women subjugated. It is in this same sense that we must understand Robin Morgan in *Going Too Far* when she likens women to a "colonized people," with the theft of territory involved in any colonization being translated here by a theft of their bodies.

The problem of women's control of their reproductive function is therefore, according to radical feminist theory, inseparable from the problem of sexual class. The body and the reproductive capacity are here posed in terms of property. For Ti-Grace Atkinson, the woman is to the fetus what the sculptor is to a work of art. For both, the right of property implies an essential freedom: the choice to destroy the work in progress or to complete it. Thus, any woman can accept the donation of sperm—which becomes her property—and can decide whether or not to exercise her reproductive capacity with regard to this donation and whether or not to carry the process through to its full term. The right of property ceases at the point when the work is completed and begins its own independent existence, when the process ends of either artistic production or biological reproduction. In the latter case, this point is reached when the pregnancy reaches its full term and the fetus becomes an autonomous human being to whom the woman has chosen to give the status of child.

The woman is seen as the property owner of her reproductive capacity, over which she should have total liberty to exercise her own free will. The social function of reproduction as conceived in the patriarchal society, that is, having a political purpose (to maintain the birthrate) and governed by abortion legislation, is seen as denying women's liberty to exercise their own free will and property rights, and therefore, as oppressing women. Following this reasoning, in order to state her claims in terms appropriate to the situation of her American sisters, the radical feminist theoretician takes a position in the national legal framework. Here, she necessarily follows the same process as the egalitarian or liberal feminists and denounces the abortion laws as unconstitutional. She alleges that these laws violate the Fourteenth Amendment of the American Constitution for the reason that they attack the rights of women to life, liberty, and property. These laws have only one reason for their existence: to enable the patriarchy to perpetuate the categorization of women as a sexual class.

The radical feminists are interested in the notion of class not only for its sexual implications but also because of the mentality it represents. The most serious contribution on this point comes from the lesbian group called the Furies. Since their analysis is not based on lesbianism but on general feminism, we will examine it in this chapter. Rita Mae Brown, for instance, denounces the inadequacy of the Marxist definition of class because it sees class only in terms of the means of production. The concept of class implies, according to her, a certain behavior, a set of basic ideas about life and a set of experiences that confirm these ideas. Although, by their sex, women all belong to the same sexual class, they also belong, through ties of marriage or family, to different social classes, whose ideas and behaviors they reproduce.

In this way, middle-class women engaged in the movement have a class behavior toward their militant sisters which they refuse to recognize. Within the primary sexual class, they constitute a subclass, which Ti-Grace Atkinson calls an identification group because of the imitative behavior that characterizes it. According to Coletta Reid and Charlotte Bunch,[17] this behavior is oppressive for women from modest backgrounds, since it is anchored in an essential idea: the supremacy of class. This arrogance can be expressed as pity for their militant sister's difficulties in public speaking, as an hysterical fixation on their own feelings, as affectation, or even as ultrarevolutionary behavior involving utter scorn for material goods. This imitation of poverty is perceived by the poor as gratuitous mockery and the worst kind of insult.

The feminists of the group called the Furies state that it is essential for middle-class militants to recognize their mistakes in acting in this way, and correct their behavior. In their view, refusing to allow self-criticism within the movement would perpetuate the divisions between women that are so useful to the patriarchy; in contrast, rejecting learned class behavior would mean refusing to perpetuate the socialization process undergone in the family, one of the major themes of radical feminist thought.

Marriage and the Family. The family is perceived as the basic cell of the system of oppression. Kate Millett defines it as follows:

a patriarchal unit within a patriarchal whole. . . . [It] effects control and conformity where political and other authorities are insufficient. As the fundamental instrument and the foundation unit of patriarchal society, the family and its roles are prototypical.[18]

As a "patriarchal unit," the family is seen as the site of a triple oppression of women: sexual, economic, and psychological. First, it is the site of sexual oppression because, as a biological family, it is essentially a reproductive cell, set up on the basis of the social function expected of women. The radical feminist protest, again, is not aimed at the reproductive *capacity* but at the *function* which, by means of the family, has drafted women into the service of institutionalized reproduction. Thus, for Marilyn Salzman Webb,[19] the woman in the reproductive cell is a "sow." At first sight, this expression appears to refer back to the physical violence done to women in past generations by multiple pregnancies, rather than to the present situation of contraception. The reference to animal nature is nevertheless expressed in the present to denounce, it seems, the psychological and cultural cost exacted by "THE" function, and the fact that science, undeniable proof of the superiority of the human race but manipulated by men, has not sought earlier to control biology and has left women essentially on the same level as the females of animal species.

As a "patriarchal unit," the family consecrates a relationship of possession. Founded on a division of labor—paid outside work for the man, unpaid domestic work for the woman—it is the site of the economic oppression of women. But the proof of the allegation that the family is the basic economic cell in a patriarchal society had already been demonstrated by Engels, who recognized the man as the owner, the woman as the means of production, and the child as labor. Although radical feminists deem it unnecessary to dwell on this fact, they take care nonetheless to point out the inadequacy of the classic socialist analysis. For them, it is important to go beyond the economic facts, since there exists a level of family reality that is not directly related to economics.

According to Shulamith Firestone, it is a matter of the psychosexual reality, that is, the psychology of power that develops along the lines of a domination/submission scheme, characteristic of relationships between the sexes and between the generations within the nuclear family. For her, as a good radical, to protest against the psychosexual reality of the nuclear family is to attack at the very roots of the psychology of power and the class system. Hence, she gives a feminist reading of the Oedipus and Electra complexes, in terms of power and adaptation to sexual politics. The author explains the initial identification of the little boy or girl with the mother as being the perception of belonging to an oppressed community, with the mother and children being under the domination of the head of the family. Conversely, the later identification with the father is to be interpreted as the desire to imitate the one who is in a position of power. The son then betrays the mother and leaves the oppressed class; however, from this betrayal, he will retain a sense of guilt, which will affect his behavior toward women. The daughter also rejects the mother, a figure who is too familiar and without prestige in comparison with the father, who seems covered with glory. Two attitudes are then possible: either she tries to rob power from the father by seducing him with feminine wiles, or if she has a brother, she imitates him and becomes a tomboy, until she reaches puberty. Then, however, recognizing that the trick is not working, she chooses conformity; she identifies with women. In this way, the process of socialization has once again done its work. The psychology of power has operated in the sense desired by the patriarchal state, which governs its citizens through the intermediary of the heads of families.

It is this socialization function of the nuclear family which, in the view of the radical thinkers, must necessarily entail a recognition by revolutionary feminists of the problem of the oppression of children, with whom Shulamith Firestone says women themselves are identified, as "ex-child[ren] and still oppressed child-women." Let us note that, again, the idea is expressed in terms of power and oppression, for the radical feminist is essentially oriented toward a political and social upheaval that will be the work of women and that will end in a situation of nonpower.

The evaluation of the nuclear family as the basic cell of the system of oppression was to lead to another debate, in which marriage was defined as "a construct of the family"; that is, in Ti-Grace Atkinson's sense of the word *construct,* "a kind of sub-institution within another institution." Founded on the theory of the maternal instinct—another myth created by men and put into service regarding "THE" function of women—marriage is one of the intersexual alliances that divide women from each other. It wrenches them out of their primary class and, through a process of identification with the oppressor with whom they share certain privileges inherent in their economic class, it prevents the confrontation between the sexual political classes that is called for by the radical feminists. Marriage is thus seen as antifeminist, and from 1970, Ti-Grace Atkinson began pushing for urgent debate on this question in the name of logic and coherence. The problem of coherence naturally refers back to the basic proposition that "what's personal is political." However, in spite of this assertion, militant women, including some of the most implacable advocates of hate for all men, continued to take husbands, and the debate was avoided. One original attempt should nevertheless be mentioned. Members of a group called the Feminists, preserving their own logic internally, inserted their opposition to marriage into the group's organizational structure by recourse to a discriminatory quota system limiting the number of married women to one-third of the group's total membership.

In spite of this initiative, the great debate on marriage has not yet been fully accomplished. The question seems to arouse considerable embarrassment among radical feminists, to judge by their elaborate evasions; marriage ought to be abolished, but not before replacement structures have been found for women. By definition, their position is hardly any clearer or more comfortable than that of the egalitarian feminists who proclaim, without recognizing the massive dismantling effort implied: "let's keep the institution but abolish its excesses."

Prostitution. It was inevitable that the debate about marriage should lead to a discussion of prostitution, since that is seen as a corollary of marriage in the patriarchal society: "As long as you're going to have compulsive marriage and compulsive families, I think you're going to have prostitution."[20]

This declaration from a former prostitute acknowledges the double standard of ethics that reigns over patriarchal marriage—the desire for change experienced by the man is recognized and accepted, while the same desire experienced by the woman is rendered illegitimate—as well as the more tolerant attitude of the wife who finds that, if her husband is going to cheat anyway, a prostitute is less threatening to her marriage than a mistress would be.

For radical feminists, prostitution is an integral part of the patriarchal system, one of the main gears that makes all the wheels go round smoothly. Following the lead of Simone de Beauvoir, Mary Daly and Ti-Grace Atkinson recall, in particular, the support given by the Christian religion to prostitution as a necessary evil whose suppression would lead to debauchery and thereby entail a complete breakdown of society.

A creation of patriarchal man, prostitution is presented as the institution *par excellence* exemplifying a system based on "two weights, two measures," for it not only supports the double standard in marriage but also integrates it into its own structure: although it is masculine demand that creates the feminine supply, the opprobrium does not attach to the man but to the woman. Thus the proof is furnished, once again, that in a patriarchal society, man is judged in terms other than sexual, whereas woman, "the daughter of Venus," is forever mired in sexuality.

Cynically evoking American values, Ti-Grace Atkinson denounces another aspect of the system of "two weights, two measures," inherent in prostitution: financial success and social ostracism. Prostitution is successful financially. According to "J.," the ex-prostitute speaking out in "Prostitution: A Quartet for Female Voices," a professional working in chic neighborhoods annually took in $40,000 more (in 1972) than the average salary offered to a woman who was not "on the game," more evidence of the value attached to prostitution by the patriarchy. Nevertheless, in spite of their financial success, earned through the fruits of their labors in return for services rendered, prostitutes are kept apart from the visible economy and forced into a hidden market.

Prostitution, as an incarnation or support of the system of double standards and an integral part of the patriarchal society, therefore has a political function. For the man who uses its services, it signifies the acquisition of power, simultaneously putting down both women and sex. Ellen Strong[21] reveals the torrents of hatred that flow from the mouths of her distinguished clients. "J." denounces the violence of the words and acts of the men of the South, murdering the prostitute in the flesh and heaping her with abuse in the language of their shame. This will to power over women thus has psychosexual roots, going back to man's ancestral misogyny in the face of woman's occult shaman force or woman as the incarnation of impure, filthy sex.

It is through the act of purchase that patriarchal man humiliates the prostitute whose services he acquires. Letting oneself be bought implies accepting all the humiliation imposed by the buyer. Thus the prostitute sells not only her services, but her soul as well. It is probably this aspect of prostitution which, in the eyes of the radical feminists, reveals the true nature of what has been the political position of women within marriage. For the ex-prostitutes converted to radical feminism, the prostitute is freer and more honest than the wife. In exercising her profession, the prostitute can refuse her client; within the patriarchal marriage, the wife cannot. The prostitute recognizes the reality of the transaction; the wife pretends not to see it.

Through the purchase of power and the degradation of the prostitute, the political function of prostitution hides another aspect: that of dissuasion. In the view of Ti-Grace Atkinson, prostitution has always been presented by men as the only alternative to the feminine role. In other words, women have been subjected to the following blackmail: either respectability in a life confined to the home, or opprobrium in a life of independence and violence. The woman must pay with her body and soul for autonomy and economic success, and the streetwalker is there as a constant reminder of the price that has to be paid.

Prostitution is the specter of economic success for women: institutionalized rape in its most public, brutal form.[22]

In denouncing prostitution as a crime, radical feminism is rising up against the thesis that it is a form of antisocial, regressive feminine behavior. As a crime of the patriarchy, prostitution, like rape, is the quintessential expression of the class relationship existing between the sexes, and the key to all economic and political analysis of the categorization of women as a class.

Love

In virtually identical terms, Shulamith Firestone and Ti-Grace Atkinson insist on the necessity of dealing with the issue of love, since they see it as central to the oppression of women. Love, they say, has a political function, which is to persuade the oppressed one to accept her or his oppression. To be convinced of this, says Ti-Grace Atkinson, one only has to consider the importance of love in the political structure of religion, where the innumerable poor who are followers of the Judeo-Christian tradition are exhorted to love their neighbor and where slaves are told to respond to their slavery with love and nonviolence. In this case, love is unilateral in nature, being directed from the oppressed toward the oppressor. Considering the insane incongruity of the couple formed of oppressed/oppressor, and the consequent isolation of the victim, the author concludes that the woman in love can only be in a psychopathological state resulting from the man's exercising his prestigious power of magnetism over the woman deprived of her humanity.

The woman is drawn to→ attracted by→desirous of→in love with→the man. She is powerless, he is powerful. The woman is instinctively trying to recoup her definitional and political losses by fusing with the enemy. "Love" is the woman's pitiful, deluded attempt to attain the human: by fusing, she hopes to blur the male/female role dichotomy, and that a new division of the human class might prove more equitable. She counts on the illusion she has spun out of herself in order to be able to accept the fusion, to be transferred to the whole and, thus, that the new man will be garbed now equally in her original illusion.[23]

This search for androgyny is equivalent to suicide since, in its unilateralness as proposed by Ti-Grace Atkinson, it consists, for the woman, of abandoning the last vestiges of her identity, an identity that has become contemptible according to the image of herself that she has internalized.

From this analysis comes the radical feminist idea that the feminist solution requires the rejection of love. In this view, there can be no amorous solution to the feminist dilemma, for a woman cannot put love into practice unless she is a woman in the sociological sense of the term, that is, subordinated. However, there is an ambiguity that Ti-Grace Atkinson does not really resolve, since she does not specify whether this rejection refers only to love as it now exists in the patriarchal society, or to love in the absolute. In other words, is she denying love itself?

The position of Shulamith Firestone is undoubtedly less equivocal. For her, there are indeed happy couples, and love does exist. She defines it as a situation of total emotional vulnerability in which the self seeks fulfillment in merging with the other, and vice versa. For her, this does not mean becoming incorporated in the other, but "an exchange between two selves" and mutual fulfillment. However, happiness is rare, since for every ephemeral experience of fulfillment, there are ten painful experiences of destruction.

Shulamith Firestone here adopts Theodor Reik's analysis, but is careful to make a distinction: the love that is analyzed by Reik and studied here is the destructive form of this emotion, that is, the distortion of it made by our society; therefore it is not really true love. In its destructive aspect, love comes from dissatisfaction within the ego, born of a conflict between the perceived self and the ideal self, this tension being temporarily resolved by a transferred ego-identification and substitution of the beloved for the ideal self. Love inevitably dies because neither the beloved nor the lover can live up to the imagined ideal ego. Why does it have to be this way? Firestone's answer is that there is a political explanation. In our society, she suggests, love is corrupt because it takes place in a context of inequality. This unhealthy form of love is romantic love in which the man must place the woman he loves higher than all others in order to justify his own descent into the lower, unworthy caste. By definition, says the author, men are incapable of loving; but her radical feminist observation seems to refer less to biological man, influenced by his male hormones, than to sociological man, affected forever by his early relationship with his mother. In her insistence on the psychosexual cost of this early trauma, the militant writer seems to be suggesting a new argument justifying the elimination of the nuclear family.

As for women, their emotion is seen to be perverted by the same class phenomenon that renders men incapable of loving. In a patriarchy that defines females as an inferior parasite caste, women are nothing without the approval of men. Thrown into a manhunt, women seek emotional security and identity as well as economic security. For them, love and status are inseparable, and, as Shulamith Firestone remarks objectively, men have good reason to say that women do not love them for themselves but only for what they can offer. In addition, stress is laid on the destructive effects suffered by the woman. Seeking to resemble the ideal image that the man worships in her, she strives not to be her real self even while measuring the cost of the overpriced deception. Here we reencounter the thesis of suicide proposed by Ti-Grace Atkinson.

One last question remains to be asked: would there still be idealization if the political context of love disappeared? Yes, in part, replies the author, referring to the lover's perception in the beloved of qualities that other people do not see. But, she adds, we must not mistake keen perception for idealization. What is destructive is blind idealization: "Thus it is not the process of love itself that is at fault, but its *political,* i.e. unequal *power* context."[24]

This is a particularly important conclusion, for radical feminism has often been lumped together and simplistically misinterpreted as a pure and simple rejection of love. Admittedly, the *SCUM Manifesto* condemns men as genetically incapable of loving. Granted, there were proclamations of hate for all men. And certainly, even after recognizing that women, in their vulnerable situation, need love, Shulamith Firestone declared that men were not worth the trouble of being loved. But before jumping to hasty conclusions based on literal interpretations, it is important to resituate all these radical declarations (except for the *SCUM Manifesto*) within the context of the works in which they appear. As we said above, doing so demonstrates that the term *man* is never taken in its strictly biological sense —an interpretation which would forcibly lead to the conclusion that the heterosexual dilemma is insoluble—but rather is loaded with sociological implications, leaving the door open for hope and change. In recent years, it has become evident that radical feminists are aware of the danger implied in an outright rejection of love, if it is defined as an equal vulnerability of two interacting partners. In this regard, significant proposals are offered respectively by Joyce O'Brien and Patricia Mainardi, who both claim to follow the "pro-woman" line:

If a women's revolution is possible, why not love? . . . There was a certain sector of the movement at one time that encouraged women to break the chains of that oppressive union because love between men and women was impossible. Wouldn't it be ironic if, among those women now leaving their marriages, it turned out to be because they now saw love as possible, not impossible, and they decided to go out after it?[25]

I believe women—and men—would like love, security, companionship, respect and a long term commitment to each other. Women rarely get much of this, in marriage or out, but we *want* it.[26]

Culture. The most serious study of culture vis-à-vis feminism is that of Shulamith Firestone in her book, *The Dialectic of Sex.* Her study analyzes three main facets: the subculture of romantic sentimentalism, the aesthetic aspect of culture in its present state, and the historical dialectic between the aesthetic mode and the technological mode of dealing with the world around us.

The subculture of romantic sentimentalism, as spread by the media, is, *par excellence,* an instrument for the socialization of women. For this reason, it increases proportionately with women's demands for liberation. It is organized around three main components: eroticism; "sex privatization," or the identification of personality with sex; and the beauty ideal. Through the mutual reinforcement of these three factors, romantic sentimentalism has acted to operate a double denigration of women, who, as the focus of an "erotomania," are depicted by an image that is not only unrealistic but is also the very embodiment of sex appeal.

Eroticism is thus made a fundamental value. Sex and desire are turned into a sacramental ritual, with man for its beneficiary and woman for its cult object. Consecrated as a ritual love object, a woman cannot be sexually fulfilled except through identification with her owner. Eroticism thereby maintains both the dependent status of women and the system of sexual classes. These two phenomena are likewise maintained by the second component of romantic sentimentalism, sex privatization.

The process is insidious. When a man exclaims, "I love blondes!" all the secretaries in the vicinity sit up; they take it personally because they have been sex-privatized. The blonde one feels personally complimented because she has come to measure her worth through the physical attributes that differentiate her from other women. She no longer recalls that any physical attribute you could name is shared by many others, that these are accidental attributes not of her own creation, that her sexuality is shared by half of humanity.[27]

Thus, these women have become incapable of distinguishing their own individual personalities from their sex. Sex privatization, which rests on a confusion between sexuality and individuality, is seen by Shulamith Firestone as a manipulation technique that is consciously used by men as a means of blinding women to their common interests as a class. The third component is the fashionable ideal of beauty, which drives all women to look alike. This standardization in itself has a political function since it stereotypes women into a class with predictable reactions. "They look alike, they think alike, and even worse, they are so stupid they believe they are not alike."[28]

Shulamith Firestone's discussion ends with an important point, corroborating the fact that the radical feminist position on love, as seen in the previous section, had been misinterpreted. The point she makes is a warning against any simplistic or extremist interpretation, and is addressed to both militants and the public. To the radical feminist who gets riled by sexual provocation, Firestone says that it is not a question of putting beauty itself on trial. The issue is not denying the beauty of a face on the cover of *Vogue,* but knowing whether the beauty of this face is individually human or is a stereotyped object. Likewise, she says, what is demanded is not the elimination of emotion, but rather its redistribution. This problem will be looked at again when we study the implications of the sexual revolution, but already we can see that the proposals of the radical feminists contain more nuances of meaning than the public likes to admit.

As for the aesthetic aspect of culture in its present state, it presents us with the image of the patriarchal reality in the sense that it replicates male supremacy. Our culture is essentially male for two reasons: first, because it has been fueled by the love of women, as its "creative muses"; second, because women have never had the chance to see themselves culturally, through their own eyes.

In this domain, then, our culture is accused of presenting a masculine vision of things: even though some men have tried to capture the spirit of the entire range of human experience, they have done so from a male point of view. The accusers charge that this treatment not only reflects a male-dominated reality but also perpetuates it and is the propaganda agent for it. In the aesthetic aspect, as in the aspect of romantic sentimentalism, our culture has been corrupted in order to perform a political mission. Shulamith Firestone inevitably cites those who have come to be viewed as bastions of virility, such as Mailer, Heller, and Donleavy, but a more original target was attacked by the members of a female rock band devoted to women's liberation. A group of feminist musicians from Chicago denounced the sexist connotation given to rock music by leftist intellectual men in order to fraternize with men from the working classes. Seeking a means of common cultural expression, they could only find this in a shared privilege, that is, their masculine domination and hate for women. From this it followed that rock music became a refuge for sexism, a male counterrevolution in which aggression and rape were substituted for love.

In the radical feminist view, such developments can only aggravate the rampant imbalance in the patriarchal culture. Art is suffering a mutilation: the sexual schism has provoked an inauthentic women's art and a corrupt men's art. A healthy art must integrate both halves of human experience. Women need to bring their contribution to art as men have previously done, and Shulamith Firestone, writing in 1970, expressed great hope for the decade that was just beginning.

The same idea of a sexual schism is emphasized in her study of the historical dialectic of culture. With a skillful use of all the radical feminist concepts, Shulamith Firestone makes a distinction between the aesthetic mode, in which the individual denies the limits of reality by creating an imaginary illusion that substitutes for it, and the technological mode, in which the individual overcomes the constraints of reality by effectively controlling its workings. From this distinction arises a comprehensive definition, according to which culture, in the abstract, is the result of the synthesis and the dialectic between these two modes. This abstract definition of culture is presented as a vision of the ideal, which serves to highlight the perversion of our present patriarchal culture, subject to sexual duality. In the patriarchal system, in fact, the dialectic of sex has played a cultural role, to the degree that aesthetics have been sexually identified as women's domain, while technology belongs to men. The aesthetic mode has thus been relegated to a secondary level, to the benefit of the technological mode, from which women are excluded. Modern man has specialized in science, which has been made purely objective, the perfect symbol of "a long cultural disease based on the sex dualism."

The radical feminist author has thus proposed to demonstrate the political corruption of culture, as a patriarchal institution that has been perverted in the same way as all the others. As the ultimate manifestation of sexism, the dialectic of culture crowns the patriarchal edifice, superimposed on the dialectic of sex and the dialectic of class. Therefore, in her view, it will require nothing less than a radical feminist revolution to put an end to these three evils.

The Radical Feminist Revolution

According to the scheme envisioned by Shulamith Firestone, the radical feminist revolution would occur in three phases: sexual revolution, economic revolution, and cultural revolution.

The Sexual Revolution. The sexual revolution is to be the result of the feminist rebellion, whose troops will be joined by the young and ethnic minorities, that is, all those whose oppression has a biological basis in age or race. The feminist revolution therefore poses the problem of separatism, with the appearance, in particular, of the notion of "sisterhood." This notion implies two concepts: an assumption that it is born out of oppression, and a connotation of militancy.

"Sisterhood" is the notion of sisters uniting in their oppression, with their union based on transcending the economic class differences that divide them, and on recognizing their common status as members of the same sexual class. Sisterhood is distinguished from brotherhood in that the notion of males sharing fraternal feelings is never the result of men's being oppressed solely for being men as such, and excludes any participation in male-dominated organizations. The latter point is made by Mary Daly, the feminist theologian, addressing herself to nuns. One could also imagine that she is criticizing those women whose first allegiance is to the political Left and not to feminism.

Consequently, and it is this which constitutes its primary militant aspect, the unity of sisters means separatism, "a qualitative leap into the new space and time of radical feminism."[29]

This definition is accompanied by a reinterpretation of religious terminology, loading it with different semantic connotations. Here we have an attempt at linguistic liberation, illustrating the effort made by new feminist militants to put words into the service of their ideology. For example, in Daly's text, the year marking the beginning of the era of radical feminism (dating from the publication of her Feminist Postchristian Introduction to *The Church and the Second Sex*) becomes 1975 A.F., for the Latin *Anno Feminarum* (era of women). However, the year the book was written is designated in traditional terms as 1968 A.D., *Anno Domini* (the year of Our Lord), the Christian era, when feminism and Catholicism had not yet appeared to her to be mutually inconsistent. In another example, *sisterhood* is defined as *an exodus community,* to emphasize the notion of leaving the mainstream and the implication of separatism. The prototype of this was a group of nuns who walked out of the Harvard Memorial Church on 14 November 1971 at the instigation of Mary Daly. Separatist radical feminism situates itself in a "space/time" (the two concepts cannot be disassociated) located outside the boundaries of the patriarchal space/time where the community of men is still living in *Anno Domini*. For another writer, Dana Densmore, the exodus of women is also the best medicine for women as an antidote to the problem of men.

Men are not our "enemies," and we should refuse to play "enemy" games with them. If they ridicule us . . . we must laugh and walk out.

Only the march of the whole movement can force the deep reevaluation that will enable such men to adjust to the reality of women as people and learn to deal in an adult way with their fears and insecurities.[30]

While Mary Daly and Dana Densmore were exhorting women to exodus, the Redstockings called for women to unite against male supremacy. This is the second militant aspect: *sisterhood* means struggle against sexist institutions, whose downfall implies their replacement by other structures under the sole aegis of women. How would feminists manage to destroy the existing institutions? No clear answer is given, but the militants believe in the development of a broad mass movement of women and the emergence of new mental attitudes favoring the demolition of the old power structures. It is on this issue that radical feminism differs from egalitarian feminism and feminist socialism. Radical feminists are not at all interested in the "power sharing" so dear to the hearts of egalitarian feminists; instead, they are demanding an all-out effort to uproot all domination and elitism in human relations. The true sexual revolution, in the view of the radical feminists, is the one that will abolish the very notion of power.

Once that is accomplished, it seems that separatism is to end. It can be ended by the pure and simple elimination of men; this is the extreme case implied by the *SCUM Manifesto*. For other theorists, it will end because women, strong in their new identity and solidarity, will have accomplished the sexual revolution in their primary concerns, and can then begin again to interact with men, individually and collectively. Therefore, separatism is supposed to last only through the phase of sexual revolution; it must necessarily end so that the next phases of economic and cultural revolution can be accomplished.

But what should the sexual revolution be, in order to guarantee the destruction of sexist institutions? For all radical feminists, it begins with the body, since it is through woman's body, encumbered with the social duty of reproduction, that patriarchal man has been able to create the sexual class of women. Robin Morgan envisages women reconquering their own personal bodies, a speculum in one hand and a mirror in the other. For Shulamith Firestone, the sexual revolution must liberate women from the tyranny of their reproductive function, and gestation and child rearing must be shared throughout the whole of society, between men and women. An interesting gradual phasing is set up starting from existing means, with family planning and child care centers belonging to a transition period; but it is equally clear that the utopian postrevolutionary society will have to find a radical solution to the problems of gestation and child rearing. This solution is to be artificial reproduction.

As drastic as it might sound, such a solution has been seriously proposed, not only by the militants of the *SCUM Manifesto* in an antimale pamphlet on eugenics, but also by numerous other radical feminists. However, this proposal is not made without some qualms. Shulamith Firestone, for instance, recognizes the danger that such a solution would represent in society as presently constituted, governed by the psychology of power. But the door cannot be closed on innovation by pleading the excuse of an imperfect present; the solution of artificial reproduction must be considered to have a place in a postrevolutionary future, when attitudes will have changed and the notion of power will have quite another meaning. This same idea is defended by Marge Piercy in *Small Changes,* denouncing the damage done by Aldous Huxley to the cause of artificial reproduction in his novel *Brave New World,* and the readiness with which our society has accepted his pessimistic conclusions in order to perpetuate the status quo. As for Ti-Grace Atkinson, she orders the entire society to go back and face its responsibilities in the matter of childbirth. From now on, men can no longer impose gestation on women. Society, says she, should decide on the necessary birthrate, but it should leave women free to choose gestation or not. To achieve the desired birthrate, therefore, society should fulfill its needs by using the method of test-tube babies! Here we have an outright refusal to consider reproduction as a duty to society. This is coupled with a will to use science for the purpose of increasing "the natural contingence of women's reproductive capabilities," in Shulamith Firestone's phrase. Besides recognizing women's right to nonmotherhood, this suggestion offers an essentially political proposal: the destruction of the very foundations on which rests the categorization of women as a sexual class.

In this same attack, a serious blow is dealt to the family as the basic unit cell of reproduction. The sexual revolution also implies the destruction of the family in its other roles as the basic unit cell of economic and psychological oppression. We must abolish the division of labor and the economic dependence of women and children on which the family is based, since this abolition is the necessary prerequisite for the disappearance of the psychology of power and its psychological and cultural consequences. At this point, the phase of cultural revolution begins.

To replace monogamous marriage, a whole gamut of options is proposed. Among those listed by Charlotte Bunch are women's communes, group marriages, cooperative houses, and extended families. To these, Shulamith Firestone adds celibacy, cohabitation, and a detailed catalog of new-style households. It is extremely important for the radical feminist theorists to throw off the shackles of the nuclear family, the basic unit of patriarchal power.

The elimination of the family as the nurturer of the psychology of power is to be followed by the total integration of women and children into all sectors of society. All institutions based on sex or age segregation are to be forbidden. As for the employment sector, we shall have to be content with temporary measures while waiting for the socialist revolution, but the idea of a salary for the housewife is rejected outright, since this would not rectify the fundamentally sexist division of labor.

When cultural distinctions between the sexes and the generations have been abolished within the family and in society, sexual repression, which keeps women and children in their place, would no longer have any reason to exist. Now we arrive at the fourth implication of the sexual revolution, sexual freedom—that is, the freedom for women and children to live sexual lives however they wish. Paradoxically, this can include a rejection of sexuality. Such, for example, is the drastic option proposed by the *SCUM Manifesto*, while Dana Densmore calls for removing the "stigma" attached to virginity, invented, she says, by patriarchal man to drive women to perform their social duty of reproduction. The sexual revolution, according to her, must deprogram women from their conditioning, which has brainwashed them to feel the sex drive as a powerful urge, and retrain them to see it as a minor need. Ti-Grace Atkinson goes even further, asserting that if feminism is to maintain its own internal logic, it must work toward a society without sex.

Here again we see a number of radical statements that have been taken literally but which, like those about love, acquire more varied nuances when seen in context. In rejecting sex, what these feminists are referring to is sex as an institution, that is, sex as it has been corrupted in the patriarchal society, either as a symbol of male power or as a technique of reproduction. Indeed, it is dehumanization and depersonalization of heterosexual relations that Valerie Solanas attacks: "Sex isn't part of a relationship, but is, to the contrary, a solitary experience . . . and a gross waste of time."[31]

Likewise, Dana Densmore condemns sex outright as a heterosexual relationship based on the expectation that the woman should be "docile and cute and sexy and ego-building."[32] All these rejections, in fact, rather than being renunciations of sexuality as such, are intended to counter misconceptions of the sexual revolution, which has sometimes been misinterpreted as meaning that now women are always available for coitus. The militant spokeswoman for Cell 16, for instance, specifies that her appeal to chaste celibacy is meant less as a literal encouragement of it than as a proposal for its acceptance as an honorable choice, and concomitantly, for the demise of the male fantasy image projected onto women. For once the idea of celibacy is accepted, a woman no longer will fear being abandoned, and if she is loved, it will be for herself and not as the reflection of a depersonalized, alien image. In other words, the asexuality envisioned by Dana Densmore is not a final solution but rather forms part of a survival strategy. It is a sort of sexual strike tactic in the old tradition going back to the Greek play *Lysistrata,* but this time used for the purpose of rescuing love.

As for Ti-Grace Atkinson, she prescribes unequivocal revolutionary action. The primary goal, she says, is to eliminate all institutional aspects of sex, that is, to make a clean break separating sexuality from reproduction by turning to the method of "test-tube babies," extra-uterine conception, and artificial incubation. Sexual intercourse, she says, would then become simply a practice; but a practice without any justifying structural motivation eventually dies out. Therefore, other options must be explored to discover what will become of sexuality when all of its institutional aspects have disappeared. Ti-Grace consequently places herself among the sector of radical feminists who interpret sexual liberty as meaning the freedom to explore new forms of sexuality that take account of women's desires, as revealed by *The Hite Report:*

Not only were women tired of the old mechanical pattern of "foreplay," penetration, intercourse, and ejaculation, but many also found that *always* having to have intercourse, *knowing* you will have intercourse as a foregone conclusion, is mechanical and boring.[33]

Touching ought to precede caressing and union. While men are in a hurry to reach climax, most women prefer slow lovemaking and a broad range of sexual stimuli. Ti-Grace Atkinson even speaks of a "sixth sense" or a "sense organ" open to receiving these stimuli:

> Our understanding of the sense of feeling, or intuition, is almost non-existent, and few people probably even realize that there is such a sense. It is as if our understanding of the sense of sight were modeled on the experience of being punched in the eye instead of on experiences such as seeing a Tunisian water color by Paul Klee.[34]

What she is asking for is a new spreading of sex throughout the whole body. It is clear that she views this type of heterosexual intercourse—"the punch in the eye"—not as a fact of nature but rather as yet another institution with a political function. It therefore appears that the redefinition of sexuality, or the refusal to accept limiting definitions of it, is actually a rejection of the institutionalization of sex. The radical feminists' views on sex follow two separate but not necessarily contradictory lines of thought: one is to react against misconceptions of the sexual revolution and to attach less importance to coitus; the other is a seeming desire to rediscover the "lost golden age" of uninhibited female sexuality whose prehistoric existence is postulated by Mary Jane Sherfey, in a world that would be entirely eroticized, where all human beings enjoy completely free sexuality, and where sexually, "anything goes." Either way, the radical feminists call for tearing down the barricades around feminine sexuality, which the patriarchy is found guilty of erecting, and demolishing the mythology surrounding it, whose crowning expression is Freudian theory. In both cases, sexuality would be removed from the brutally political context and be accepted as an ordinary fact of life.

The Economic Revolution. In the economic phase of the revolution, as the radical feminists see it, women will leave behind the marginal status that had been necessary while women developed a new identity and solidarity among themselves and while the sexual revolution was being accomplished. In the economic phase, the time will have come for a reconciliation between feminism and the political Left. Not that the radical feminists had ever questioned the basic tenets of socialism; according to its own internal logic, radical feminism, with its concern for social justice and equality, had always perceived itself as socially radical or socialist. But in earlier phases, in their view, it will have been thought necessary for the cause of feminism to go forth on its own, independently of socialism, to leave behind the "wardship" that had prevailed until the 1960s, and to form an alliance, such as described by Linda Seese,[35] based on the recognition by leftist radical leaders that no revolution would be possible without a strong feminist collective. Kate Millett speaks in terms of a "coalition" when she prescribes a national union of blacks, young people, women, and the poor. Shulamith Firestone's scheme goes farther, envisioning feminist troops on a worldwide scale, their ranks swelled by youths and racial minorities, joining forces with the proletariat and the third world to combat imperialism.

There is no extensive description of the economic revolution in radical feminist writings. Like the dialectical theory of economics, this is not the strong point of radical feminism. Shulamith Firestone nevertheless gives some useful guidelines and foresees a postrevolutionary society which, in ensuring the economic independence of children and providing for the needs of all people, whatever their contribution to society, would achieve the first egalitarian distribution of wealth in the history of the world. By the inclusion of children, her scheme belongs to the great tradition of utopian socialism. Although the concept of "the dictatorship of the proletariat" does appear in Firestone's revolutionary scheme during the transition period, it must be noted that for her, just as in classical Marxism, this period is supposed to lead ultimately to a planned anarchy in which the state would wither away.

In the absence of clearly defined programs for economic revolution, the main idea on this subject that emerges from the writings of radical feminists is this: they consider that socialism not only has never been achieved historically, but also, and especially, that it cannot be achieved without the prerequisite of the sexual revolution. Therefore, in their view, today's existing socialist people's republics cannot be taken as authentic examples of socialism.

The Cultural Revolution. Like the economic revolution, the cultural revolution will depend on the prior elimination of the sexual dialectic. In the radical feminist view, it is to be not just a quantitative advance, a search for more knowledge, but also qualitative, aiming for the "achievement of cosmic consciousness" in a more well-rounded culture. The aesthetic mode, that is, our way of perceiving, interpreting, and creating images of the world, will be more firmly anchored in reality; the technological mode, that is, our way of controlling temporal and material aspects of the world, will be less dominated by a false obsession with objectivity. In the cultural revolution, these two dichotomous modes of perception will be integrated to form an androgynous culture; the lines between the two segregated cultural categories will be blurred. Whatever we can conceive, we can achieve. Furthermore, an underground culture or alternative "counterculture" will no longer be necessary, because its aims will have become reality.

This theory developed by Shulamith Firestone seems to have found early application in the example of a feminist rock band from Chicago who attempted to develop a revolutionary feminist culture. They declared themselves pioneers seeking to "bring to life a dream of the future" and to make rock music one of the vehicles of the new feminist culture during the prerevolutionary transition phase in which we are now living. The lyrics of their songs are not focused on stereotypes of "bad girls" or "sexy chicks," nor on the eternal female complaint, but rather on an affirmation of women's worth and a denial of the necessity of suffering. In addition, by the mere fact of being competent musicians with a mastery of their instruments, they were stepping outside the bounds of culturally imposed sexual roles and destroying the myth of the "priesthood" of instrumentalists. In the rock music world, eliminating the inherent cleavage between the male instrumentalist and the female singer is tantamount to destroying sexism. It also makes the music more democratic by breaking down the barriers between the worshiped musician and the adoring fans, at last establishing a relationship of equality, with audience participation.

However, to change the world, as the feminist rock band from Chicago discovered, it is not enough to have a visionary concept of culture; one must also have a power base—that is, in this case, the support of a mass feminist movement that would one day ensure the achievement of this cultural revolution. We can therefore see this inspired attempt as an early forerunner of the cultural revolution envisioned by Shulamith Firestone. The effort of these feminist musicians from Chicago to be a vehicle for a new feminist and socialist vision reveals the dynamic role that radical feminists want to play in bringing about the future utopia. It is up to women, they believe, to propose a redefinition of the culture and the world to come; or even to propose an absence of preconceived definitions, if we adhere to Shulamith Firestone's theory.

The concept of the destruction of sexism, with the world being redefined, or rendered undefined, by women, is pure metaphysics. It has often been said that women are not capable of being good philosophers. Ti-Grace Atkinson is convinced that the traditional language of metaphysics has no relationship to women's experience. Hence, in her own terms, she has sketched a theory of identity, as follows:

> an elaborate and intact theory restructuring life as self-justifying in and of itself. . . . What if identity were built from the inside? What if one's life were like a work of art, created by a dialogue with one's surroundings, whether animate or inanimate?[36]

Here we reencounter Shulamith Firestone's prescription for eliminating the barrier between the conceptual (the aesthetic mode) and the real (the technological mode), this time applied to the self. Building the identity "from the inside" also implies the refusal to accept the constraints of obtaining the approval of society, the supreme reward of recognition by others. This same refusal is expressed by Shulamith Firestone when she foresees a society in which the conceivable is acted out in reality, desire is immediately satisfied, and therefore the whole process of sublimation and repression of the id will disappear.

It seems that the radical feminists see the free expression of each individual's id as a necessary guarantee of protecting one's own personal identity against falling into the trap of a collective identity. For Ti-Grace Atkinson, any system of "humanist metaphysics and epistemology" ought to be based on the principle that each individual's primordial concern is the realization of his or her human potential. This same concept of total fulfillment of each human being is expressed by Shulamith Firestone. She believes in "the fully sexuate mind," in an androgynous cultural environment; will this perhaps prefigure the "achievement of cosmic consciousness?"[37]

This cosmic consciousness will be based on three components that will put an end respectively to the sexual, economic, and cultural dialectics: total sexual freedom, individual self-determination, and the transformation of the conceivable into the real. In Firestone's utopia, "artificial cultural achievement would no longer be the only avenue to sexuate self-realization;

one could now realize oneself fully, simply in the process of being and acting."[38]

The honest question mark that follows the phrase *cosmic consciousness* is a confession of Firestone's difficulty in pinning down this concept. It seems that the presiding spirit in radical feminist metaphysics and epistemology tends toward a synthesis between two hypotheses: one, total mastery of reality achieved through acting out the dream—the ultimate achievement of integrated culture; the other, a state of nature synonymous with equality and the absence of predefined roles, with any system of codification being suspect. The paradox is a challenge in itself.

The Personal Utopia of Shulamith Firestone. *The Dialectic of Sex* ends with a valiant effort by the author to propose a coherent sketch of what the future household might be like for people who choose the option of belonging to a social entity organized for procreation.

The household (Firestone prefers *household* to *family*) would be grouped around ten or twelve adults of various ages, bound by a contract for an initial period of seven to ten years. At the end of this time, the contract would be renewable. This arrangement would guarantee a certain amount of stability in the short term, considered necessary for child rearing. The children themselves would make up one-third of the household. During the transition period, these children would be the genetic offspring of couples living in the household; later, the household's children would be conceived and born using artificial means, to ensure that the household would be "a totally liberating social form." No doubt this must be seen as a veiled allusion to the elimination of the taboos of incest and the Oedipus and Electra complexes, the generators of the psychology of power. The children would be the responsibility of all the members of the household, in such a way that the relations between adults and children would be established purely on the basis of personal affinities. Thus, as previously suggested, love has its place in a radical feminist utopia:

> Thus all relationships would be based on love alone, uncorrupted by dependencies and resulting class inequalities. Enduring relationships between people of widely divergent ages would become common.[39]

In addition, children, women, and men would all enjoy the same legal rights and have the same option to transfer from one household to another. There would no longer be such a thing as being underage; the status of minor or adult would be abolished, thereby also eliminating the generation gap.

In utopia, the domestic tasks would be shared among all by an equitable rotation system, until such time as cybernetics perfects household automation. City planning would naturally have to adapt to these new household structures. The author suggests the college campus as the image most resembling the potential future community habitat. Clustered around certain basic collective structures—lounge, library, study center—there would be small private housing modules, where people would go to lead their private lives or to retreat from communal activities.

The economic system, during a transition period, would still be based on money, and a scheme would be set up in which everyone, men, women and children, would receive a guaranteed annual income distributed equitably by the state. There would also be a leveling out of class differences. In addition, the notion of work would be separated from that of salary, with cybernetics freeing human beings from all obligatory tasks. Thus purified of the corruption that is inseparably linked to considerations of salary, prestige, and power, work would be done for its own sake, according to each individual's tastes and curiosity. According to the author, the concept of work and education would become something like the medieval system of apprenticeship in a given discipline, where people of all ages worked together at all levels.

By putting an end to conflicts based on biological, sex, and age differences and to economic cleavages based on employment and salary, the utopia proposed by *The Dialectic of Sex* brilliantly reconciles feminism and socialism.

Internal Dissension and Self-Criticism

The two issues that have most tragically divided the radical feminist movement are *internal structure* and *the use of violence*. These are problems of organization and strategy rather than of theory. Writings on these issues belong under the heading of self-criticism, as militants either pass judgment on their own previous opinions or condemn certain options of other radical feminists.

In her article "The Liberal Takeover of Women's Liberation," Carol Hanisch,[40] a member of the Redstockings, points out an early error committed by the young Women's Liberation movement: the underestimation of male supremacy, leading feminists to believe that masculine dominance could be overcome in only a few years. This, she says, was a "naive, silly idea," which was translated into a second error: the priority given to questions of structure to the detriment of the fundamental issue of the "phallocracy." This is how the New York Radical Women were caught in the structural trap which, according to the author's facile alibi, was laid by the liberal, or egalitarian, feminists, who wanted to take over the movement. The main structural problem was that of leadership. The guiding principle, which Hanisch confesses having adhered to unreservedly, was "equality without leadership." It cost the unity of one group, the New York Radical Women (NYRW), when it reached a membership of thirty and this number was considered too unwieldy to give everyone an equal chance to be heard. In the name of structure, therefore, it was decided to split up the members into two groups chosen by chance and not by affinity; the result was a separation between the founders that, for a time, deprived the NYRW of its effectiveness.

Out of this split came the Redstockings, who from the beginning drafted a code of principles in order to discourage membership applications from any feminists who did not feel at home in their organization. This effort was in vain, for the "structuralists" did not waste any time in dominating the new organization. Belonging simultaneously to both the Feminists (Ti-Grace Atkinson's group) and the Redstockings, they condemned the Redstockings as antidemocratic. Carol Hanisch sees this maneuver as a diversionary tactic, aimed at distracting the thinkers of the "pro-woman" line from their policy of concentrating on communication with the feminist masses. Calculating the damage done by the refusal to accept any leadership, Carol Hanisch asserts that it ended in a shameful star system, with the fanatics of "nonleadership" paradoxically themselves being cast as leaders of the rank and file because of their fanaticism! This feud additionally cost the Women's Liberation movement the services of many sincere and competent feminists, who were ahead of their time in their consciousness-raising, but whose talents were sacrificed in the name of democracy. Here we reencounter the criticism made by Betty Friedan.

As for identifying those who were primarily responsible for this schism, the Redstockings' attempt to blame the egalitarian feminists for having manipulated the antileadership "structuralist" feminists seems wide open to attack. First of all, the liberals had never made any secret of the fact that they favored strong leadership; second, this accusation appears to contradict one of the principles of the *Redstockings Manifesto,* by which they proclaim themselves to be always on the side of women. In this sense, the liberal feminists, who never promised any such commitment, provide the Redstockings with a lesson in militant solidarity, blaming the schism on the CIA and FBI, which they accused of infiltrating and dividing the movement.

The second issue causing dissension, the use of violence, divided the radical feminists in two ways. First, their disagreements stretched the tolerable limits of differences of opinion in their debates on the use of violence as a strategy against oppression. Second, dissension took a self-destructive form when violence broke out within the movement, ranging sister against sister.

The feminist charter on violence is certainly the *SCUM Manifesto.* It legitimizes hysteria as a terrorist force.

If SCUM ever marches, it'll be over the President's face; if SCUM ever strikes, it'll be in the dark with a six-inch blade.[41]

In 1971, Robin Morgan also supported violence as a strategy of the Women's movement, rooted in the historic tradition of women fighting for liberty. In the sense that armed struggle requires competence, violence also represented for her a set of technical skills that are so many "tools for liberation" in the hands of women. As tools, they are means and not ends: this is the implied distinction by which she rejects the accusation of imitating male behavior. Hence her proposal for a crash program to teach fighting techniques in six-week sessions, in a special training camp complete with child care centers, where women martial arts experts would teach other women who would then go into the community and teach others: "each one teach one." The inspiration for this project is unquestionably the old Amazon dream of a feminist army. However, six years later, in her critical introduction to *Going Too Far,* Robin Morgan reversed herself and lamented her earlier article as false, a blend of feminist stridency and leftist rhetoric, naively plagiarizing war games. Upon mature reflection, playing soldiers seemed just as childish as playing house.

This was already Ti-Grace Atkinson's conviction in 1971. For her as the theoretician of the group called the Feminists, radical feminist discussions on the strategy of armed struggle were perpetuating a mutual voluntary illusion, while most individual feminists felt in their hearts that they themselves were not the least bit capable of violence. Her lucid observation of this flaw was based on her definition of violence as a "class function," that is, as organized pressure brought to bear by the oppressor for the purpose of maintaining the status quo within the class system. Therefore, in her judgment, violence was unacceptable as a strategy for the oppressed. Joseph Colombo, Valerie Solanas, Angela Davis, all the fanatical revolutionaries whom she admired because they incarnated the pure spirit of rebellion, were not to be seen as agitators, troublemakers, and fomenters of disorder, but as victims of the oppressor's violence whom the Women's movement should not condemn.

Consequently, in the name of their common oppression, Ti-Grace Atkinson censured the diatribes that radical feminist groups were heaping on revolutionaries of every stripe. For her, the movement had simply chosen the wrong target. Besides, as a victim of its own inconsistency, it was condemning violence in others while practicing it in words, or even acts, against its own militant sisters. In 1971, Ti-Grace was physically attacked by her feminist sisters in the debate on violence when she defended the memory of Joseph Colombo. In response, she wrote an open letter to "collaborators"—her term for women who claimed to hate men but still went to bed with them—in which she proclaimed her disgust and announced her decision to break with the Women's movement. She chose black for the pages of her letter as a symbol of mourning for the Women's movement, which, for her, had died on 6 August 1971. The contents of the black pages of *Amazon Odyssey* show that, like Kate Millett, the militant Ti-Grace Atkinson had paid dearly with her body and soul.

Radical Feminists Judge Liberal Feminists

The leading theoreticians of radical feminism criticize the views of their liberal sisters, the egalitarian feminists, on three specific issues: the patriarchal reality, feminist strategy, and organization.

As Ti-Grace Atkinson sees it, the liberal, or egalitarian feminist, underestimating the degree to which women are oppressed, is attacking the most superficial aspect of oppression, that is, sex discrimination in employment. For Ti-Grace Atkinson, to attack only this aspect is to misdirect the battle against the roles instead of the institutions, just as if the black slaves struggling against oppression in the 1850s had based their cause on a charge of racial discrimination in employment! Robin Morgan, also taking the historical perspective, sees the National Organization for Women (NOW) evolving toward the same "bourgeois feminism" as the suffragists of the long-defunct National American Woman Suffrage Association (NAWSA). Pragmatism, so often invoked as a virtue by the egalitarian feminists, is itself questioned. In Morgan's view, NOW, by concentrating on single-issue political goals, has had far too great a tendency to sacrifice its political principles, and compromise has become surrender. Besides, as Shulamith Firestone recalls, the unfortunate example of NAWSA, taken over by conservative feminism, proves that "the attempt to work within and placate the white male power structure" is untenable and self-defeating in terms of immediate political gains.

These diverse judgments made in 1970 are part of the great democratic debate that was then going on within the Women's movement, the same discussion that the Redstockings labeled as a structural dispute. As early as 1968, this movement-wide debate had produced a schism in NOW, in which Ti-Grace Atkinson and her followers quit the organization to found the October 17th Movement, later renamed the Feminists. The affair caused a great stir and had important repercussions, since it shook up the most important chapter of NOW, the New York chapter. Ti-Grace's principal criticisms were aimed at the centralized hierarchy of NOW and what she saw as the excessive powers of its president. Admitting that she was calling for nothing less than a revolution, she tells how she had proposed to replace the hierarchical structure of the organization with a system of drawing lots for offices, leading to an anonymous "nonmanagement." This proposal was rejected at a meeting where, according to Ti-Grace, the NOW officers had bought the votes with bribery, "in the worst American tradition."

All these criticisms of egalitarian feminists respect the rules of mutual tolerance. They even appear less acrimonious than the internal conflicts within the radical feminist wing, between such groups as the Feminists and the Redstockings. But it was this latter group which, here again, took the initiative in hardening the lines of the debate. Indeed, grave charges were brought by the followers of the "pro-woman" line against the staff of *Ms.* magazine, all the graver in that they took a personal turn, making Gloria Steinem their target.

The Redstockings undertook to demonstrate that *Ms.* was not a feminist forum but simply the product of a commercial operation exploiting feminism to serve its own ideology. As a commercial operation, *Ms.* was attacked first for its style of journalism. Pat Mainardi and Kathie Sarachild,[42] citing their personal experience, accused the editors of being authoritarian and watering down articles they had submitted. Far from being a vehicle for radical ideas, Ms. was accused of being a traditional women's magazine dressed up in new trappings, in which, according to Ellen Willis,[43] the image of the "liberated woman" was substituted for that of the "sexy chick" or the "perfect homemaker." It is clear that for the Redstockings, the editors of Ms. were impostors masquerading as feminists. But this masquerade, as Ellen Willis presented it, went much farther than a simple commercial operation; she accused it of being a political tool in the service of the existing powers. On this premise, the Redstockings denounced the Ms. ideology as a perversion of feminism on four essential counts.

First, the Ms. ideology was attacked as being founded on *individualism,* consisting in the belief that each woman individually could liberate herself, with a further corollary, seen as paternalistic, that so-called liberated women should then help their unliberated sisters to do likewise. It is evident that the Redstockings were twisting words, distorting one of the liberal feminist options—taking charge of one's own destiny—and presenting it as the only option they offered. If the liberal feminists really believed individuals could liberate themselves, why then would there be an organized liberal feminist movement?

Revisionism was the second count in the charge that the Ms. ideology was a perversion of feminism. Kathie Sarachild accused the liberal feminists of having distorted the process of consciousness-raising by cutting it off from its roots in action and transforming it into personal therapy aimed at erasing the negative self-image that women had internalized. Ellen Willis asserts that the liberal feminists also had a faulty interpretation of *sisterhood,* which forbade any criticism of another feminist. Such a position, says Willis, could only further obscure the political conflicts between women. This last point sheds light on clause VII of the *Redstockings Manifesto:*

> We will always take the side of women against their oppressors. We will not ask what is "revolutionary" or "reformist," only what is good for women.[44]

While such an assertion works in the context of a confrontation between the sexes, it also allows for confrontations over differences between feminists. One must acknowledge the soundness of this logic, but bitter, fruitless feuds must not be mistaken for exchanges of views.

In a third count of the charge of perversion of feminism, Ellen Willis reproached the Ms. ideology for attacking only *sexual roles and not fundamental male power,* labeling as antifeminist sophistry the Ms. argument that men and women are co-victims of sexual conditioning. The Redstockings' theoretician seems to be forgetting how far this criticism can reach; in fact, to judge from some of the proposals of Ti-Grace Atkinson or Dana Densmore, the staff of *Ms.* is not the only one guilty of this particular "perversion" of feminism.

Finally, in the fourth count of the accusation, which comprises and outweighs all the others, *Ms.* was said to be compromising American feminism by *links with conservative elements* hostile to the Left, in the service of the existing power structure. Here is where the attack becomes personal, with Gloria Steinem being charged as primarily responsible for the perversions and denounced as a former CIA agent who had worked for the Independent Research Service. These accusations were hurled into public attention by the Redstockings in a pamphlet distributed 9 May 1975, and were widely taken up and repeated when Steinem herself remained silent. Naturally, the charges did not stop with her past history; as a consequence of this past, the Redstockings tried to cast doubt on the genuineness of Steinem's commitment to feminism. The clinching proof of this is the heading over the list of charges: "Agents, Opportunists and Fools."[45]

All these accusations are among the most painful pages of militant feminist literature. They leave no door open for another hypothesis, the possibility that someone from outside the movement was attempting to discredit an influential feminist. Such a case occurred when Kate Millett was forced into a public admission of her bisexuality under pressure from parties who intended to smear her, not among feminists, but rather, in public opinion, and through her, to discredit the whole Women's movement. The context the Redstockings chose for alleging Gloria Steinem's past association with the CIA was the 1975 International Women's Year Conference in Mexico City, which was surrounded by antifeminist elements. The international forum might have inspired them to more prudence; but in the framework of radical feminist reaction to the liberal feminists' return in force, the Redstockings seem to have decided to be the scavengers of the new feminist movement. In somewhat the same way, the lesbians seem to have wanted to be the avant-garde of the feminist unconscious.

LESBIANISM

As an unequivocal sexual option, homosexuality definitively polarizes the sexes. Therefore, when lesbianism is offered as a political solution, it cannot help but pose a dilemma for feminism. This is in fact what happened in the United States when militant lesbians began proselytizing in the years 1970–73, in the name of feminism itself. The most interesting analyses of this phenomenon are the writings of the Daughters of Bilitis and those of more recent groups born out of the new feminism, particularly the Radicalesbians and the Furies.

First, these theoreticians take care to offer their definition of lesbianism:

We are the extrusions of your unconscious mind—your worst fears made flesh.[46]

A lesbian is the rage of all women condensed to the point of explosion. . . . The perspective gained, . . . the liberation of self, the inner peace, the real love of self and of all women, is something to be shared with all women—because we are all women.[47]

The LESBIAN in each one of us is the part of us, or the whole of us, that puts women first—the part of us that is working for a better world for all women.[48]

One cannot help but be struck by the broad inclusiveness of these definitions. According to the first one, based on the psychoanalytical theory of repression, every heterosexual woman is a latent lesbian who does not know it. The second and third definitions present lesbianism as a political solution, since they perceive it as a revolt. Lesbianism is therefore not only a sexual option between women, but also an act of self-assertion and of primary identification with women. Such is the double implication of the expression used by the Radicalesbians, "woman identified woman," which is both a lesbian version of feminist sisterhood and a claim of an individual female identity. The lesbian version of feminist sisterhood is presented as the only possible way to achieve love, since lesbian love unites two equal persons, equal by virtue of the fact of their common oppression by men. It is easy to recognize here Shulamith Firestone's postulate of the necessity for equal vulnerability between two partners in love. In addition, the Radicalesbians' definition of themselves rejects the strictly sexual label of *lesbian,* which they say was conceived by men as a weapon against female homosexuals, who are thereby deprived of individual human identity and stereotyped as an anomaly. According to the order set up by Phyllis Lyon and Del Martin, the founders of the Daughters of Bilitis, every lesbian perceives herself first as a human being, next as a woman, and only in third place as a lesbian. Lesbians are said to be the product of the patriarchal society, falsely categorized in a sexist society which casts people into "rigid sexual roles." This latter expression must cause some wonderment among "straight" feminists who are aware of the distinctions established by lesbians themselves between the "butch," or virile lesbian, and the "femme," or feminine lesbian. Can lesbianism offer itself as a model for liberation when it thus apes heterosexual sexism?

To raise this question is no doubt unfair to the Radicalesbians, who could not be convicted of such a heresy since they assert that, in a sexually free society, the categorization of people as homosexual or heterosexual would not exist. In their view, the strictly sexual label *lesbian,* conceived by the patriarchy, has a dual political function. First, it is a way of dividing women among themselves, as heterosexual women accept society's conventional process of depersonalization and perceive the lesbian not as an individual but as a stereotyped role or potential sex object. Second, it is a means of dissuasion, condemning heterosexual women to remain strictly within the boundaries of the male-defined feminine role.

Lesbianism, not the label but the actual choice, here perceives itself as the true feminism, for the reason that as an act of self-assertion and solidarity between women, it responds to repression precisely by rejecting the degrading role imposed on women by men's definition of them as dependent, relative beings that exist not for themselves but for men.

In popular thinking, there is really only one essential difference between a lesbian and other women: that of her sexual orientation — which is to say, when you strip off all the packaging, you must finally realize that the essence of being a "woman" is to get fucked by men.[49]

On this premise, it is easy to postulate that a feminist ought to refuse "to get fucked by men" and that lesbians therefore, incarnating this refusal, are the avant-garde of feminism. Paradoxically, lesbians who refuse to allow the patriarchy the right to define them in terms of their sexual option are themselves defining their own feminism by this choice. Obviously, they are operating on the idea that "what's sexual is political." While heterosexual radical feminists interpret this phrase as meaning that sex has become a symbol of power, the lesbian interpretation is that heterosexuality is itself an institution which oppresses women. A new notion appears here, "heterosexism": an extension of sexism rooted in heterosexuality and in the assumption that every woman is, or wants to be, linked to a man, economically and emotionally. Hence the rejection by lesbian feminists of any solution other than pure lesbianism, including bisexuality and celibacy.

Hence, concurrently, their ultimate assertion that lesbianism is not just A solution but THE political solution, the only guarantee of women's liberty, since no woman is free to be anyone at all if she is not free to be a lesbian.

This assertion provides another illustration of the refusal of all sexual categorization, as the Radicalesbians prescribe, and it is in this perspective that lesbian proselytizing must be viewed. Martha Shelley calls for the harassment of heterosexual women, in order to make them aware that homosexuality is part of the normal sexuality of every human being and is not an anomaly.

As long as you cherish that secret belief that you are a little bit better because you sleep with the opposite sex, you are still asleep in your cradle, and we will be the nightmare that awakens you.[50]

Lesbian feminists thus seem to have taken on the mission of awakening women from their amnesia and freeing the repressed desire latent within every feminist. Within the feminist movement, they took various approaches. Heterosexuals of the liberal or egalitarian faction were exhorted to dare to talk about lesbianism, and not to set it aside as a secondary issue out of a concern for damaging the movement's reputation. As for young radical feminists who had no qualms about discussing a taboo subject, they were told they must stop perceiving lesbianism as a sexual variant from the norm of women's relations with men, since such a position still defines women in terms of men, and therefore, as relative human beings. Seeking the deep causes of the profound hostility that heterosexual feminists showed toward lesbian proselytizing, the lesbian theorists are unanimous in diagnosing it as self-hatred: women have been brainwashed to detest themselves and detest other women; therefore they prefer to identify with the oppressor. Again, we find the theory of the pathology of oppression being applied to love, as Ti-Grace Atkinson had done, to show how love has been corrupted in the political context of the patriarchy.

How did radical feminists, either bisexual or heterosexual, react to lesbian proselytizing? The presence of lesbians in the movement never posed any problems until their proselytizing raised the question of the role of lesbians as such within the movement. We have seen how they sometimes perceived themselves as the avant-garde of feminism, or even identified lesbianism as the only true feminism.

The radical feminist theorist Robin Morgan, first addressing the notion of the avant-garde, recalls that as a rule, a true avant-garde must represent the point of view of a majority which has given rise to it. However, she

says, although lesbianism might have been enabled by the Women's movement to flourish publicly and undertake militant activities, it nonetheless
remains an unrepresentative minority point of view. As for Ti-Grace Atkinson, with her particular talent for sensing fine nuances, she proposes that
lesbianism is a variant form of the claimed avant-garde function. She does
not deny that, in a future phase of the feminist revolution, the lesbian
troops might become a reserve corps of leaders of the rank and file; but
given the nonrevolutionary present, she perceives them as having essentially
a strategic value in a "buffer zone," protecting the flanks of the main
feminist movement against attacks by the patriarchy in the same way that
in the McCarthy era, the Communist party served as a "buffer" protecting
the labor movement. Atkinson's appraisal therefore acknowledges that lesbianism is necessary to the survival of the Women's movement.

There is much less agreement among heterosexual feminists' responses
to lesbian allegations of the political value of lesbianism as the optimal
feminist solution. Nonlesbian feminist theorists make a clear distinction
between the two aspects lesbianism claims to cover: the sexual fact and the
political fact. While lesbians lump them together, the heterosexual radical
feminists break them apart. It is impossible, they say, to define a given
militant's degree of feminism by her sexual choice. To do so would be to
fall back into the same old heresy and deny the very essence of feminism as
a movement to end the use of sexual categorization as the definitive criterion of human identity and destiny.[51] As Anne Koedt[52] puts it, lesbians, in
politicizing sexual choice, are distorting the slogan What's Personal Is
Political. While it is true, she says, that on the basis of this militant
proclamation, women's lives have been wrenched out of the private realm
and opened up to political analysis, it is false to say that every militant
feminist's personal life, including her sex life, therefore becomes the political property of the Women's movement.

It is in this same spirit that Ti-Grace Atkinson presents lesbianism as
distinct from feminism: "Lesbianism is a 'sexual' position, whereas feminism is a 'political' position."[53]

Admittedly, says Ti-Grace, the very concept of lesbianism depends on
the identification of a counterclass: men. Thus, one might be led to believe
that lesbianism is a political concept. But lesbianism, both as a theoretical
concept and as a practical reality, is entirely dependent on male supremacy.
Ti-Grace therefore turns the lesbians' accusation of "relativity" back on
themselves. She pursues this line in asserting that lesbianism is "reactionary" while feminism is "revolutionary." Feminism, she says, is revolution-

ary in that, even though it is separatist, it confronts oppression and combats it. In contrast, lesbianism is reactionary because it represents a flight from confrontation with male oppression; this flight, since it amounts to a refusal to fight, is therefore equivalent to recognition and acceptance of male oppression. We must admire the adroitness of Ti-Grace Atkinson's logic in asserting that lesbianism recognizes and accepts male oppression, when we recall that lesbians themselves proclaimed that love has a greater chance to succeed between lesbians than between heterosexuals since it involves two people who are equal in their oppression by men.

The best argument demonstrating that lesbianism is neither "the only true feminism" nor the political panacea for all women's problems, but is purely a sexual choice, comes to us from Robin Morgan, revealing that the majority of lesbians are married women. This means, she says, that secretly, they have chosen the sexual option of lesbianism, but publicly, they are all for the political option of the patriarchy, clinging to the privileges of security that heterosexual marriage provides. According to Ti-Grace Atkinson, some of these women are also militant in the movement:

> There are women in the movement who engage in sexual relationships with other women, but who are married to men. These women are not lesbians in the political sense. These women claim the right to "private" lives. They are collaborators.
> There are other women who have never had sexual relationships with other women, but who have made, and live, a total commitment to this movement. These women are "lesbians" in the political sense. [54]

Ti-Grace is catching lesbians in their own trap: politics. Her response to their claims is that, if lesbianism is political action, then it can only consist of a woman's primary and total commitment to the cause of women, with no sexual implication whatsoever. Whereas lesbians want to sexualize political combat, Ti-Grace Atkinson pushes feminist logic to the extreme and desexualizes this same combat — and foresees the necessity for such desexualization lasting as long as the patriarchal system, and lesbians themselves, imprison sex in the political context.

FEMINIST RADICALISM

Double or Triple Allegiance

Feminist radicalism (that is, feminism within radical socialism) is distinguished by double or triple allegiance: the double allegiance of white militants to the political Left and to feminism; the triple allegiance by minority women to the political Left, to the struggle for ethnic liberation, and to feminism. However, the feminist radical's fundamental commitment is to socialism, particularly in the form of the Socialist Workers party, which united all these struggles in the name of revolution. Naturally, the feminism of these women could not but be influenced by their other primary allegiance; they therefore reject any idea of feminist separatism, even as a temporary tactic, as some radical feminists advocated. The SWP view is stated by Caroline Lund:

> My concept before I joined the YSA was that all the various struggles going on would be fought separately, and then when it came time for the revolution, we would all somehow get together and make the revolution. But this did not seem sufficient. . . . You have to build a unified revolutionary organization . . . not as a federation of separate struggles but a united, cohesive group with the common aim of helping to lead a socialist revolution.[55]

The anticapitalist premise is always assumed, contradicting this assertion of all-inclusiveness. Thus, the black militant Frances Beal[56] considered that the adherence of the Women's movement to socialism was a necessary precondition before the movement could claim to represent minority women. In fact, among black women, there were many who preferred to give their sole allegiance to socialist radicalism rather than feminism, Angela Davis being the most famous example.

For feminist radicals, on the contrary, there is no doubt that feminism helps socialism just as much as socialism helps feminism. This double proposition sums up the argument by which feminist radicalism, on the one hand, has justified its autonomy from the Left, and on the other hand, vis-à-vis other feminist currents, has justified its allegiance to socialism.

The task of persuading feminists to support socialism was undertaken by Caroline Lund. Granted, she said, the socialist revolution will destroy the apparatus of oppression; nevertheless, in order for it also to destroy the institutions that specifically oppress women, the revolution must have the participation of a strong feminist movement, with the weight of a powerful organized force. The allegiance of a powerful feminist movement to socialism will guarantee the feminist revolution within the socialist revolution. On the other hand, as the SWP women's liberation platform recalls, feminists alone will not be able to bring about the anticapitalist revolution that is the necessary prerequisite for women's liberation.

Conversely, persuading socialists as such to support feminism was the goal of feminist militants who underlined the valuable assistance that a strong feminist movement would bring to the socialist revolution. Minority women were the ones who felt the greatest need of legitimizing their feminist autonomy in the eyes of the men of their community. The Chicanas, particularly, pleaded their own cause with a great deal of conviction, arguing simply for the fundamental right to take responsibility for themselves and to fight for freedom.

> Chicanas are determined to fight. . . . The issue of equality and freedom for the Chicana "is *not negotiable.* Anyone opposing the right of women to organize into their own form of organization has no place in the leadership of the movement. FREEDOM IS FOR EVERYONE."[57]

There were two concepts of the Women's movement that Mirta Vidal denounced as distortions invented by male Hispanics who were hostile to the feminism of their women: first, that the Women's movement is an affair of white people; second, that the Women's movement, by being directed against men, saps the strength of the Chicanos' own revolutionary struggle. Mirta Vidal responded to the first accusation by recalling that the ultimate goal of the new feminist movement is to destroy specific sex roles universally throughout society. To the second accusation, she retorted that basing socialist unity on the eternal submission of women was a sham.

The Feminist Radical Analysis of the Patriarchal Reality

True to its primary allegiance to socialist radicalism, feminist radical theory is a faithful reflection of Marxist ideology. If we compare the theoretical analysis of feminist radicals with that of radical feminists, we immediately see a fundamental difference on the issue of assigning the blame for women's oppression, since the feminist radical lays the principal burden of guilt on the capitalist system.

Social Class and Sexual Oppression. The term *class* consequently takes on a different connotation here. Whereas radical feminists spoke of sexual classes, the feminist radicals adhere strictly to the Marxist concept of economic classes. According to them, it is not the *patriarchy* that changed the course of history; it is *capitalism.* In primitive society, they say, there was equality between men and women. For Evelyn Reed,[58] the original form of human society was the matriarchy, whose historical existence she believes has been authenticated by Johann Bachofen and Lewis Morgan, and which she conceives, in keeping with the political theory of Engels, as a sort of primitive communism. Women held high positions; legal marriage and monogamy did not exist; people cohabited on a temporary basis according to their own desires; the community looked after everyone's needs. But the agricultural revolution, carried out by women as their ingenious solution to the problem of feeding society, freed men from their duties as hunters, thereby enabling them to learn the techniques of agriculture and industry that women had invented. At first working as skilled laborers, men went on to conceive of new techniques. However, women's honor is saved, in the author's view, since she emphasizes that women had started from nothing, whereas men built on the previous conceptual work of women. "First came the women, biologically endowed by nature. Then came the men, socially endowed by the women."[59]

This assertion appears to be intended as the first feminist contribution to socialist theory. The version of feminism expressed here contains a whiff of revenge, since it speaks in terms of superiority. In addition, it verges on heresy, since it is based on a claim that there is such a thing as natural, biological superiority.

Pursuing this retrospective view, the feminist radical anthropologist reveals how the takeover by men of the means of production brought about a social and political mutation resulting in the class society. This society, whose avatars reoccur throughout history in three forms—slavery, feudalism, capitalism—entailed the relegation of women to an inferior social position. Evelyn Reed thus reaches the same conclusion as Engels:[60] that is, the root cause of women's oppression is the emergence of a class society based on private property. This theory can be distinguished from that of radical feminists in two ways. First, it exonerates men from the charge of collective guilt inherent in them as a sexual class; at most it lays blame on the limited class of plutocrats. Second, as a corollary, it assumes that economic classes existed prior to the sexual oppression of women, the latter having arisen to serve the needs of the former, since the confinement of women to the home was conceived by husbands as a guarantee of their own paternity of their children so as to be sure they were leaving their worldly goods to their genetic heirs. This same chronology is the basis of the feminist radical theory proposed by minority women. If we can believe Mirta Vidal, the aboriginal inhabitants of North America practiced sexual equality before the patriarchal system was imported by European imperialists.

Although the feminist radicals assert that the sexual oppression of women was born out of the economic class system, they are forced to recognize that this oppression exists everywhere in the world. An objection therefore arises: how do they reconcile the existence of sexual oppression under socialist regimes with the theory that it was a product of capitalism? It seems that the answer must be sought in the institution of the family, which is the basic cell of capitalist societies, and which still remains as an anachronistic vestige of capitalism in people's democracies, since they have not yet been able to carry out the feminist revolution.

The Family. It goes without saying that, for the feminist radicals, the institution of the family was born out of the economic class system. Like the radical feminists, they assert a causal relationship in the development of the family. As further proof of this, they point out that the institution of the family arises only when economic surpluses and the individual accumulation of goods reach a point requiring the transfer of social and economic functions from the clan level to a smaller structural unit. Therefore, in this view, the family is above all an economic institution, centered around domestic labor and the rearing of children. In the beginning, say Marie-Alice Waters[61] and Dianne Feeley,[62] agreeing with Evelyn Reed, the family functioned mainly as the best way to conserve private property and pass it along within blood lines. Its economic function was thereby considerably increased since, by caring for the material well-being of its members, it relieved the capitalist state of any social responsibility for the working class. In this way, a heavy economic burden was placed on the poor under the pretext of family responsibilities.

Besides being an economic institution, the family also has an ideological function. It becomes the vehicle for a reactionary ideology, as its hierarchical structure develops in family members the docility required by the class society. This insidious conditioning is particularly aimed at women, since it prepares them for servitude. If the family is indispensable to the economic class society, the subjection of women is, therefore, indispensable to the family. Here the feminist radicals reach the same conclusion as the radical feminists.

The oppression that women endure through the institution of the family is not simply a wart on the nose of an otherwise healthy system. This oppression is the very essence of the institution of the family.[63]

According to feminist radicals, this oppression lies first of all in the relegation of women to domestic slavery, this being the least costly means found by society in the capitalist state to rid itself, as stated above, of any responsibility for the nonproductive population: children, old people, the handicapped. This relegation, in addition, gives rise to all the many aspects of the oppression of women: their exclusion from higher tasks providing more personal fulfillment, discrimination in employment, their economic dependence maintained through the nonremuneration of domestic labor, and their cultural death. Women have thus been kept apart from any participation in activities outside the family by means of the double myth of maternity, which has two antithetical but converging aspects: on the one hand, the denigration of gestation as a biological affliction; on the other hand, the exaltation of maternity as a mystique.

The hostility of feminist radicals to the family is the most authentically feminist aspect of their theory, not that it is distinguished from traditional Marxist analyses, but rather because it counters the revisionist attempts expressed by the Left in this matter. Of all efforts at Marxist revisionism, feminist Marxists judge that the most dangerous for feminism is the communist viewpoint, such as it is revealed by Fern Winston in her article, "The Family—Is It Obsolete?"[64] Wishing to rationalize the status of women in the Soviet Union, the Communist party has presented the family as "a revolutionary force in society" and an emotional safe harbor providing comfort and security to its members. Such a concept is denounced by feminist radicals as being in flagrant contradiction with the positions of Marx and Engels. Besides, they judge it to be unrealistic. For the first time, in fact, society has developed enough resources to be able to assume all the social and humanitarian responsibilities for its members. The isolated household cannot alone supply such a variety of resources and is an anachronism that condemns women to domestic slavery.

In the capitalist society, therefore, women are doubly oppressed, both as women and as workers. Even worse is the status of minority women, since they suffer from racial oppression as well.

The Triple Oppression of Minority Women. The minority woman has no trouble convincing her man that she is as much a victim of racism as he is. They also share the same fate in terms of economic oppression. Frances Beal, in a feat of logistical acrobatics, takes care not to separate the economic exploitation of black men from that of black women, or even from that of the entire working class, while simultaneously attempting to prove that the most oppressed of all are women laborers, in particular, black women laborers.

Where minority women come into conflict with the men of their community is when, claiming a legitimate right to their own feminist struggle, they protest their sexual oppression as women and accuse their men of being the primary offenders. For Frances Beal, the black woman is "the slave of a slave." The first implication of this slogan is that the black woman, just like the black man, is a victim of the racist capitalist system. Thus she refutes the accusation that the black man has been castrated by society with the collusion of the black woman. Frances Beal's phrase is therefore a feminist follow-up to Angela Davis's demolition of the myth of the black matriarchy.[65] "Let's not mistake our oppressors," say the black feminist radicals; the oppressor of both the black man and the black woman is the white capitalist. In the second implication of Beal's little phrase, the black woman is "the slave of a slave" in the sense that her immediate oppressor is the oppressed black man. Not that he is basically to blame, but that, once again, the pathology of oppression leads the oppressed to imitate the behavior of the oppressor; in this case, the only way open to him is in the domain of sex, because he has no identity except in terms of his virility. Once again, sex becomes equated with power, and the black man is guilty of supporting the "phallocracy."

While recognizing that two hundred years of oppression and discrimination in a white capitalist regime cannot help but have disturbed the psychosexuality of the black man and have led him to be a "phallocrat," we must nevertheless regret that Frances Beal's analysis does not go so far as to explain the origin of the role model, that is, the white man's phallocratic domination over the white woman. Certainly, for Beal as a black woman, this is not her problem; but if we admit that the white man's phallocracy over the women of his race is just plain phallocracy, pure and simple, then it becomes a problem for Beal as a woman. It also seems curious to us that the author lets pass without comment the fact that the rise in black power coincides with an increase in black sexism. The black male radical of the 1960s, attacking white capitalism, showed himself to be uncontestably a greater phallocrat than the black man had ever been before; might not this be taken as proof that the sexual relationship is perceived as a power relationship, certainly exacerbated by capitalism, but not caused by it? If so, how is this to be reconciled with socialism?

In contrast to black women, the Chicanas, although admitting that the system is to blame, are much less sparing of their men's touchiness on the subject of feminism, and they fume with rage at the hypocrisy of the Chicano who camouflages his sexism behind a mask of fidelity to the ancestral culture:

When Chicano men talk about maintaining La Familia and the "cultural heritage" of La Raza, they are in fact talking about maintaining the age-old concept of keeping the woman barefoot, pregnant, and in the kitchen. . . . Women who do not accept this philosophy are charged with betrayal of "our culture and heritage." OUR CULTURE HELL![66]

The first sentence poses the problem of "bedroom politics." This phrase, repeated by Frances Beal, refers to the violation of women's free will regarding their reproductive capacity. This violation, according to minority women, has operated in two ways. The first one is attributable once again to the white capitalist system. White plutocrats, wishing to maintain a demographic balance in their favor, have continually reduced minority women to the ranks of guinea pigs in their experimentation with contraception and sterilization techniques. Frances Beal describes this as a macabre "surgical genocide." Nonetheless, in the second aspect of "bedroom politics" which minority women oppose, the liberalization of abortion laws and access to contraception must not be interpreted as genocide.

[A black woman has] the right and the responsibility to determine when it is in the interest of the struggle to have children or not to have them and this right must not be relinquished to anyone.

It is also her right and responsibility to determine when it is in her own best interests to have children, how many she will have, and how far apart.[67]

The claim is curious, as it hesitates between the cause of black civil liberties and the cause of women's liberation, and in spite of the addition of the second sentence, it makes women's right to control their own bodies subordinate to the interests of the racial struggle. This interpretation is confirmed when the author proclaims that the black woman, now that she is freed from multiple pregnancies, should use her new availability to serve the revolution. No such subordination mars the later writings of minority women; feminism has done its work. Thus, Maxine Williams claims the right, purely and simply, for women to control their own bodies, without any conditional clauses about racial commitment; Frances Flores, making the same demand, uses the hallowed word *inalienability,* thereby definitively claiming this right with no "ifs, ands, or buts" about it.

The Feminist Radical Revolution

The feminist radical revolution, we are told, will be the achievement of a grand, sweeping, unified feminist movement, a federation of organizations and groups which, up to that point, will have worked separately for liberation according to their own particular form of oppression. It is hard to see the logic of the reasoning by which radicals reject the strategy of separate struggles within the main body of socialism, but accept it within the feminist segment of their movement. It seems that logic has been sacrificed in the interests of time, which is supposed to work in the radicals' favor by allowing for an increased number of conversions of women to Marxism.

The socialist program for women's liberation, as stated by the Socialist Workers party (SWP), links the new feminist movement with the earlier historic women's struggles for democratic freedoms. The consciousness-raising process in the present struggle is presented by the SWP as going beyond that produced by the first wave of American feminism. Overlooking the fact that there was a nineteenth-century version of radical feminism, or interpreting it (like that of Kate Millett) as a class phenomenon, the SWP reduces the first wave of militant feminism to a mere outgrowth of the bourgeois democratic revolution, while it greets the current feminist movement as belonging to the true anticapitalist revolution. In both cases, the SWP viewpoint sees feminism as being dependent on the broader socialist struggle. According to this same viewpoint, the new feminist movement is rediscovering or reclaiming the primitive matriarchy, in the sense that it is putting an end to women's historic confinement. Women, we are told, are again at the center of a social and political mutation, but this time, its outcome will be women's liberation.

To prepare the way for its own revolution, the feminist movement, in the socialist view, ought to base its strategy on a transitional program of democratic demands which will be rooted in the needs of the female masses. This program specifically aimed at women can be carried out through coalitions of various feminist groups working together, in spite of their divergent ideologies, on the first common ground they can find. Among the essential issues are each woman's right to control her own body, the evolution of the institution of the family, and economic liberation by ending all discrimination in employment and education. The choice of the evolution, as opposed to the destruction, of the family as an institution, is based on the conviction that replacement structures still have to be created to perform the economic and social functions heretofore fulfilled by the family. In another example of compromise, the feminist radical program incorporates the Equal Rights Amendment (ERA), even though the ERA demands equal rights in a society that has not yet been reformed by revolution. Counting somewhat on the notion of retroactive correction, the feminist radicals consider passage of the ERA as a sort of overdue readjustment of history and democracy, with equal rights for women having been too long postponed; besides, during the transition period, the ERA will be needed to guarantee the end of sexual discrimination. Concerned about protecting the female worker masses, and not wanting to fall into reverse discrimination, feminist radicals propose that the so-called protective legislation, instead of being abolished as sexist, should be maintained, but extended to include men as well as women.

The feminist radical revolution, properly speaking, will be achieved in two phases. First, in modern industrialized countries, a sufficient degree of industrial development has now been achieved to allow full integration of women in industry. Feminist radicals, faithful to the theories of Engels, thus foresee the realization of the "first premise of women's emancipation." A necessary consequence of this initial mutation is supposed to be the industrialization of domestic labor. It is here, in this second premise of women's liberation, that the feminist radicals seem to place their hopes of seeing the socialist revolution include the feminist revolution. According to Marie-Alice Waters and Margaret Benston, the industrialization of domestic labor will effectively end the economic function of the family, and thereby destroy the material basis for the oppression of women. Hence, Marxism alone will suffice to resolve the psychosexual dilemma. We wonder whether these Marxist theorists might not have underestimated the psychological basis of women's oppression—the psychology of power—and whether, in believing that resolving the economic problem of the family will necessarily entail the disappearance of the psychic structure of oppression, they might not be guilty of excess optimism.

What will the society be like after the revolution, according to feminist socialists? We have not found any full-length portrait of utopia, only some rough sketches, in which two main features are always indicated: first, the end of all maternal responsibility for child rearing, with the establishment of free nurseries and child care centers operating twenty-four hours a day; second, the industrialization of domestic labor, including a communal system of housecleaning, laundry, and meal services.

All this was already foreseen long ago by Engels in his projections of a Marxist future. We have also encountered this concept in the liberal feminist utopia. Here, therefore, feminist social radicalism is not introducing innovations. What it really seems to be proposing is a return to the pure sources of Marxism, with the primary aim of countering the antifeminist aspects of the views of communist revisionists. Inspired by faith in socialism, and proud, for the most part, of belonging to the SWP, the only political party to have developed a program platform in favor of women's liberation, the feminist radicals honestly admit their intention to undertake active socialist proselytizing within the new feminist movement.

Feminist Radicals Judge the Women's Movement

The feminist radicals' judgment of the Women's movement is conditioned by the two main focal points of their strategy: in the long term, the development of a grand, unified feminist movement, and in the short term, the formation of vast coalitions for the achievement of particular goals.

In her essay "Women and Political Power," Betsey Stone[68] attacks the *raison d'être* of the National Women's Political Caucus (NWPC), which is to promote access by the greatest number of women to positions of political power. Although the NWPC claims to be nonaligned, its candidates, remarks Betsey Stone, always run for office under the label of one of the traditional political parties. Such a policy, she believes, is derived from false pragmatism, consisting of wishing to attend to the most urgent things first. Furthermore, it overestimates the moral value of women, leading some militants, Gloria Steinem among others, to dream of a world where politics are made suddenly cleaner by the arrival of women in power. In so doing, says Stone, the liberals, or egalitarian feminists, are mistaking the target and are aiming their fire at the "masculine mystique" instead of directly attacking capitalism. Finally, says Stone, their cooperation with the existing parties and their electoral propaganda constitute a deviation which is harmful to the special interests of women. For example, in 1972, in order not to risk hurting the chances of the Democratic party, the NWPC avoided any debate on abortion, even going so far as arranging campaign rallies on the same day that the Women's National Abortion Action Coalition (WONAAC) had organized a national abortion day. There, says Betsey Stone, we have a case of the politics of last resort, comparable to those of the black civil rights movement in the 1964 election of Lyndon Johnson, or of the pacifist movement in the 1968 campaign of Eugene McCarthy.

On balance, these criticisms are remarkable for their moderate tone. Certainly, the SWP denounces the liberal feminists for cooperating with the capitalist system, but it does not question that the majority of them are acting in good faith. It even congratulates them on their ability to mobilize their troops.[69] It is clear that the feminist radicals hear a familiar chord in the liberal feminists' will to action. Besides, in the short term, the feminist radicals themselves are limiting their strategy to merely reformist objectives, as witness their support for the Equal Rights Amendment. In the long term, they have hopes of winning over some liberal feminists to the socialist cause. The criticisms expressed by the women of the Young Socialist Alliance (YSA) become personal and bitter only when their target is the now-legendary pair of politicians, Bella Abzug and Shirley Chisholm, whom they denounce as capitalists and opportunists of feminism.

The feminist radicals converge with the liberal feminists in their will to action toward specific short-term objectives or reforms; however, this same will to action distances the feminist radicals from some groups among radical feminists, whom they identify as "parlor feminists" or "utopian idealists." These derisive labels are attached to those women who remain caught up in the personal, who are hostile to any effort to indoctrinate women into a mass organization, and who try to live lives free of any alienation, within the cozy comfort of their in-group. Feminist radical critics cite the example of Cell 16; it is easy to imagine that they are also aiming at the group called the Feminists. As for the charge of "utopian idealism," the feminist radicals find the radical feminists guilty for their involvement with alternative institutions. They criticize these women for refusing to take a stance calling upon the government to face up to its social responsibilities, believing instead that women themselves have the necessary resources to create child care centers, family planning clinics, food cooperatives, and so forth. In the view of the feminist radicals, such initiatives belong to the "utopian bourgeois mentality"; they are only available to rich women and risk veering the movement toward the tradition of volunteer charity work.

In both cases, the radical feminists are presented as being caught in the trap of the personal. In fairness, this reproach can only be applied to a minority of radical feminists, and furthermore, let it be recalled that radical feminists themselves, in their efforts at self-criticism, denounced these weaknesses within their own ranks. It also seems that by their disavowal of alternative institutions, feminist radicals are indirectly attacking lesbians. The lesbians' genuine problems (which extend even to their very survival, they claim) are entirely dodged by feminist radical militants, who are more concerned with socialism than with sexuality or ontology; but the feminist radicals deserve tribute for having refused to enter into any personal polemics.

Proselytizing by YSA Women Again Raises the Problem of Internal Organization

Many liberal and radical feminists would raise the objection that a moderate tone is always effective in any effort at political infiltration or conversion. In fact, this was proven in the years 1970–72, when socialist proselytizing by women of the YSA caused some problems for both liberal and radical feminism. The militants of these two tendencies discovered the danger of political takeover and control that threatens unstructured groups when faced with a well-organized entity having a strong central power structure, such as the Socialist Workers party.

Among the most severe denunciations are the report written by Lucy Komisar for the NOW governing board,[70] and the protests made by the young radical feminist group known as the Chicago Women's Liberation Union.[71] A consensus was established condemning the coercive methods used by the women of the YSA. These methods were perceived as being essentially intended to manipulate feminist organizations so as to promote the Socialist Workers party (SWP), and according to the charges, they ranged from taking over control at meetings to embezzling funds. A purge followed, which considerably weakened the influence of socialists within the Women's movement. Happily for the YSA women, however, a new outlet for their energy presented itself in the form of the Women's National Abortion Action Coalition (WONAAC).

The conversion campaign by feminist radicals, like the proselytizing by lesbians, served to expose the vulnerability to which the feminist movement was condemned by its lack of strong internal structures. Many feminist groups learned the lesson: some, like the Seattle Radical Women, retained their identity through a dissuasive program, while others, such as the Chicago Women's Liberation Union, opted for a stronger organization, forming themselves into chapters under the authority of a central executive committee.

It is not surprising that feminist social radicals chose to concentrate on the struggle for abortion rights, operating within WONAAC. Such specialization furnished them with a specific fundamental objective: to eliminate the biological oppression of women. This specialization was in perfect harmony with the two main traits that define feminist radicalism: pragmatism and radical socialist orthodoxy. The feminist radicals are hostages of socialism, in the same way that egalitarian feminists are bound by their primary allegiance to Americanism, and both are thus somewhat imprisoned by their orthodoxy and condemned to imitative behavior and noninnovative theory.

Militant lesbians appear to have the greatest autonomy, in the sense that they have broken off relations with the other sex. While we must applaud their proposal for a society in which categorization by sexuality would not exist, we cannot help wondering if this proposal is not inherently in contradiction with the irreversibility and polarizing character of homosexuality. Although female homosexuality has appeared in recent years as a political choice and a somewhat voguish trend from which feminism keeps a wary distance depending on changing circumstances, lesbianism in its older and more authentic form is a way of life whose deep roots evade easy explanation. From a theoretical viewpoint, the lesbian analysis, such as it was developed openly at the time of new feminist resurgence, has been more imitative than innovative, being grafted onto radical feminist theory.

A simplistic view of radical feminist theory sums it up as follows: a refusal of love, a rejection of the dominant culture, hate for men, and separatism. In the media, literal interpretations of these positions have attained remarkably wide distribution. We believe that this exposure has had a positive effect, in the sense that it has considerably shaken up the smugness of male chauvinists among all men, particularly on the political Left. It is thanks to the radical feminists that feminism has been able to exist as an autonomous movement, to have escaped from being coopted by socialism and to have had a universal reach.

Nevertheless, the time has come for these same radical feminists to explain their declarations and to reveal to the public that their rejection of love, culture, and men are specifically aimed at the *corruption* of love, the *corruption* of culture, and the *sociologically defined behavior* of men. The radical feminists should give their utopian revolutionary program the same widespread media exposure that others have given to caricaturing feminist philosophy. The task will be harder, since it will not necessarily have the sympathetic cooperation of the media. But it seems to us to be vital, if these militants want to avoid having radical feminism, already torn apart by internal conflicts, being turned into no more than a butt of crude jokes, a scarecrow with which to frighten women away from feminism.

FIVE

A Feminist Theory of Androgyny

Feminist philosophy is constantly evolving. The androgynist point of view was yet another theory that developed within the new feminist movement of the 1960s, and it found its best expression in literature.

Androgyny is certainly the most revolutionary concept in contemporary feminism. The philosophy of androgyny specifically addresses the psychic structures of sexism. For Mary Daly, at the time when she wrote *Beyond God the Father* (1973),[1] this philosophy meant the repudiation not only of sexism, but also of its root cause: the Divine Plan. For in her view, the traditional interpretation of the Divine Plan, under whatever name it is called, is the original source of alienation of the two sexes. The philosophy of androgyny has thus been perceived as an adventure in ontology, the systematic study of being, which addresses the great existential questions. Androgyny offers a new perspective rather than a strictly codified theory.

Carolyn Heilbrun, in *Toward a Recognition of Androgyny*,[2] embarks on the ontological quest by tracing the flow of "the hidden river of androgyny" in our heritage from the past. Myths, heroines of turn-of-the-century novels whose actions oppose the "anti-androgynous world," the life-style of the Bloomsbury Group, all of these are beacons lighting the voyage to "ontological salvation." Heilbrun's book is an appeal for recognition of androgyny not just as a fantasy, but as a truly possible psychic identity.

THE FEMINIST CONCEPT OF ANDROGYNY

In the introduction to her book, Carolyn Heilbrun makes an important distinction intended to dispel any misunderstandings about the concept of androgyny as it is interpreted by feminists and presented in this chapter. Heilbrun says, "One danger perhaps remains: that androgyny, an ideal, might be confused with hermaphroditism, an anomalous physical condition."[3]

Carolyn Heilbrun's feminism consists in rendering the concept of androgyny devoid of any bodily connotations. In so doing, she breaks with the Freudian conception of psychic bisexuality, which is supposed to be grounded in physical bisexuality. Androgyny in her meaning is not a matter of fantasizing about new kinds of sexual union or wishing to have the organs and bodily functions of the opposite sex, but rather it is the pursuit of an ideal "unlimited personality," based on the refusal to sexualize human traits or to link psychic identity with biological sex.

What is this ideal of "unlimited personality" and "universal human traits"? Carolyn Heilbrun, following Euripides, sees its prototype in Dionysus, as the "embodiment of universal vitality." It is defined as "woman-in-man or man-in-woman." Here we find ourselves at the heart of the issue raised by feminism. Man, having set himself up as the "norm," as the ideal and superior being, has perceived the feminine principle as "other," that is, inferior; hence, he perceives woman as something nonhuman, alien, an object. The perspective of androgyny, which sees the "feminine" in the "masculine" and vice versa, rejects the notion of "otherness" which, by definition, depersonalizes some humans as alien beings. Instead, it demands recognition of "the importance of the 'feminine' principle, not as 'other,' but as necessary to wholeness."[4]

Note that the feminine principle is considered "important" but not "superior," since there is no presumption of any ideal sexual norm in the egalitarian reciprocity of androgyny. Sexual labels become purely conventions, and the terms *feminine* and *masculine* have completely equal value. While Germaine Greer warns women against blindly trying to imitate men (who are themselves victims of mutilation in their own quest for a superhuman self), Phyllis Chesler reproaches some feminist theorists for exalting so-called feminine virtues, such as intuition and compassion. These traits, she says, should not be considered solely the privileged attributes of women; they are universal human traits. If they have been more developed in women than in men, this is a compensatory adaptation, because other traits have been repressed. Their importance in feminine psychology must therefore be seen as "the price exacted by sexism."

The feminist concept of androgyny contains not only ontological connotations; it also has social implications. For in providing for total realization of the self, it additionally opens the way for a reconciliation between the sexes, with every sort of being participating in the full span of human experience. The quest for oneness of the human personality expresses a refusal of what psychology calls sexion,[5] or sexual cleavage. This is meant not only in its biological implications, as in the myth portrayed by Aristophanes, but also in its psychic and social implications: sexion of the psychic identity, and sexual polarization of behavior in keeping with the biological sex. This quest is a challenge to gender identity which, as an assigned or learned sex role, is based on the individual's repression into the unconscious of all psychic manifestations of the opposite sex.

The feminists who support the androgyny concept are pleading innocent to the accusation Juliet Mitchell launched against her radical sisters in *Psychoanalysis and Feminism,* of having forever closed the door on an exploration of the feminine unconscious.

THE PROBLEM OF PSYCHIC IDENTITY

The feminists of the androgyny theory are picking up the old debate about nature versus nurture, or natural heredity versus cultural environment. Germaine Greer and Zella Luria, among others, postulate that culture is primary in forming the psychic identity of both men and women, who are cultural beings by nature.

The "normal" sex roles that we learn to play from our infancy are no more natural than the antics of a transvestite.[6]

The definition of masculine and feminine is not a closed biological definition but rather a social division that is wide open.[7]

The androgynists therefore refute the notion of an innate, universal masculine or feminine nature, placing the emphasis instead on the learned character of behavior. They take great care to reveal how the learning process occurs through the predominating environment, as demonstrated by various experiments in psychology. Zella Luria, for example, supports her theses with the research findings of John Money and Anke Ehrhardt, who revealed that starting from the same biological substratum (infants of type 46.XX, with female chromosome structure but the anomaly of male external genital organs, in pairs of identical twins), it is possible to develop two alternate forms of behavior, identified with either the feminine or masculine gender. The process consists simply of labeling the child as a boy or a girl, and raising it in keeping with the label.

The children who had lived many years with the assigned masculine gender chose to keep it. Those who had lived a long time with the assigned feminine gender chose corrective surgery toward female characteristics. They had in fact become what they had been assigned to be. This can aptly be called the "Pirandello effect."[8]

Zella Luria belongs to the feminist school of psychology, which also includes Phyllis Chesler, Eleanor Maccoby, and Naomi Weisstein,[9] whose work is used as a reference by feminists of every tendency. These feminist psychologists are somewhat of an antidote to women psychologists of the post-Freudian school, whose advocates have been Marie Bonaparte, Helene Deutsch, and Marynia Farnham.

For instance, Eleanor Maccoby's research[10] with young children led her to conclude that there is a great similarity psychologically between the two sexes in the first two years of life, with differences in social behavior beginning to appear in the third year. The underlying implications are twofold. First, there is neither a masculine nor a feminine nature, in the sense that there exists no psychological trait that exclusively belongs to one or the other sex. Secondly, there exists a sort of apprenticeship in gender identity, which begins to show results around age two.

The androgyny theorists stress that it is not a question of attempting a block rejection of sexual differences, but rather of restoring them to their true proportions. Admittedly, say Eleanor Maccoby and Zella Luria, there are sexual contributions from the genetic program, but these are "relatively mitigated." On this point, Eleanor Maccoby underlines the notion of "average difference," that is, difference between the statistically defined general psychological profiles of the two sexes. Statistical averaging should not make us forget that individual variations exist within each sex, with some women presenting a "masculine" psychological profile and some men showing a "feminine" psychological profile. At the current stage of research, say the feminist psychologists of the androgyny theory, the mind has no sex.

The new balance achieved by the feminists of the androgyny theory between genetic and cultural influences, between innate and acquired characteristics, challenges not only the exaggeration of psychosexual differences, but also another distortion. This is the pretended claim of women's "inability to adapt," which is often stated to be linked to their reproductive capacity, without any recognition of sociological and cultural realities, that is, the quasi-immutable feminine role in society.

In terms of feminist androgyny theory, our society is accused of reducing psychic identity to gender identity, narrowly polarized between "masculine" and "feminine," and achieving this result through a long series of violent aggressions against each individual personality. Parents—fathers more than mothers, according to Zella Luria's research—stereotype their children in keeping with the sexual differences perceived by society. The parents' perceptions are reinforced when they are internalized by the children, and thus become self-fulfilling prophecies. In this way, through subtle conditioning, individuals become walking stereotypes, matching the ideal definitions that have been assigned to their genetic sexual group. But, these feminists ask, assigned by whom?

WHO'S RESPONSIBLE FOR SOCIALIZATION? OR, RELIGION AND PSYCHOANALYSIS ON TRIAL

Parents, friends, teachers, textbook authors and illustrators, advertisers, those who control the mass media, toy and clothes manufacturers, professionals such as doctors and psychologists—all contribute to the socialization process. This happens through dynamics that are largely uncalculated and unconscious, yet which reinforce the assumptions, attitudes, stereotypes, customs and arrangements of sexually hierarchical society.[11]

"Largely uncalculated and unconscious" . . . This statement absolves a lot of individuals from responsibility and definitively shifts the blame back on the socialization process itself. For feminists of the androgyny theory, stereotyping people is an inveterate tendency of human nature; that is, our species is not content to see itself as it is, but must stereotype. Therefore, androgynists believe not that there has been a masculine conspiracy in history, but rather that, from the interaction between biology and culture, a set of myths have been born, which together constitute, according to Phyllis Chesler,[12] "the psychology of modern history," in the sense that they mold our personalities.

Men nonetheless are not entirely pardoned in the eyes of the feminists of the androgyny theory. Many of these feminists state that once the process of stereotyping was underway, certain masculine power groups intervened in it early, taking advantage of it opportunistically, according to Phyllis Chesler, so as to create a sexual caste system, which preceded the creation of racial and economic classes. Here we are approaching the radical feminist viewpoint, with the variation that the expression "feminine caste"—a group systematically stigmatized solely for being born female—is substituted for the expression "feminine class"—a group resulting from economic, political, and social exploitation decreed by men and based on sex.

For Mary Daly, a particularly heavy burden of responsibility lies on

Judeo-Christian theologians, the fathers of Western culture. Their ideas on the spiritual mission of man and the intrinsically evil nature of woman have been reflected and enlarged upon by women themselves in a society where, according to Virginia Woolf, women have always acted as magnifying mirrors for men, reflecting back an image of them that is larger than life. In order to understand the androgyny theorists' hostility toward the Judeo-Christian tradition, it suffices to consider how far Judaism has gone in repressing bisexuality—the most striking example doubtless being the ritual of circumcision—and how much Christianity has rationalized it in religious ceremonies.

In this repression, presumed to be imposed by divine law, Georg Groddeck even saw one of the reasons why the important issue of masculinity and femininity in human beings has been relegated to the background in psychoanalysis and everyday life. Indeed, although psychoanalysis recognizes bisexuality during "anamnesis" (the clinical practice of probing the patient's memory), psychoanalytic therapy does everything possible to stifle it. It is therefore understandable that feminists of the androgyny theory do not look for any extenuating circumstances in putting psychoanalysis on trial, but instead make it their favorite target, as the "new theology" of modern times, which has substituted the terms *mental health* and *mental illness* for the religious concepts of good and evil.

Attacks are waged on two fronts: in the field of academic research, and in the field of clinical psychology and psychiatry. The latter field is characterized by a primarily feminine clientele being treated by primarily masculine therapists. The problem raised by Naomi Weisstein and Phyllis Chesler, therefore, is that male practitioners have internalized our society's prejudices about the two sexes, which have been rationalized by modern psychology. Among the five false preconceptions that Phyllis Chesler denounces in the field of psychology, she stresses one in particular: the tendency toward the belief that only men can be mentally healthy. The amount of study she devotes to this prejudice is explained by the fact that it reveals modern psychology as discriminatory in its very essence, based on a double standard in measuring mental health. In particular, Chesler reports an interesting experiment conducted by Inge K. Broverman at Worcester Hospital in 1968. Identical lists of 122 character traits were presented to three groups of psychologists that included both men and women. The first group was asked to draw up a list of character traits that would be found in a clinically sane man; the second group was to do the same thing for a clinically sane woman; the third group's list was supposed to describe a clinically sane adult. When the three lists were compared, it was found that the first and third coincided perfectly, but the second and third were in total contradiction to each other. The experiment demonstrated that for these particular psychologists, believed to be representative of their colleagues, the idea of a clinically sane woman contradicted their idea of a clinically sane adult, thus lending support to the thesis that the ethic of mental health is masculine in our society.

It is easy to see what ammunition such an experiment can provide to feminists. It enables them to point to the fundamental paradox in the classic position of the psychology profession regarding women, as follows: a dependent, fearful, emotional woman is not recognized as a mentally healthy adult, *but she is a mentally healthy woman;* conversely, a woman who has qualities defined as appropriate to a mentally healthy adult or a mentally healthy man—being enterprising, outgoing, and independent—is *not a mentally healthy woman,* but a neurotic!

This experiment also exposed the fundamental false premise on which modern psychology is based: the belief in the existence of a feminine nature, and as a corollary, a masculine nature. Here, Naomi Weisstein's position converges with that of Phyllis Chesler. Weisstein even identifies this preconception as the cause of the failure of psychology, since it leads most psychologists to postulate that human behavior flows from an individual inner dynamic.

That psychology practitioners and students approach every experiment with conventional ideas about the two sexes is illustrated by tests of sex identification. During a Harvard graduate seminar that Naomi Weisstein attended, participants were asked to examine two piles of tests and identify the sex of the persons tested, one pile having been written exclusively by women, the other by men. Only four persons in twenty were able to identify correctly the two piles. The error, Weisstein specifies, was not attributable to the students, but rather to erroneous psychology teaching; the students had learned their lessons all too well.

Her conclusion is clear: founded on a double standard of mental health and a set of preconceived beliefs, psychology as it is practiced in academic research is nothing but a pseudo-science, with no value whatsoever in the search for a liberating solution for women.

In the field of psychoanalysis and psychiatry, feminist androgyny theorists emphasize the dialectic between the two phases of anamnesis and therapy. As stated above, although bisexuality is recognized in the first phase, the phase of thorough exploration of the patient's unconscious, it is repressed in the subsequent therapy phase, when psychoanalysis reinforces the patriarchal system by reintegrating women in their "normal" roles, that is, into a system based on sexual bipolarization and not on bisexuality. Whether in private therapy or a psychiatric hospital, a woman who rebels against the "normal" feminine role is treated as an anomaly and "cured" by a form of therapy that is a reflection and magnification of the very patriarchal order that the rebel is rejecting. In addition, psychiatric hospitals, by being organized around a sexually stereotyped division of labor, condoning coquettishness and even sometimes being the scene of physical or sexual molestation, function as "mirror images of the female experience, and as penalties for *being* female, as well as for desiring or daring *not* to be." [13]

In the same way, private therapy operates as a buttress of the patriarchal structure, in the sense that the therapist/patient relationship not only mirrors the situation of power and pretended protection in the father/daughter or husband/wife relationship, but also supports the institutions of marriage and the family. The most telling example occurs when the therapy includes a sexual relationship between the middle-aged male therapist and the young female patient (questionable ethically, but not unknown to happen). This relationship is conceived, according to Phyllis Chesler, as a violation of the taboo of incest, intended to reinforce the attraction, and therefore the domination, of the prestigious masculine figure, first the father, and later the husband.

At this game, women are beaten before they start. Far from liberating the woman patient, the therapist/patient relationship projects the therapist's neurosis on her. This idea is not new; in 1926, Karen Horney was already pointing out how much the psychoanalyst's idea of women's development simply reproduced the typical idea that boys have of girls. Far from liberating the woman patient who is suffering from a desire to rebel, psychiatry even prides itself on being antifeminist. Mary Daly in fact remarks that there is a coincidence between the emergence of a second wave of popularity of psychosurgery and the second wave of feminism, citing Barbara Roberts's analogy with genocide, calling psychotherapy the "final solution" of the woman's problem.

The indignant tone and the forceful comparisons are felt necessary to adequately express feminists' outrage over the way in which women are victimized by the virtuosos of psychoanalysis. These warnings are thought all the more urgent since, twenty years after the reign of the feminine mystique, the psychoanalyst's couch continues to exercise its charm. Psychoanalysis is perceived by the woman patient as the solution to a problem she poses in individual terms, in keeping with the feminine role; and the analyst responds in kind, by lending masculine aid and protection. In the early years of new feminist activism, Phyllis Chesler reveals, the total number of American women in psychiatric facilities increased from 479,167 in 1964 (1,079 more women than men) to 615,112 in 1968 (50,363 more women than men).

The publication of statistics on psychiatric institutions and the exposure of the underlying imposture of private therapy are the direct consequences of feminist militancy. Feminists were attempting a rescue operation and recruitment campaign to convince women candidates for the psychoanalyst's couch that the best therapy was feminism itself. It is in the context of this rescue operation that one should interpret Phyllis Chesler's remarks:

Up to a point, women's liberation was more 'therapeutic' than either marriage or psychotherapy: it made women happier, angrier, more confident, more adventurous, more moral—and it produced a range of behavioral changes. [14]

Phyllis Chesler's 1972 book even foresees the development of radical or feminist psychotherapy, a possibility which, she admits, inspires an uncertain or even uneasy reaction. In bringing that about, the psychologists of androgyny will have played a heuristic role, in demanding that, in the frame of reference of future researchers, "normal" human beings shall have both "masculine" and "feminine" personality traits.

THE FEMININE SOCIAL ROLE

Self-Sacrifice

According to Phyllis Chesler, mythology is the psychology of modern times, in the sense that myths shape our personalities. For this feminist psychologist, the formative myth of the feminine social role is that of Demeter and Persephone, centered, as it is, on self-sacrifice:

Neither Demeter nor Persephone *acts*. They *react*—to rape or to the loss of a daughter or virgin self. Demeter and Persephone are not Amazon figures. Their cult is essentially one of Earth-Mother-worship: mothers who produce more mothers to nurture and sustain mankind with their "miraculous" biological gifts of crops and daughters. The inevitable sacrifice of self that biology demands of women in most societies is at the heart of the Demetrian myth. [15]

Chesler's distinction between action and reaction implies the perception of women as submissive and dependent. Women, as reactive creatures, are not capable of initiative, and therefore can neither attain the highest levels of culture, nor achieve the full realization of their own humanity. The sexual act to which both goddesses in the myth are reacting, the rape and kidnapping of Persephone by the god of the underworld, or perhaps even by Dionysus or Zeus, both, in various versions, presumed to be her father, is the model for a concept of sexuality founded on the triad of rape/incest/procreation. The myth reproduces on three levels—cultural, ontological, and sexual—the renunciation that women are expected to accept in marriage. The "flowers of forgetfulness" gathered by Persephone prefigure, in Chesler's view, the loss of individuality in conjugal union. Unfortunately, the modern Persephone no longer has her mother to save her; the modern mother, having been socialized in the maternal function of self-abnegation and devotion to the male, prepares her daughter to submit to the same subordination. Deprivation of maternal solicitude and sexual harassment: these are the two factors which, according to Phyllis Chesler, condition the daughter to accept her submissive role.

The self-sacrifice that the feminist psychologist denounces, in both the myth and the reality of the feminine social role, refers to motherhood, since the patriarchal system dictates that the maternal function is *the* social function of woman, on the premise that gestation inevitably imposes on the biological mother the responsibilities of child raising. Chesler denounces the anachronistic distortion by which, through Freudian psychology, what once was a necessity for the survival of the species has been transformed into a salvation myth aimed at twentieth-century women. We begin to see a consensus forming that the maternal function is the crux of the separation between male and female roles on reaching adulthood.

Referring to recent research carried out by Feldman and Nash on the degree of interest in young children manifested by adults of both sexes, Eleanor Maccoby recalls that the people showing the most sensitivity, whether men or women, were those who had already been placed in a position of responsibility for children. Here we are witnessing not only the usual effort to establish a new balance between genetic and social factors, but also, particularly, a refutation of any sexually differentiated response between men and women regarding children. Both "masculine" and "feminine" traits are associated with nurturing behavior. Clearly, the feminists of the androgyny theory are not rejecting the whole idea of the maternal function, but rather the theory that women have a monopoly on the maternal instinct.

The issue is not stated in political terms or in terms of the right to work, but in existential and philosophical terms, as witness the series of open questions posed by Eleanor Maccoby. Why, in the name of a supposed aptitude for nurturing, are women forbidden to participate in other aspects of adult life, and thereby prevented from achieving self-fulfillment? What effect would there be on men if they were to take on part of the responsibility for the so-called maternal function? In recent experiments to test this thesis, the results showed reduced tendencies to aggression. Might that not be, asks Eleanor Maccoby, a potential remedy for the violence in our society? In this insistence on the need for an equitable sharing of responsibilities between both sexes, feminist androgyny theorists reveal their profound conviction that only a redistribution of the so-called maternal function can provide the premise for sexual depolarization, with the first image presented to children being that of happy cooperation between the sexes.

Symptomatology

In Chesler's view, the modern Persephone, abandoned by her mother, presents three fundamental psychiatric symptoms: a state of depression, frigidity, and suicidal tendencies. Depression in women is a perpetual "state of mourning" for something that they have never had; frigidity, which is the renunciation of sexual pleasure in return for economic security and maternity, will persist as long as the institutions of prostitution, rape, and patriarchal marriage still thrive; as to the expression *suicidal tendencies,* Chesler says it refers to the fact that women usually do not actually kill themselves, as men do, but merely make *suicide attempts,* since the essence of femininity, acquired through cultural conditioning, is to lose in order to win. Ironically, Chesler points out, the women who succeed in suicide thus manage, in one way, to reject the feminine role of being predestined to failure, but they do so by paying the only price possible: death. The central focus of the author's organizational scheme is obviously *lack,* whether in terms of privation, lack of self-realization, or failure. From this sense of failure, there emerges the self-destruction that accompanies self-hatred. Mary Daly and Germaine Greer recall that self-hatred is the female victim's internalized reflection of the male oppressor's own self-hatred; the male purges his guilt by turning his self-hatred against the female as a scapegoat.

The feminine choice of failure characterizes what feminists of the androgyny theory call "the dread of happiness" or "the fear of freedom," perceived by Thomas Szasz as the "indirect forms of communication" characteristic of "the slave psychology,"[16] and which are in fact forms of rebellion against the oppressor. The feminist psychologist develops this thesis in an effort to prove that women's psychiatric symptoms are not linked to specific feminine traits, but instead arise from the pathology of oppression, and are, by definition, signs of rebellion against oppression. They express aspirations, still unformulated but quite legitimate, to be authentically and fully oneself. In the final analysis, as we have seen in the Housewife's Syndrome, they are really signs of mental health, indicating that there could still be every possibility of self-realization if the "final solution" of psychiatry did not drag the rebel back, "cured" and docile, to the abhorred role.

Castration and Madness

Germaine Greer's thesis is that women's socialization into the feminine role has resulted in their "castration." Such an assertion is contrary to Freudian theory, because if there is such a thing as castration of women, the Freudians would only be able to find a place for it by categorizing it crushingly as a physical defect owing to an interruption of the biological process. However, Greer's "female eunuch" is not the same as the emasculated man defined in Freudian terms, with the clitoris being considered an aborted penis. Instead, the term "female eunuch" describes the psychological condition imposed on women by society's defining "femininity as meaning *without libido,* and therefore incomplete, subhuman, a cultural reduction of human possibilities."[17]

The refusal to be "subhuman" and the claim of the individual's right to realize her full potential fit into the perspective of the "unlimited personality" inherent in androgyny. This full potential is to be freed, says Germaine Greer, by the reintegration in women of the libido, an energy which is not the monopoly of masculinity but is essential to every living being. The fact that Germaine Greer studies four aspects of feminine castration—body, soul, love, and hate—reaffirms the libido as a force diffused throughout every aspect of the personality. She thus removes it from the narrow limits imposed by the patriarchal view of sexuality, that is, coitus between the active male patriarch and the passive female eunuch, or in other words, a relationship characteristic of sadomasochists.

Women have been castrated in the flesh in the sense that all signs of vigor and independence have been erased from the female body. The traits which earn women compliments from men are those typical of the castrate: soft curves, languor, delicacy. Castrated in their flesh, women have been taught to perceive sexuality as passive; therefore, their own sexuality has been distorted and denied. Kept in ignorance, they have become alienated from their own sexual and reproductive organs. In her study of the female body, Germaine Greer has chosen to give special attention to the primacy of cultural factors. This choice lies in feminist logic: after so many centuries in which sociological woman has been perceived as purely a product of biology, one would expect to find that woman's bodily aspects are malleable by socialization. Hence Greer's patient cataloging of the factors which, following the whims of fashion, have intervened to modify the work of nature and to turn the female skeleton into a feminine frame: corsets, pantyhose, high heels, eurythmic gymnastics, etc.

Likewise, women's souls have been subject to castration by conditioning, which has consisted of suppressing or diverting women's energy. As Freud observed—rightly, in this case—repression consumes energy that might otherwise be expressed in creativity. In this way, women are mutilated by the destructive action of unconsumed energy, which they turn against themselves.

The perversion of love, says Greer, is the consequence of the perversion of the libido into a male monopoly and into heterosexual relationships, which are by nature sadomasochistic. The three perversions of love are altruism, egotism, and obsession. The altruism of the "female eunuch," for example, is not genuinely altruistic, selfless concern for another, since it has a vested interest: in exchange for self-sacrifice, it demands security, as compensation for the loss of the self, that is, castration. Castration, again, under the aspect of loss of self-respect and a feeling of insecurity, is at the origin of jealousy, since jealousy is a form of amorous egotism. As to obsession with the object of one's love, this is "an aberration from the norm," "sickening," "a cheap ideology," and women must become aware that this is so because it is destroying them. Obviously, for Germaine Greer, love does not exist in the patriarchal society. What we call love, she says, is contrary to the very essence of love. Here we reencounter the opinion already expressed by the radical feminists, such as Shulamith Firestone and Ti-Grace Atkinson. Greer cites, without disagreeing, Ti-Grace's brutal phrase: "Love is the victim's response to the rapist."[18]

Perverted love engenders hate, in whose most profound depths there stagnates men's disgust for the facile and sordid sexual relationship. This disgust, of which one sign is the association of the sexual organs with those of excretion, makes men feel guilty, and they take out their guilt feelings by avenging themselves on the internal nature of women's genitalia. As a secret concavity, Mary Daly and Phyllis Chesler remind us, the vagina becomes a spittoon or a sewer. In Germaine Greer's view, the extreme expression of men's fixation and disgust with feminine genitalia is the clitoridectomy. For Phyllis Chesler, the culmination was the bloody episode of the witchhunt, a projection of a "sexocidal hatred of women." To be sure, the best proof of the success of the socialization of the "female eunuch" is women's internalization of this masculine hate for their genitalia, demonstrated either as deadly violence, which some women inflict on their own sex organs, or as nymphomania, which is nothing more than a compulsive need to degrade oneself.

As a new critical evaluation of women and their sexuality, Germaine Greer's theory of female castration seems to be a deliberate rebuttal of the post-Freudian view expressed by Freud's disciple Marie Bonaparte in *Female Sexuality*. Specifically, Greer's theory is the feminist antidote to the post-Freudian view that women's bodies and psyches are filled with the passive influences of the ovum. Marie Bonaparte wrote:

> Throughout the whole range of living creatures, animal or vegetal, passivity is characteristic of the female cell, the ovum whose mission is to *await* the male cell, the active mobile spermatazoan to come and *penetrate* it.[19]

Marie Bonaparte furthermore sought to ascribe the causes of frigidity to two factors supposedly inherent in the nature of women's bodies: weaker libidinal energy, and a greater acceptance of bisexuality; the latter, said she, made it even more difficult to adapt the patient's libido to the passive, that is vaginal, role. Bonaparte's post-Freudian diagnosis becomes, for Greer, a diagnostic error, since this diagnosis is itself the cause of the frigidity of the "female eunuch." In reading the two opposing theorists' descriptions of feminine social behavior, many will find the similarities more striking than the differences. But one crucial difference remains, which must be remembered from the start: the semantic content of the word *woman*. For Marie Bonaparte, the word refers to a biological being who, by her very nature, cannot become other than what she is. For Germaine Greer, however, the word refers to a product of culture, and in her introduction, she declares her basic assumption that "everything that we may observe could be otherwise." It is nature versus nurture again.

Phyllis Chesler's work *Women and Madness* contains many echos of Germaine Greer's thesis. The "female eunuch" and the mythological Persephone are both appellations of the same feminine artifact, that is, woman as an artifact of the patriarchal society. The first presents a face that is society's image of normality; the second is seen as pathological. The theory of women's madness proposed by Phyllis Chesler follows Germaine Greer's thesis, not only in picking up the theme of feminine castration, but also in the three perceived elements of this castration. "Such madness is essentially an intense experience of female biological, sexual and cultural castration, and a doomed search for potency."[20]

Here, madness functions as a partial or total rebellion against the sexual stereotype; in this form, it is called schizophrenia. It can also appear as a total acting-out of the devalued feminine role; in this form, it is called neurosis.

At the extreme, therefore, if we do not allow ourselves to be influenced by the labels assigned by the patriarchal experts, madness is a positive reaction, in the interpretation given to it by feminists of the androgyny theory. This is so in the sense that both cases above reveal a nonadaptation to an artificial role. The woman who totally acts out the devalued feminine role is manifesting a form of rebellion just as much as the one who violently rejects the stereotyped role. This acting-out process, in fact, is perceived by the victim as a ruse that will enable her to escape from the semi-existence of femininity; this is the interpretation Phyllis Chesler gives to the madness of Ellen West, Zelda Fitzgerald, and Sylvia Plath. There is no question that, in feminist terms, this is an erroneous choice, since seen by psychiatrists as crippling, self-destructive immaturity, it condemns women to the "bell jar."[21] of the psychiatric hospital, which offers neither refuge nor liberty.

Phyllis Chesler's theory can be classified with the famous "anti-psychiatry" of Ronald Laing. Feminists of the androgyny theory propose that feminine "madness" ought no longer to be treated by thwarting its progress, but on the contrary, by letting it take its normal course. It would appear then that feminine "madness" is not illness but the beginning of the cure, a step on the road toward the woman's return to being authentically herself, in the ontological quest for her own identity.

THE ANDROGYNOUS FEMINIST REVOLUTION

The androgynous feminist revolution will mean liberation for both sexes. From the outset, the principle of individual liberty applies doubly, calling for human beings of both sexes to have the right to spontaneous self-expression and free interaction of sexual characteristics. The androgynous feminist revolution will therefore be essentially a spiritual one, a revolution in ontology, that is, in confronting the fundamental spiritual questions of human existence. Androgynous feminism will thereby transform human consciousness and will generate "a human becoming, pointing beyond the idolatries of sexist society."[22]

Mary Daly, in her book *Beyond God the Father,* which she defines as a work of philosophy, redefines the semantics of the old patriarchal theological concepts in new humanist terms, and sees in the Women's movement hope for a new potential in human development. This is so in the sense that the Women's movement accomplishes a synthesis between the individual's ontological dimension and society's ontological dimension, by linking the individual's journey of self-discovery with her revolutionary participation in history. This synthesis involves a journey of self-discovery for each woman, from the isolation of the "non-being of the separation"— rupture with the patriarchal society—to the return voyage in community, to forge a new reality with other human beings. This reality will be revolutionary, for each woman, as a member of a movement, is participating in history, and is struggling not only to overturn those who are in power, but also to destroy the masculine and feminine models that restrict the human potential of both men and women.

Founded on the theory that energy lost will ultimately be regained, the androgynous feminist revolution is perceived as joyful. Germaine Greer exalts "joy in struggle," and Mary Daly, in her "Feminist Postchristian Introduction" to *The Church and the Second Sex,* salutes the "ludic cerebration" represented by women's rediscovery of their brain power.

Although this revolution, in the long term, is to be the work of all men and women, it will begin by the self-liberation of women. This priority is explained by the fact that women, suffering from greater alienation as a consequence of their relegation to an inferior status, have intuitively recognized the dehumanization of which both sexes are victims in the context of current society.

Using different formulas, all the theorists of androgynous feminism prescribe the same break with the paternalistic experience. Phyllis Chesler speaks of each woman's redirecting her feelings of love toward the realization of her true self. This love would no longer be the kind she grants to a man in return for security and protection, but rather a new kind, love of her own strength and self-confidence. This is what Germaine Greer calls "personal security," enabling women to discover that insecurity is the first prerequisite for liberty. Greer exhorts women to break away from the old sexual model of rape/incest/procreation; the entire system is open to question.

Women must learn how to question the most basic assumptions about feminine normality in order to reopen the possibilities for development which have been successively blocked off by conditioning.[23]

These theorists do not hide the difficulties each woman will encounter on the road to her own personal liberation. The process of becoming oneself demands all one's existential courage to face the experience of nothingness, whether it is called entering non-being or "explor[ing] the dark without any guide." According to Mary Daly, the ontological quest first involves a descent "into the depths," an experience that will not be suicidal if it is carried out in "sisterhood" within the feminist community.

The philosophy of *Beyond God the Father* invites women to an initial phase of collective exorcism of the patriarchal presence that has been internalized by women ever since the Original Sin as feelings of guilt, inferiority, and self-hatred. This is the significance that Mary Daly gives to her feminist reading of the myth of the Fall. Removing the image of the Fall from its context in patriarchal religion, she sees it no longer as "a Fall *from* the sacred" but as "a Fall *into* the sacred and therefore into freedom," beyond the dichotomy of good and evil.

At this point, the second phase of the ontological experiment can begin: the return journey, founded on an intuition of the integrality of human experience, when androgyny will ultimately become a reality. This new ontological quest is perceived by Daly, the ex-theologian in the second stage of her commitment, as being based on women's refusal to accept the finite limits imposed until now by a supernatural entity that we have called God. As implied by the title of her book, Mary Daly is calling up women to take part in nothing less than a movement for deicide: a feminist version of "God is dead." She calls for deicide against "God the explanation," held up imperiously as the answer to all questioning; deicide against the "God of otherworldliness," presented as the promised reward for virtue; deicide against "God the judge of sin," who makes all women intrinsically guilty. Nor is it a question of preaching the coming of a woman divinity. Even though Daly's exhortations to reconcile former antitheses, such as thought and matter, spirit and flesh, might remind theologians of the doctrine of Saint-Simonism, we are a long way from the dogma of the Male-Female Godhead expounded by some of its disciples. In spite of her choice of words, there was no mysticism in Daly's androgyny. The only God[24] in *Beyond God the Father* is the potential for creativity inherent in each human being. God should be perceived as the power to be, a verb and not a noun. Just as the noun has implied that God's creatures are finite, that is, finished and static as they were created, so the verb implies the infinite, continuous fulfillment of each individual human being, and above all, of each woman. The author solemnly salutes "feminine ontophany," that is, the emergence of a new process of "women's becoming":

> Women's becoming is something more like a new creation . . . the arrival of New Being.[25]

With the arrival of this "New Being," new types of interactions and syntheses will occur between individuals of both sexes. Men will rediscover tenderness; women, energy. Other various liberation movements will crystallize around the Women's Liberation movement, which is already acting as a catalyst, since it frees both women and men from self-destructive dichotomies. This was the ex-theologian's real meaning—and not a sacralization of women—when she spoke of a "Second Coming," in contrast to the "First Coming," which was the sacralization of men. Inspired by this androgynous vision, and in Phyllis Chesler's phrase, after the entire social drama has been acted out, individuals of both sexes belonging to all the various liberation movements will together develop new institutions.

In the androgynous utopian society as seen by Germaine Greer, there would be no marriage, since any formal legalization ruins the chances for spontaneity and tenderness in relationships. Greer dreams of self-governing communes in the countryside, where parents would come and go depending on their job responsibilities, also sometimes moving in for long periods, and where the stable element would be the farm couple. The children would have all sorts of space to explore, while the adults would pass on to them their manual skills and intellectual knowledge. Juvenile sexual experimentation would not be discouraged. The child might not even know the identity of its genetic mother, while she could also have loving relationships with other children. Here we see that Greer is discarding the type of possessive relationships that develop in the nuclear family. A certain vagueness remains about how young adults would take their place in society, but this is perhaps inevitable in a proposal that does not pretend to be more than a first sketch. The problem is evaded by a half-joking reference to the number of socially maladjusted individuals regularly produced by the nuclear family.

In spite of Greer's opposition to the notion of a contract, her proposal is nonetheless based on a conviction that some form of stable structure is necessary to every social being. This is the same conviction that has led other feminists of the androgyny theory, Gayle Graham Yates, for example, to speak not of the abolition of marriage, but rather of a new pluralism in the types of marriage contracts available. This concept, which accepts the need for both legality and relative permanence, covers a whole range of solutions, including the single-parent family, communal marriages, and legal recognition of homosexual marriages. The need for legality is based on a recognition of the individual as a social being; the family unit would function "as a microcosm of social values, as a location for economic distribution."[26]

The requirement of permanence would ensure the stability that is necessary for the well-being and education of children, as well as the emotional security of all the members. Of course, it is understood that these types of marriage would be based on reciprocal contributions, as envisaged in Letty Cottin Pogrebin's experimental marriage,[27] or in Alix Kates Shulman's marriage contract.[28] This fundamental principle is judged necessary to end the sexual stereotyping that now confronts young children from the earliest age and which they internalize for a lifetime. The issue of the family is thus posed in terms of child rearing, that is, in terms of the training of future adults.

The androgynous feminist utopia also finds a place for love. Germaine Greer sees love as the relationship between two individuals who help each other find self-fulfillment, as described by Abraham Maslow. Very similar is the approach of Mary Daly in *Beyond God the Father,* for whom love is an attempt at oneness. It must be specified here that it is not a question of burying oneself in the other, as in the current interpretation of love in the patriarchal society denounced by Ti-Grace Atkinson; it is a question of aiming together, as a couple, to find a new way of being, which is to be born out of the energy of psychically androgynous women.

At that point, sexuality would no longer be the sadomasochist relationship that feminists condemn, but rather true interaction between the sexes: "a form of communication between potent, gentle, tender people."[29]

For Germaine Greer, the new heterosexual relationship, central to the life of every human being, would be just as much a liberation of men, who are tired of bearing all the sexual responsibility, as it would be of women. Women, from now on, must learn how to "humanize the penis," granting less importance to a man's male genitalia than to his human sexuality—a change that will only be possible if women's genitalia regain the same rights —without, however, falling into the constraining emphasis on technique of the sexologists Masters and Johnson.

Lastly, what sort of political regime is envisaged in the androgynous utopian society? Germaine Greer refrains from making any declarations of allegiance, so we must proceed by deduction. Her categorical rejection of reformism and her comment that "it might be possible . . . to arrive somehow at liberty and communism without strategy or revolutionary discipline"[30] suggest that her personal utopia would be linked to a nonbureacratic, decentralized form of socialism. Gayle Graham Yates, without making categorical assertions, nevertheless enlarges on the subject of "androgynous politics." This would be the fruit of equal cooperation between men and women. Women's contribution, at first, might be limited to specific fields, such as ecology, social services, and peace; but the author foresees a second phase when interactions would develop between the contributions of both sexes. Such an experiment, she tells us, would probably have its greatest chance of succeeding under a democratic socialist regime, with "androgynous democratic socialism" influencing the state toward decreased production of goods and increased production of services. Furthermore, in the androgynous democratic socialist state, excessive centralization would be avoided through a distribution of power among operational entities that would control the utilization of funds.

As we can see, the androgynous revolution is based on extreme generosity. However, generosity is one of the least-known aspects of feminism. The Women's movement has often been denigrated for the extravagance of its demands, the aggressiveness of its militants and the sensationalism of some of its demonstrations. But rarely is attention given, in return, to the humanist philosophy inherent in the androgynous perspective. In an age of the mass diffusion of ideas, this is one of the best-kept secrets of all contemporary philosophical movements. Could this be because, with a conscious will toward universality, the androgynous approach goes to the very heart of the problem between the sexes, and in questioning the identity of every man and woman, it makes us feel very insecure, at least in the short term? The question remains open, surrounded by an intriguing silence.

THE FEMINISTS OF THE ANDROGYNY THEORY
JUDGE THE WOMEN'S MOVEMENT

The feminists of the androgyny theory have not thrown themselves into the fray of criticism within the movement. Admittedly, Germaine Greer reproaches Betty Friedan for condemning women to equal opportunity under the status quo; furthermore, while she acknowledges her interest in Ti-Grace Atkinson as a person, she expresses her disagreement with the condemnation of sexuality by Atkinson's group, the Feminists. Nevertheless, the pages of *The Female Eunuch* devoted to the Women's movement are more of a cursory retrospective history than a strictly ordered critique.

The most serious criticism is expressed by Phyllis Chesler. For the author of *Women and Madness,* the American feminist movement has unquestionably reproduced the negative traits inherent in the acquired feminine role, specifically, the mutual feelings of antipathy and rivalry between women. The author lists a long catalog of griefs committed by women against each other. Within the movement itself, accusations have included the claimed "elitist arrogance" of professionally successful women, the supposed "pushiness" of black women, the so-called renegade cowardice of heterosexual women, and the pretended idiocy of the happy housewife! For Phyllis Chesler, the vindictiveness expressed against the "elitists" is simply a reflection of the patriarchal system's double standard, in which men can and should succeed, but not women.

However, on balance, the feminists of the androgyny theory render a favorable judgment on the Women's movement. Germaine Greer interprets the numerous subdivisions of the movement as a sign of its dynamism, or even its strength. Phyllis Chesler sees the movement as experimentation in new ways of being for women, and welcomes the proliferation of groups as an effort to institutionalize "sisterhood." In a note, she even praises the work accomplished by the egalitarian feminist organizations which, because of their pragmatic orientation, have suffered less from paranoid internal splits. In spirit, feminist androgyny theorists are in favor of integrating all the tendencies of feminism to achieve a synthesis, so as to put this synthesis into the service of women and all humanity.

SIX

Feminist Literary Criticism

Feminist literary criticism is one of the latest manifestations of feminism to arrive on the scene. A frankly political approach, it arises because of the emergence of a feminist school of literature, and it gives rise in turn to a literature of commitment, for which it defines the criteria.

Feminist literary criticism at first was limited to the original contributions of a few individuals, such as Katharine Rogers, author of *The Troublesome Helpmate,* published in 1966, and Mary Ellmann, whose book *Thinking about Women,* published in 1968, immediately earned her the status of a leading expert in the field. Admittedly, in many universities, from 1966 on, women lecturers gave courses on women authors or on women's history and issues, but their approach was entirely empirical. The beginning of an organized effort at feminist literary criticism in America dates from the formation, in 1970, of the Modern Language Association Commission on the Status of Women. This commission established contacts with feminists on university faculties, and published their essays and research papers in its review *Female Studies.* Other organizations have appeared since then, such as the Women's Caucus for the Modern Languages or the International Institute of Women's Studies; other reviews have also been published, enabling feminist literary critics to compare their ideas. In particular, we can mention the *Women's Studies Newsletter,* the *Women's Studies Quarterly, Feminist Studies, Signs,* and two of the more recent, the *Women's Review of Books,* published at Wellesley by the Women's Research Center, and *Belles Lettres, A Review of Books by Women.* One of the first symposiums to explore the links between feminism and literature was held at the University of Kentucky in April 1973. The symposium presentations were subsequently published under the title *Feminist Literary Criticism,* edited by Josephine Donovan, and this collection should be recognized as a precious work of classification and synthesis, which attempts to resolve the dilemmas facing feminists in the matter of literary criticism.

Feminist literary criticism is a daughter of the Women's movement. It is engaged in political action, since it is inseparable from feminist philosophy, like any other demonstration for "Women's Lib." Having perceived the underlying foundation of the patriarchal society, that is, the power relationship between the sexes by which the male group officially enthroned as "superior" exercises its domination over the female group classified as "inferior," feminists became aware that existing literature and literary criticism, up to that point, were based on a substratum of sexual politics.

Consequently, according to the editors of *Female Studies*, the feminist approach to literature and to literary criticism needs to serve two essential functions. The first is to awaken women to the fact that literature is a masculine institution, which, throughout history, has never ceased transmitting a patriarchal image to women. This image, which is ever more sophisticated, is the ultimate objectification of the emotions of the primitive male, perceiving woman as the personification of the mystery of the menstrual cycle and the manna of fecundity, and therefore, as being strange and disturbing—in a word, *other*. Therefore, literature as a masculine institution must be denounced as an institution of socialization, responsible for offering to both sexes behavioral models and roles that match the sexual hierarchization and polarization of our patriarchal societies.

This primary function of feminist literary criticism is therefore founded on a double refusal typical of feminist philosophy. It is first a refusal of the alienating conformity that for centuries has condemned women to a sexually defined identity and to an existential impoverishment as a consequence of the arbitrary polarization of human traits into sexual stereotypes and roles. The second refusal is even more radical: it is a rebellion against women's status of "otherness," in the sense that this "otherness" has been spread throughout every aspect of life, and is synonymous with inferiority in patriarchal terms, since to be other than man is to be less than human. Particularly interesting here, as Bonnie Zimmerman[1] suggests, would be the views of lesbian feminist critics, since the lesbian, as both a woman and a homosexual, has been seen as doubly "other" in the patriarchal stereotyping and mythology.

A second function of feminist literary criticism will be, at some future time, to raise the fundamental issue of generic human consciousness. It is true, feminist critics admit, that at present there exist specifically masculine and feminine perceptions; but, they ask, aren't these precisely the result of sexually biased socialization?

Feminist criticism raises implicitly that fundamental question to which we are just beginning to address ourselves—need women and men have distinctly different consciousnesses? The answer is obviously yes insofar as we are socialized human beings—two genders separated experientially from birth, given different attitudes and self-images. But whether the differences in our reproductive organs are accompanied by natural differences in temperament and consciousness is a question to ask, if not yet to answer.[2]

The question asked here reflects a major concern of feminist philosophy, which is to participate in ontological research, that is, research into the nature of being and of human existence. This ontological experimentation is to transcend the sexual dichotomy, which destroys men as well as women, and is supposed to lead toward psychic androgyny in a society where the word *androgyny* itself would no longer have any meaning, since it refers to a psychosexual duality that would by then be archaic. Sexual politics would have definitively yielded to humanism.

Feminist literary criticism is therefore undertaking the task of liberating both sexes, in wishing to show how, in innumerable cases, the word *sex* refers purely to an abstraction. There is no question of imitation; any sexual integration process that consists of women's imitating men would be fatal to the desired ontological experiment. We see also to what extent feminist literary criticism here perceives itself as the spearhead of feminist philosophy, since it is assuming the responsibility for resolving the most fundamental problem raised by feminists. In so doing, as some critics remark, it is continuing the work of Virginia Woolf, the first feminist literary critic, for whom psychic androgyny was both an ideal and a truly practical possibility.

THE STUDY OF THE MASCULINE GESTALT

The realization of the androgynous ideal, according to the theorists of feminist literary criticism, will be the culmination of the third phase of their process. In fact, all of them perceive three phases in the long term. The first phase consists of studying the image of women in existing literature. This is obviously the easiest task and the one to which, until now, most feminist critics have devoted their attention. It must be noted, however, to their great credit, that feminist critical essays do not boil down to just a study of sexist works, but are a real effort at theoretical classification, with a trend toward an awakening of political consciousness. Thus, the first feminist critics had the task of detecting and classifying the various ways in which women have traditionally been represented in literature.

For Katharine Rogers, for example, there is a literary tradition of misogyny, which has developed under three influences. The first was the patriarchal tendency of the Greeks to deprecate the feminine character and mind, which were presumed to be universally characteristic of the whole gender. Next came the Roman dichotomy between conjugal love and sexual passion, with its two stereotypes of the wife and mistress. On the one hand, there is the respectable matron, far too domineering, who in the Middle Ages and Renaissance became the shrew, like the one we know from Shakespeare, and on the other hand, the lascivious, bewitching mistress, who later became the whore: courtesan in the Renaissance, femme fatale in the nineteenth century, and "witch-bitch" in the twentieth century. This dichotomy divided the stereotypes between two opposite poles. The first was idealization, masking male scorn for the sex which asked for its protection; the most edifying examples of this process are the medieval Virgin and the Victorian lily, united in the same vocation of martyr. The second pole of this stereotyped dichotomy is deprecation of women for their dangerous affinity with the animal world, as witness the biblical story of the Fall. Virulent disparagement of women attained its paroxysm in the twentieth century, when misogyny finally dared be proclaimed openly, and for the first time, even motherhood itself was attacked. The groundwork laid by the Greeks and Romans was climaxed by the third factor, Christian asceticism and the Christian hostility toward women expressed from the earliest centuries, as in the writings of Saint Paul, who associated women with forbidden carnal desires and blamed them for enticing men into committing sins of the flesh.

In this retrospective glance at literary misogyny, there already appear the feminine stereotypes that Mary Ellmann lists in an exhaustive catalog, according to the various attributes that literature has traditionally assigned to women:

- Formlessness
- Passivity
- Instability
- Confinement
- Piety
- Materiality

- Spirituality
- Irrationality
- Compliancy
- Two incorrigible figures: The Shrew and the Witch.[3]

Besides pointing out the universality of the list, applicable to all sexist works, Ellmann also highlights its lack of plausibility. Above all, she draws our attention to the impossibility of lending credibility to a classification scheme characterized by such profusion and so many contradictions. Similarly, she observes the contrapuntal implications, as each feminine virtue implies a feminine vice. She offers us some examples of these contrasting pairs of opposites: thus, chastity implies, alas, frigidity; intuition implies irrationality; motherhood implies domination. In the same manner, Paula Marshall, in *Keeping the Faith*, deplores the two poles between which the black woman has always been agonizingly torn in literary portrayals: the "nigger wench" and the "Negro matriarch."[4]

In this uneven depiction of the feminine character in sexist literature, the norm is, of course, negative, while virtue represents the ideal toward which the weaker, depraved sex is always being encouraged to strive. The converse relation, says Mary Ellmann, illustrating her idea with a diagram dear to feminists, takes account of the view that the masculine author has of his own sex:

> Super-sexual IDEAL
> ↑
> WOMEN = DEFECT   MEN = IDEAL
> ↑
> Sub-sexual DEFECT[5]

The political merit of the theories just described is, first, to demonstrate the permanence and universality of the domination of one sex throughout all of literature; and next, to reveal the force of a tradition which, rooted in ancient mythology, has become not only a literary convention but also a habitual way of thinking. One might, therefore, suppose that many authors accept it unconsciously, and that one of the goals of feminist literary criticism would be to awaken them to their sexism. As for feminine readers, they would be expected to conclude that the image of women perpetuated by a masculine tradition for more than two thousand years can only be artificial and cut off from all sociological reality. Finally, these interpretations have the political merit of demonstrating to what extent the denounced schemes are collective, in the sense that the masculine clique perceives women in terms of generic identity, and whether acting out of patriarchal feelings or pure misogyny, relegates them to a subhuman status.

Katharine Rogers and Mary Ellmann did a good job of preparing the path for a political approach to literature, as it is practiced now by feminist critics. But Kate Millett is the one to whom we owe the first introduction of the concept of "sexual politics" in literature, through her study of the works of D. H. Lawrence, Henry Miller, and Norman Mailer, showing how these authors' descriptions of copulation reproduce and reaffirm the power relationship between the sexes in our patriarchal society. Kate Millett's assessment has the interest of looking both backward and forward in time. Her correlation recalls the role played historically by the sexual act, transformed by the male into an act of power, which is at the origin of the patriarchal hierarchy. It also prophesies the role coitus would eventually play in making phallocracy the norm, as preached by the apostles of virility. Coitus as described by Lawrence partakes of an "elaborate political code" and sanctifies the mystic communion of the exalted male and the subjected female united in the cult of the phallus. The sexual broadsides of Henry Miller's heroes culminate in the dehumanization of the woman by "reducing her to a cunt," saleable sexual merchandise. Here appears the climactic rite of the phallic cult: sodomy, the coup de grâce with which the virile champions of Miller and Mailer, worthy emulators of the heroic rapists that we have earlier seen demystified by Susan Brownmiller, finish off the object of their disdainful domination. For, in Mailer, coitus is always combat, and because of this, it incarnates the only possible relationship between the sexes, that of a deadly war over "a curious cause, none other than male supremacy."[6]

Kate Millett's thesis, therefore, is that these bits of sexual bravado must no longer be interpreted as merely the personal fantasies and wild imaginings of certain authors, but as an outrageous exploitation of literature as an instrument of socialization, with the sole aim of putting women back in line. For Millett, these heroics are the aggressive reactions typical of a ruling caste that feels its privileges threatened and is making last-ditch efforts to preserve them. D. H. Lawrence reacts against the modern woman, as represented by Hermione and Gudrun, who are irremediably "lost," in *Women in Love,* or by Ursula and Kate Leslie, who are "saved," in the nick of time, by their submissive love for the male. As for Henry Miller, he dehumanizes women and transforms sexuality into a cheap marketable commodity. Meanwhile, Mailer, obsessed by what he considers a sissifying feminization of America, launches his ideology of "sexistentialism" in the service of a frantic battle against homosexuality, masturbation, impotence, and capitulation to women. Kate Millett says,

> *Machismo* stands at bay, cornered by the threat of a second sexual revolution, which, in obliterating the fear of homosexuality, could challenge the entire temperamental categories (masculine and feminine) of patriarchal culture.[7]

The preceding extract thus identifies literature as an emanation of the political and social context of sexuality. The return to this correlation is one of the essential traits of feminist literary criticism, which sees itself as engaged in political action. This political/social correlation is also quintessential to all feminist literature. Therefore we must examine the uses that are made of it. They are twofold.

The return to the social argument first enables militant feminist critics, like the radical feminist historians, to explain the causes and modus operandi of an upsurge in phallocracy. The causes lie in the cultural and social factors contemporary with a given literary work. Katharine Rogers and Kate Millett agree in recognizing that every step in social or political progress for women is accompanied by a corresponding crescendo of misogyny in literature. The conjunction of a cultural factor, Freudianism, with a social factor, women's victory in obtaining the vote as a result of the first wave of feminism, inspired D. H. Lawrence's cult of the phallus. In the same way, more recently, the second wave of feminism provoked Mailer to embark on his personal crusade, declaring a holy war against the sexual revolution.

Every new rise of phallocracy is expressed by a tendency to revised versions of myths and stereotypes, and the feminist critic's emphasis on the social argument thus points out the ways literary portrayals of women are contingent upon their era. The most recent example, cited by Katharine Rogers and Mary Ellmann, is the twentieth century's demolition of the stereotype of the mother. They present this demystification as belonging to the purest tradition of misogyny. It is in the same vein as previous revisionist efforts concerning matriarchal myths, for example, those of Pandora and Hera. This time, the revisionism has coincided with the two factors mentioned above, that is, the victorious conclusion of the first wave of feminism and the popularization of Freudian theories. Early feminism brought woman down from her pedestal. Freud completed this process when, in 1920, in his *Essays on Psychoanalysis,* he stressed the overwhelming influence of the mother/child relationship throughout the adult's lifetime as a prototype (not always a healthy one) for all subsequent love relationships. After this, society abandoned the attitude of veneration for the mother, which had been the Victorian ideal, and instead, the mother became anathema, in the castration scenario of momism.

A good feminist critic, however, even though she denounced the defamation campaign being spread against mothers, did not wholly deny the existence of the personality type of the abusive mother; she recognized here an element of truth. But her mission consisted of seeking the causes for the development of this personality, and this research was not restricted to the prejudiced world of psychology, but belonged instead to the domain of sociology. The second function of the feminist critic's return to the social argument is to explain women literary characters, by taking account of the lot of the average woman in the society of her time. Three examples of this type are provided in *The Troublesome Helpmate,* applying to the medieval shrew, the seventeenth-century pedantic female, and the Victorian old maid. According to Katharine Rogers, the shrew can be explained by the financial dependence of wives on their husbands, which has led to the mercenary attitude of the rapacious wife, so decried in literature, who sees her husband only as the source of money. As to the seventeenth-century stereotype of the pedantic female, ridiculed in the classical age, she was the natural result of the fact that society only approved of a limited education for women and forbade them to pursue higher learning. Likewise, in the nineteenth century, the old maid, mocked for her frustration and her shameful avidity for marriage, was purely the product of a society that offered no approved role to the unmarried woman.

The same process of sociological explanation can be applied to the attitudes of women authors. Thus, in response to those who accuse nineteenth-century women authors of confining themselves to popular romances and novels with narrow horizons, Cheri Register in her "American Feminist Literary Criticism" points out two external factors: the cultural conditioning of women that led many of them to believe they were not competent to write in any other medium than popular fiction, and the economic pressures of an age when a market existed for sentimental literature and when writing novels was one of the rare permissible means for a woman to earn an honest living. These two points seem important to us to prevent anyone's drawing a hasty conclusion that a "feminine nature" exists in which sentimentality is one of the essential features. To do so would place a burden on all future literary work by women.

In view of the interest that feminist literary critics accord to the social context, it is easy to understand their tenacious hostility to "new" criticism. The latter, which places the accent on form rather than content and emphasizes atemporality and universality, is incapable of judging a whole gamut of women's work.

This insistence on the social context, as in all feminist philosophy, rests on the idea (as Simone de Beauvoir said in *The Second Sex*) that "one is not born a woman, one becomes one."[8] The critic's aim is to persuade every woman that she is a socialized creature, trained to accept a man's world. Consequently, the critic calls upon women readers to exercise critical judgment about how literature relates to their own lives. In this way, after having set forth the fundamental rhetoric of *The Romance of Tristan and Iseult*, Phyllis Franklin warns against the myth of love in Western society and asks:

What is the significance of this rhetoric for us? A crucial one, I think. Men as well as women are carried away by passion, but women much more than men are defined by the terms of their sexual participation and so passion can have a more devastating effect when they make decisions "under the influence."[9]

Likewise, after examining Strindberg's play *Miss Julie*, which presents the misogynist author's conception of the male as "sexual aristocrat" and his dramatization of the woman's fall in sex, a group of students in a course taught by Phyllis Franklin reached similar views. They compared the two poles between which women have been driven and drew the conclusion that women need to avoid both the Scylla of idealization and the Charybdis of degradation. Such a reaction might seem naive, recalling the identification of a young girl reader with a romantic heroine. But this is not really the case here. The process is not one of identification; besides, these readers are not confining themselves to the subjective but are establishing a relationship between the personal and the political. The lesson learned in the reading is, in fact, to bring a critical judgment regarding the effects of sexist manipulation, and the message is that an entire sex has, until now, been subjected to such manipulation. This teaching, which rests on a utilitarian conception of literary criticism, attacks the manipulator/manipulatee relationship and participates in a quest for both identity and survival, like all feminist literature.

Feminist literary criticism therefore represents a rupture with existing literary criticism, and perceives itself as such. At this point, we are embarking on the second phase of the process followed by feminist literary critics: the battle against "phallic criticism." This is Mary Ellmann's expression, by which she means to denounce the merger in the minds of male critics between an author's sexual denomination and an evaluation of her work. Here again, "anatomy is destiny"! "Books by women are treated as though they themselves were women, and criticism embarks, at its happiest, upon an intellectual measuring of busts and hips." [10]

"Phallic criticism," also called the testicular theory, is not satisfied merely with morphology. It even plagiarizes bodily functions to produce an "ovarian theory of literature," [11] as described by Kimberley Snow, who recalls that one eminent male critic went so far as to offer an interpretation of Emily Dickinson's poetry linked to the poet's menstrual cycle. [12]

The attacks against "phallic criticism" are inseparable from feminist philosophy. First of all, they reveal a rejection of sexism. Sexism does exist in literary criticism, since male characters or authors are never reduced to being nothing more than their bodily functions. Sexual discrimination, as would be expected when the art of criticism emanates from a patriarchal society, strikes against women. A further element of feminist philosophy inspiring feminist critics is the rejection of a solely sexual identity and the claim of a fully dimensioned personality for women. Refusing to be reduced to a sexual identity amounts to saying "No" to the subservience that every feminist sees implied by an artificial norm of femininity. This "No" not only has an existential value; it also bears directly on literary works by women, since it means a refusal to see such works burdened by outdated cultural presumptions, like Dr. Johnson's verdict on the woman preacher. [13] In a similar way, women authors in the past have often been judged on the basis of their conformity to traditional norms of femininity. A woman was expected to "write like a woman." Nevertheless, as Mary Ellmann reminds us, the situation was not always easy for a woman who conformed to the rules. Admittedly, the male chauvinist critic was satisfied and reassured since the woman author had written a "woman's book," proving once again women's incapacity to do any better. But the very label *woman's book* expressed all the phallocratic critic's disdain for this "minor" genre.

For, in the domain of literary works, as elsewhere, the ideal norm has always been masculine. This is the second aspect of "phallic criticism" that feminists denounce. Mary Ellmann recalls how Mary McCarthy, after having been complimented for her "masculine mind," aroused the immeasurable jubilation of Norman Mailer when she wrote *The Group*, a "female novel." For Mary Ellmann, Mailer's exaggerated jubilation, expressed in terms of defecation, betrayed the sexism of an author who was jealous of seeing a woman regularly depart from the feminine sphere, thus flouting sexual literary conventions, and was triumphing in his belief that she had finally capitulated, "getting back in line," so to speak, and revealing her true nature.

Needless to say, feminists do not consider *The Group* to be a capitulation. At most, we ourselves might be slightly tempted to speak of commercial opportunism. What feminist literary critics protest is the deprecation of so-called women's books and their relegation to the minor ranks of literature. Here we reencounter the rejection of the status of "otherness," which, by definition in terms of an arbitrary ideal norm, that is, *men's books*, is synonymous with inferiority. Long ago, in *A Room of One's Own*, Virginia Woolf had denounced the arbitrariness of critics who judge any book on war to be an important work, while they automatically class as insignificant a work dealing with women's feelings in a parlor. According to the judgment she was incriminating, men's experience is thought to be universal and essential to the human condition, while women's experience is considered a minor accessory to the existential struggle of human beings, the central theme of literature. On this point, it suffices to read the literary production of women and feminists of the last ten or fifteen years, both in Europe and the United States, to see to what extent women writers deal essentially with universal human themes.

In so doing, women authors are carrying out feminist literary critics' prescriptions, in keeping with the critics' second mission, the final step in their process. Feminist critics have already accomplished their first mission: that is, by the two-step process of analyzing the way women are represented in literature and denouncing the inherent sexual discrimination of "phallic criticism," they have revealed the "masculine gestalt," thereby exposing existing literary works as an instrument of socialization and showing literature to be a reflection of sexual politics. Just as radical feminist historians, in the same war for liberation, have studied male ideology so as to be better able to combat it, so feminist critics have analyzed the masculine gestalt so as to be better able to correct it. This correction, fulfilling the second function of feminist literary criticism, will raise the issue of generic human consciousness, which is to be accomplished by praising and encouraging the creation of literary works by women.

DEVELOPMENT OF A NEW GESTALT

What should be the norms for a new gestalt, according to feminists? As stated above, it is the final step in feminist literary criticism—"prescriptive criticism," in Cheri Register's expression—that provides an answer to this question. "Prescriptive criticism," the decisive element in feminist criticism, aims to guide women authors striving to create a feminist genre of the novel, stage plays, or poetry, as well as critics wishing for measures to evaluate the feminism of a given literary work. In this sense, any feminist literary critic can become an author, and every feminist author is doing the work of a critic in developing a new gestalt. For authors and critics, Cheri Register offers five criteria by which a personal work can be judged to participate in the broad political movement for women's liberation:

> Because of its origins in the women's liberation movement, feminist criticism values literature that is of some use to the movement. Prescriptive criticism, then, is best defined in terms of the ways in which literature can serve the cause of liberation. To earn feminist approval, literature must perform one or more of the following functions:
> 1) serve as a forum for women
> 2) help to achieve cultural androgyny
> 3) provide role models
> 4) promote sisterhood
> 5) augment consciousness-raising.[14]

From the author's detailed discussion of each criterion, we have retained only the most important, the role of literature as a forum for women. In Register's view, a work plays this role to the extent that it faithfully reflects women's experience. The key word is *authenticity*. A first requirement is therefore implied, that is, that the work must be a direct expression by a woman of her own authentic experience. A second requirement, linked to the first, is that this expression must be free from any cultural constraint or hindrance; that is, free from any notion of conformity to preconceived norms set up by men. Among the standards the author lists for judging the authenticity of the experience described, we inevitably find these concepts, that is, the writer should be true to herself and should have a critical viewpoint about her experience in relation to dominant cultural and political presumptions.

If we wonder about the deeper motives that drive feminist critics to insist on the literary requirement of an authentic expression of women's experience, we find the answer first in the desire to end women's alienation. Women have become strangers to their own experience, and to the lessons and meanings to be derived from it, because this experience has either been distorted through the phallocratic viewpoint, or has been stifled altogether. Literature must present women with true-life accounts in which they recognize their own experience during the first phase of the long march of the quest for identity. Faithful depiction of this true-life experience is also a message from women to the opposite sex revealing what it means to be a woman, with all the related trials and tribulations, in a given society. This exploration of women's reality is furthermore a necessary step toward correcting the imbalance afflicting our culture. "It is only after we have integrated the dark side of the moon into our world view that we can begin to talk seriously of universal culture."[15]

Only then will we be able to achieve the desired "cultural androgyny" that Cheri Register mentions second on her list.

If we come back to this list, it seems to call for two essential remarks. First, it implies that feminist literature ought to have political implications. For the moment, the accent is not on the conflicting tensions of a power relationship, but the vocabulary used reveals an attitude in favor of literature as public expression, acting as a consciousness-raising forum in the hope that it will lead to a united front of women represented by "sisterhood." It is easy to perceive the difficulties that each author faces in creating a subtle balance between the personal and the political, avoiding the traps, on the one hand, of narcissism or self-indulgence, and on the other, the dryness of a propaganda tract.

The second remark on Cheri Register's "prescriptive" criteria is that feminist literature and criticism have two aspects: affirmation and rejection. Each "thou shalt" implies, in effect, a "thou shalt not." Some works of criticism or literature are primarily works of denunciation. Their authors say no to the status quo, to the oppression of women and to sexism. In contrast, other works exist in which there appear new imaginative perceptions, facts and forms of consciousness, of a totally new order. Within feminist literary criticism, two tendencies can be seen, one insisting on the right to refuse, the other on the ability to imagine. As illustrated by the imaginary dialogue created by Carolyn Heilbrun and Catharine Stimpson in *Feminist Literary Criticism,* the two are not necessarily contradictory. They correspond simply to two steps in the same chronology, since proposals for new schemes often depend on denunciations of old oppressive structures. The literature of refusal bears on the present and the past, and as its advocate admits in the fictitious dialogue mentioned above, it risks, in the long term, getting "mired in anger"; if the literature of imagination does not take over, oriented toward the future and playing a prophetic role. Many authors, besides, manage to merge the two tendencies in a single work, thus placing in opposition "negations that produce transcendencies," in a phrase borrowed from Josephine Donovan.[16]

Here we have a neat definition that aptly sums up the "feminist perspective." This last expression is often used to refer to the approach militant feminists take to literature, and suggests how much feminist literary criticism perceives itself as still in the process of developing. For the woman writer, it means a feminist vision of the world, whether the author concentrates on a refusal of the past or an imaginative affirmation of the future.

Lastly, in concluding this chapter, there is another point I wish to make. Feminist literary criticism, it is often said, should, in the long term, develop a theory of literary history, genres, and techniques that does justice to the special consciousness and culture of women.[17] A number of feminist theorists have devoted themselves to the issue of whether women's writing can be an especially female form. Earlier, their predecessor, Virginia Woolf, had already admired the long sentences of the novelist Dorothy Richardson, praising the ability of "a woman's sentence" to delve into the depths of an individual human life. In 1971, Kate Millett, in her introduction to *Prostitution: A Quartet,* also called for new forms of writing, suggesting the reproduction of fluent, oral speech, in monologues or dialogues. This, said she, would exploit women's facility for oral expression, a facility they shared with all oppressed minorities to whom other forms of expression were forbidden. In addition, the political sense of this new form of expression was said to be all the greater insofar as this gift for verbal communication could be sharpened within consciousness-raising groups. Then perhaps, Millett hoped, we would arrive at a new, specifically women's form of writing. No doubt it is better, as some French feminists have suggested, to speak of *l'effet-femme,*[18] or *l'effet de féminité.*[19] Although it happens that we ourselves sometimes refer to a feminine viewpoint or principle, we must recall, nevertheless, that the terms *feminine* and *femininity* do not in any way imply the conclusion of an innate feminine nature. The predilection of women for the humanities, which Virginia Woolf observed, arises in part because of women's relegation to this area. Femininity is also the result of socialization. During the present period of mutation and uncertainty, where there is still a confusion between stereotypes and individual identity, it is important to use the concept of femininity cautiously, and always to specify the precise meaning accepted for it in the given context.

SEVEN

A Synthesis of Reconciliation

The feminist literary critics' study of the masculine gestalt, like the radical feminists' denunciations, belongs to the initial consciousness-raising phase of feminism. The critics' development of a new gestalt, on the other hand, belongs with the androgynous approach to feminism. In seeking a new gestalt, feminist literary criticism is working toward a harmonious synthesis between the diverse theories within the feminist movement, after the quarrels and internal divisions we have discussed above. There is no denying that these divisions exist. But it would be unfair of us to stress only the disagreements; this would express a lack of faith in women's ability to practice political compromises and transcend their differences outside the field of literature.

The three main ideological currents of the feminist movement that we have studied—egalitarianism, radicalism, and androgyny—contribute respectively to three different domains: social, political, and cultural.

This factor provides a basis for a first step toward peaceful coexistence. The best proof of this is that it is possible for the views of a given feminist to be a mixture of two approaches to feminism. The blend may be egalitarian/androgynous feminism, as in Betty Friedan's autobiography or Letty Cottin Pogrebin's writings; or it may be radical/androgynous feminism as with Mary Daly in her second phase of militancy, or with Shulamith Firestone, in the parts of her works dealing with the cultural aspect of feminism.

A second factor leading toward a possible synthesis is that numerous areas of consensus exist, not only between individuals but also in ideological terms. It is these areas of consensus, expressed by at least two or three voices, that we wish to emphasize here.

The effort at reconciliation is not merely a personal dream inspired by feminist zeal, but is embodied in a number of actions or position statements demonstrating a genuine will toward synthesis. In the radical feminist camp, we have the initiative of Charlotte Bunch and Rita Mae Brown in their creation of *Quest,* a journal of feminist theory, defining its purpose as follows:

> We want to be theoretical without being academic, to create theory that sustains a vision of the future and helps shape and coordinate current tactics at the same time. We've had valuable contributions from reform, radical, socialist, lesbian, and cultural feminism, but we haven't yet developed a synthesis that could provide an overall ideological framework.[1]

This is the same spirit of reconciliation that inspired the "Forum" department started by *Ms.* in 1975 as a place for dialogue within the Women's movement, to enable feminists with different allegiances to compare their views and find points of common agreement. Across the divide separating the socialist and egalitarian camps, we find the Socialist Workers party and Betty Friedan congratulating each other on the success achieved in the joint action of the women's national strike of 26 August 1970. They recommended unity in "the things that don't divide us," with joint actions becoming the roots that would attach women more firmly to the movement and enable them to transcend their ideological differences.

The blends described above persistently reveal the androgynous approach as a pattern for possible reconciliation. Indeed, it is precisely on the basis of this approach that the broadest possibility for consensus appears, that is, on the fundamental principle of defining people as human beings and not as members of one or the other sex. For feminism to remain consistent with its own principles, it must recognize the logic of the notion that if women are equal to men, then men are also equal to women. The refusal to allow women to be defined solely in terms of sex—which has always been the first tenet of feminism—must imply a corollary refusal to allow men to be defined solely in terms of sex. With only rare exceptions, feminists agree on the primacy of defining people as human beings, granting mutual equality of the sexes. The egalitarian feminists proclaim this principle when they demand passage of the Equal Rights Amendment, which would enable women to be officially recognized as "persons" within the meaning of the Constitution. They are likewise proclaiming it when they speak of "human liberation" and suggest: "Let's at least start with the assumption that men and women are human."[2]

Radical feminists apply this same assumption to women when they denounce the process by which the maternal function robs women of their humanity and turns them into baby-producing machines. They apply this assumption to men as well. For example, Dana Densmore, Ti-Grace Atkinson and Robin Morgan, like the feminist androgynists, are attacking not biological man, but rather sexism and phallocracy, when they refer to "sexual roles" and "masculine behavior." It is this expression, *sexual roles,* which causes a great cleavage within the Women's movement, says Jo Freeman:

> One perspective saw the ultimate goal of the movement as the annihilation of sex roles. By its nature this view includes the liberation of men with that of women. . . .
> The other perspective can best be described as "cultural nationalism." This viewpoint sees men at worst destructive and at best irrelevant.[3]

This is a fair analysis, but again, it must be emphasized that the second perspective only covers a couple of extreme cases: SCUM, which never really existed as a formal organization, and the minority faction among lesbians consisting of those who reject bisexuality as a legitimate option. Among other radical feminists, separatism is only talked about, as with the advocates of the "pro-woman" line, or else is sought in reality only as a temporary solution, as a radical demonstration of the rupture implied by Mary Daly's "non-being" or Germaine Greer's "explor[ing] the dark without a guide."

A difficulty might be seen to persist regarding men's and women's relative contributions to the process of cultural, political, and social change. Egalitarian feminists, who give extensive credit to the present contribution of men, nevertheless tend toward reciprocity when they address social issues, such as the educational challenge presented by the current upsetting of sex roles, or the androgyny in the working world that Caroline Bird sees existing at some periods in history or in the near future. For their part, the radical feminists, who give the major share of credit to women in the process toward change, cannot be so naive as to think that men will willingly turn over power to women and accept all their proposals for innovation. As one of them, Elizabeth Reid, says, radical feminists must accept compromise so as to make possible an alliance between feminists and other oppressed minority groups, composed of both men and women.

Furthermore, the rejection of sexual labeling does not imply the rejection of sexuality. In this domain as well, the androgynous perspective appears to provide a pattern for reconciliation, in which sex is perceived as necessary to the fulfillment of every individual and as having its best chance for interaction in heterosexuality. From here, it is only a small step to the view expressed by Betty Friedan in *It Changed My Life*:

I think love and sex are real and that men and women both have real needs for love and intimacy that seems most easily structured around heterosexual relations.[4]

If egalitarian feminists barely touch on the subject of sex, this must be seen as not only a choice of priorities but also a concern for order, the wish we have seen expressed by Caroline Bird that everything should be put in its proper place so as to straighten out the old sexist confusions: sex belongs in private life and not at the office.

Among radical feminists (except for the author of the *SCUM Manifesto*), let us repeat that although they attack sexual intercourse as an institution, defined as such by Ti-Grace Atkinson, they do not deny sexuality. It only remains to define what sexuality means, and above all, to define what it means to women. The problem therefore lies rather in a reevaluation of aptitudes and a redistribution of initiatives between the sexes, in keeping with the conclusions of Masters and Johnson and the hypotheses of Mary-Jane Sherfey, which have shown that women have an inexhaustible capacity for orgasm. However, a tendency to hindsighted reevaluation making up for past injustices is an inevitable by-product of any rebellion, among all minorities who perceive themselves as oppressed and seek their own identity.

In the domain of sexuality, in any case, there are three points of infallible consensus among feminists. The first is a firm resolution against what has been, until now, the indissociable triptych of coitus/gestation/motherhood, and an assertion that coitus in the heterosexual relationship must not necessarily be linked to the function of gestation. All currents within the Women's movement reject a morality that legitimizes the servitude of women while proclaiming respect for the right to life. All feminists agree that this view is a perversion of morality, in that it reduces a human being to a mere reproduction machine by separating the body, which is thus turned into a dehumanized object, from the individual's free will, the willingness to give life. In contrast, women engaged in the feminist struggle believe that morality is on their side, reasoning that the free willingness to become a mother implies a willingness to assume the ethical obligations of motherhood. The second point of feminist consensus is a resolution that the heterosexual relationship must no longer consist of an active male dominating a passive female, but must take account of rediscovered feminine energy. Masculine sexuality must become open to new options without giving absolute priority to coitus and orgasm, in accordance with the most frequently expressed wish of the women interviewed in the *Hite Report*. The third point of consensus is that the true sexual revolution has never taken place. The so-called sexual revolution of the 1960s has resulted in an even greater manipulation of women, more than ever debased as sexual objects. An anonymous woman quoted in the *Hite Report* confirms the condemnation already expressed by Mary Daly, Dana Densmore, Betty Friedan, Shulamith Firestone, and countless others:

If the sexual revolution implies the attitude that now women are "free" too, and they can fuck strangers and fuck over the opposite sex, just the way men can, I think it's revolting. Women don't want to be "free" to adopt the male model of sexuality; they want to be free to find their own.[5]

The fact that Shere Hite's interviewees confirm the feminist stance is not just an insignificant coincidence. This gives considerable credibility to the feminists' claims, and makes it appear that the feminist consensus on this issue can count on active support from a broad coalition of women.

Definitely, it is the first two resolutions mentioned above that will bring about the real sexual revolution and ensure a future for true love. The necessity of love, as we have seen, is reasserted by Betty Friedan, Shulamith Firestone, and Germaine Greer. We have never encountered a case in feminist literature where love was declared to be of no value. Women of all tendencies in the movement, whether egalitarian, radical, or androgynous feminist, have made the same denunciation that love in our society has been corrupted. For all of them, true love can only be restored to society by an indispensable prior condition: the access by women to human dignity, and the eradication of the old stereotypes of fragile feminine weakness and protective masculine strength. In this new context, there will come about new kinds of interaction and synthesis implied by psychic androgyny, which is the pattern for reconciliation, first, between feminists, and subsequently, between the sexes.

As for the problem of marriage and the family, the greatest hope for reconciliation comes from the fact that the differences of opinion have more to do with the personality of a given group or individual feminist than with ideological cleavages. Marriage and the family, as revised and corrected by feminism, have their proponents, not only among egalitarian feminists but also among radical feminists—the Redstockings—and feminists of the androgynous approach, Gayle Graham Yates, for example. All these women recognize the need for structures with a certain amount of stability. What they are up in arms about is the institution of the family as a cell for sexually polarized socialization.

Therefore, it is in the androgynous approach to feminism that we must look for a path toward reconciliation, as in Gayle Graham Yates's proposals for multiple formulas for the family. Such a suggestion should not pose any problem for the egalitarian feminists, who, as we have seen, leave the door open to individual solutions. This suggestion can cover the feminist political radicals' option in favor of a mutation of the family. In addition, it can resolve the dilemma of the radical feminists of whether to act within the system or opt out of it. The issue of legality remains to be worked out, but a step toward a solution can be seen in the proposal for seven-to-ten-year contracts, in Shulamith Firestone's personal utopia, which would guarantee the stability of communal structures necessary for child rearing.

We can state that, regarding the family, a unanimous consensus has already been established on the necessity for change. The family can no longer be what it once was. The fundamental change, prescribed by all feminists, will be to carry out a second separation in the previously indissociable triptych of coitus/gestation/motherhood: the severing of the gestation capacity from the motherhood function. This scission is the first phase of a new sharing of responsibilities. This phase will see women gain access to all types of employment. On this point, consensus will be reached among feminists if the issue is stated, not in terms of career success, but of personal fulfillment. This new phase will also, as we have said, end sexual stereotyping, and will be the prelude to the cultural revolution if it culminates in a system of nonsexist education, across the board, from textbooks to the curriculum.

Lastly in our discussion, there remains the issue of socialism as an option and priority.

As an option, egalitarian feminists reject it point-blank, either explicitly or implicitly. But there again, the proposals of feminists of the androgyny approach are remarkably tolerant and conciliatory. Although, in fact, Germaine Greer and Gayle Graham Yates envision a utopian socialist type of society, they both also think that we can be spared the trouble of a revolution. This refusal to dragoon the feminist troops would no doubt permit the Women's movement to retain its egalitarian wing. However, this refusal runs a strong risk of costing the movement the allegiance of the feminist radicals, for whom socialism is a priority. A gleam of hope remains in the fact that the feminist radicals hold to the strategy of a strong, autonomous feminist movement, and want to join with other militant feminists on a program specifically for women. The movement could go forward on this basis, which might well prove to be the basis for the great feminist mutation in history: sexual freedom adequately defined, eradication of sexist mentalities, and destruction or mutation of patriarchal institutions. Since feminism is fundamentally egalitarian, might we not see the emergence, in practice, of a new type of socialism, which would no longer necessarily be called socialism, and which would offer convincing appeal to both egalitarian and radical feminists? In this respect, feminism is the "torchbearer of the future" of the "social movement" spoken of by Alain Touraine.[6] It would be ludicrous, as well as a sure sign of immaturity, if feminism were to fail because of a fixation about defining itself with reference to another ideology, that is, for or against socialism.

An obstacle of this sort would reveal feminism as relative, dependent for its identity on its relationship to something else, founded on a chronological confusion between long-term and short-term problems. However, this essential point is clearly recognized by all the main feminist theorists. Now, they say, it is important to take action in the fields where there is agreement, and let the differences of opinion lie dormant until further notice. In the matter of memberships in formal organizations, this viewpoint has led to a realignment within the Women's movement. In a 1974 survey of 500 members of the National Organization for Women (NOW), 9 percent of those interviewed declared themselves as belonging to the radical Left, politically speaking, and 12 percent belonged to other feminist organizations in addition to NOW.[7] Their membership in NOW signified that this organization no longer appeared as merely reformist, but was seen more and more as a pragmatic, action-oriented association. Elsewhere, we should not forget the example of Elizabeth Reid, the Australian radical feminist, who acted for two and a half years as consultant to the prime minister for women's affairs. The coverage given to her by *Ms.* in January 1976 is indicative of a willingness toward mobility and compromise, regarding both the feminist movement and the authorities in power. Elizabeth Reid and Gloria Steinem have both urged women to become engaged in the traditional political system as well as in the feminist movement. However, this double engagement should have a mutual feedback effect, with each return to office or to the movement bringing new awareness and sensitivity gained in the other domain. In this way, it would be possible for feminists to transcend the habitual polarizations, as the temporary nature of the engagement would enable them to step back from the dual experience of power and militancy and keep an open mind. Naturally, the prior declaration of allegiance to feminism distinguishes this type of commitment from that of some other women in politics who, perceiving the feminist label as a hindrance, are caught in the trap of solidarity with the government and forced to witness their actions compromised by budgetary problems, with no other recourse but the silence of a well-disciplined party member.

The reconciliation scenario we have just established is no doubt very sketchy, a modest prototype of what the Women's movement in the United States could achieve if coordination were established between the factions to structure a formal ideology. A platform is needed, going much farther than such a general agreement as the one developed in the 1977 National Women's Conference in Houston. A synthesis is possible and necessary if the Women's movement is ever to transcend the polarizations and leadership quarrels that have considerably bogged it down. Overcoming these divisions seems to us an imperative condition for survival in the face of the reactionary backlash that has developed in recent years. It could provide the feminist movement with enough momentum to go far beyond what Gloria Steinem has aptly called "prefeminist, either/or, polarized thinking." All things considered, American feminism has not yet attained full maturity.

PART III

The New Feminist Movement in Action

EIGHT

The Instrument and Philosophy of Action

The problem of action has often been an embarrassing one for American feminists. Because of the extremely rapid growth of the feminist movement in the 1960s and 1970s, this question arose even before there was time to develop a coherent body of ideological thought. In 1970, when conscious-ness-raising appeared to have been effectively achieved, new feminism, paradoxically, had an instrument for action but no unified program or strategy. "Let's not worry about strategy, let's just get moving": this was Germaine Greer's view at that time. Others, such as Judith Hole and Ellen Levine, merely dared to speak of "areas of action," a phrase that recalls a pluralist slogan used by French feminists: "Women in Movements."

THE INSTRUMENT OF ACTION

Pluralist expression is a reflection of what the new feminist movement has always been, that is, a decentralized movement with a wide range of organizational structures. Chronologically, the first of these structures was the broad national association working toward general political goals. Here we find the oldest organizations, vestiges of the first wave of feminism, including the League of Women Voters and the now-moribund National Women's Party (NWP).[1] Among the organizations born out of the new wave of feminism, the two most important are unquestionably the National Organization for Women (NOW) and the highly active National Women's Political Caucus (NWPC), which was created in 1971 primarily for the purpose of promoting women in politics. From 1968, the Women's Equity Action League (WEAL) concentrated on the struggle against sexual dis-crimination, while the National Black Feminist Organization (NBFO), founded in 1973, was the first large autonomous feminist organization to defend the cause of ethnic minority women.

These groups are generally organized on a national scale, with a hierarchical structure. Their local chapters or committees systematically replicate the hierarchy of the national headquarters and are based on a strict distribution of responsibilities. Some organizations receive government funding and have their head offices in the national capital; for example, the League of Women Voters for many years has occupied an impressive amount of space on the upper floors of a high-rise building on M Street in Washington. Others are much more modest; I saw some, such as the premises of the NWPC, where a visitor in the early 1970s was not only warmly welcomed but also might be enlisted to help out in the task of the moment.

Another category of organizations defends the interests of more specialized groups, usually in various professional sectors. Some pioneers in this matter have been the Women's Caucus for Political Science, the Federally Employed Women (FEW), and the Association for Women in Psychology, some of whose members have provided a significant contribution to the feminist theory of androgyny. A more recent group is the National Women's Studies Association (NWSA), coordinating the efforts of university women engaged in literary or historic research under the heading of Women's Studies.

Other organizations have existed only on a municipal scale. The first feminist group of women municipal employees, Women in City Government United, was created in New York City in November 1969 to contest sexually discriminatory salary practices regarding men and women campaigning for Mayor John Lindsay. In the Boston area, the organization known as 9 to 5 began in 1972 stirring up feelings among office employees in both the public and private sectors. In many cities, various movements of this type have been associated in a citywide umbrella organization, such as Female Liberation of Boston, the Chicago Women's Liberation Union, or the Los Angeles Women's Union, which have presented themselves as radical feminist efforts to build an autonomous local women's liberation action group interested in a variety of problems.

Nevertheless, the basic cell of the Women's movement has always been the particular local group. This has been the site *par excellence* of radical feminism. Few of the pioneer groups, whose important contribution to ideology we have already seen, survived beyond the late 1970s, and the well-known names, such as the Feminists, the Redstockings, or the New York Radical Feminists, if they still existed, covered an entirely different reality, as the founders had given way to new members.

Moreover, not all groups have necessarily focused on radical feminism;

many have been formed independently of any ideological current, to address particular problems. Their duration has been a function of their intended purpose. This often happened in the early days of new feminism, when shock actions were being organized to arouse awareness; if the group achieved its goal in a short time, it immediately dissolved. This was the case with Media Women after the publication, in August 1970, of "The New Feminism," a special supplement to the *Ladies' Home Journal*. Even at that time, the action of a local cell group, like that of the broad national associations, was not necessarily revolutionary. A myriad of such groups were founded in the 1970s, engaged in long-term work or constructive feminist projects and covering the widest possible range, from Women Artists for Revolution, Feminists on Children's Media, or the Los Angeles Women's Health Center, to women's businesses or feminist retreats.[2] Lastly, we must not forget the countless anonymous cell groups that sprang up spontaneously in the 1970s on university campuses and in cities, lasted long enough to produce some consciousness-raising, and dissolved as unobtrusively as they were formed.

These diverse examples reveal the changeable character of the American feminist apparatus. The dramatic schism of the New York Radical Women in 1969 was an early foretaste of the breakup and disappearance of many groups. It is understandable that some militant feminists wound up concentrating on the problems posed by this fragmentation. In 1975, Jo Freeman deplored the fact that the movement had spread without first building a base, and criticized the radical feminist faction for their inertia and for allowing themselves to get bogged down in discussion over the same old issues. It is certain that this tendency to mutability, although it favored experimentation, compromised long-term actions. Nevertheless, fragmentation had its advantages, not least, the one mentioned by Jo Freeman, that of propagating the movement. The first stage could not be otherwise; in ten years—and this is a remarkable achievement—the new feminist movement not only drew in and radicalized millions of American women, but it also succeeded in producing ramifications in sectors that had been the most obstinate longtime opponents of feminism.

The first advantage of fragmentation appeared at the level of formal or informal membership. Within the nebulous cluster of diverse groups which together formed the new feminist movement, a newcomer was sure to find the unit for action or theoretical reflection that best matched her own desires. Furthermore, if at first she felt safest in a reformist action group, later, after the process of radicalization that usually occurred, she could turn toward the more revolutionary branch of feminism. As for formal membership, the fragmentation process, as organizations broke up and reformed, seems to have played a dual role. First, it retained women within the movement who might otherwise have left it. This is what happened in the case of NOW, when it split up over internal divisions, and new feminism was nevertheless able to retain the most conservative elements through the formation of WEAL. At first, in fact, WEAL called itself the "right wing of the women's movement." Another NOW spin-off, Woman-surge, tended to attract older women, who felt more comfortable in it than in NOW, which was becoming more politically radical under the influence of a new younger generation of militants.

In addition, the fragmentation of the Women's movement, by making a distinction between groups devoted to action and those devoted to formulating ideology, enabled women to belong to more than one organization, thereby providing an opening toward cooperation, if not unity. The same woman could simultaneously be a member of a radical feminist "think tank" and an organization devoted to practical action or even public service. A dilemma was posed for radical feminists by the dichotomy between radical theory, which refused any accommodation with the system, and constructive action, which in some way has to take account of the system; but a convenient solution to this dilemma, for the radical minority of NOW, or for women who might have been revolutionary during their student days but later joined a feminist association of professional women, was provided by the separation between thought groups and action groups. In any case, said the members of the Center for Women's Studies and Services, militant feminists should accept support from the system the better to overturn it. Moreover, from the beginning, radicalism was able to influence reformism and prevent the compromise that could have allowed the Women's movement to get sidetracked in fashionable "good works." The most obvious example is the evolution of NOW that brought it to take stands in favor of voluntary interruption of pregnancy, the right to choice in the matter of sexual preference, and decentralization of its own organization.

The second major advantage of fragmentation appeared in the impact of the Women's movement on nonfeminist organizations and women in general, by facilitating infiltration and persuasion. Regarding persuasion, there is reason to believe that the existence of radical feminist groups, which expressed the most audacious demands and were specifically set up to take aggressive actions, brought around public opinion and the authorities to accept the "reasonable" claims of the reformist organizations. Regarding the infiltration of nonfeminist organizations, this was done by pretending to break with the new feminist movement; this tactic was used for the first time, as we have seen, by women members of the Auto Workers' Union. In 1972 and 1973, many women union members[3] took temporary leave of absence from NOW in order to achieve egalitarian feminist infiltration of labor unions, with the result that the American Federation of Labor and Congress of Industrial Organizations (AFL-CIO) pronounced itself in favor of the Equal Rights Amendment, in October 1973, after forty years of the most implacable opposition.

Although, with some exceptions (office workers, teachers, self-employed professionals), women workers are hardly organized on feminist bases, individual initiatives protesting against sexual discrimination reveal the influence the movement has had on women at work. In a landmark case in 1972, Lucile Abreu, who, after twenty-one years of service in the Honolulu Police Department and despite having passed the examination eight times, had been refused any job promotion, brought legal action before the Equal Employment Opportunity Commission (EEOC) and won the promotion she deserved. In the same year, Helen O'Bannon sued Merrill Lynch for sexual discrimination and was awarded $10,000 in damages and interest, while Merrill Lynch was ordered to spend $4 million in the revision of its hiring practices. In February 1978, Paulette Barnes, having filed a complaint against the Environmental Protection Agency, received $18,000 in back salary, in compensation for the promotion she had been denied by the department head after she had refused his sexual advances. The flood of sexual discrimination claims took the EEOC by surprise, causing a severe backlog in the examination of cases.

The fragmentation of the movement also enabled ethnic minority women to address their own problems from within the framework of the Women's movement. In the large egalitarian feminist organizations, decentralization had operated in the sense of the creation of specialized committees. Thus, NOW took pride in having, from 1977, a Minority Women's Committee, while the NWPC diversified even further with a Chicana Committee and an Asian Women's Committee. The year 1977 furnished further proof of the spread of feminist ideas among ethnic minority women, with the gathering of the First Convention of Jewish Women at Cornell University, followed a little later by La Conferencia de la Chicana in Boulder, Colorado.[4]

Finally, there was even an attempt to organize rural feminism, if we can judge by the formation of another NOW committee in the late 1970s, Feminism in Rural Life.

The culmination of the persuasion and infiltration work done by the Women's movement was the National Women's Conference held in Houston in November 1977. There was reluctant attendance by radical feminists, who feared the risk of being co-opted, an inherent danger of any conference financed by the government; but in spite of the radicals' underrepresentation, the conference confirmed the strength of the new feminist movement, which held a majority in all the delegations, including those from states where the antifeminist backlash was the most virulent. Despite the efforts of the NWPC to promote an overall plan of action at the expense of "minor" groups, the conference displayed the movement's desire for representation of every sector, which took concrete form in fragmentation. The most diverse range of committees, including women students, handicapped women, ethnic minority women, lesbians, and women on welfare, were all able to make themselves heard and get their amendments adopted. Even the antifeminist delegations voted in favor of some feminist proposals.

The presence at the women's conference of an antifeminist minority— estimated at 15 to 20 percent—reveals, of course, that opposition existed. But the development of a backlash, not necessarily composed of women, is a measure of the success of the Women's movement, whose impact can be evaluated in proportion to the combativeness of its adversaries. The Women's movement by this point was perceived as a political entity, from which a majority of men and women expected a certain measure of activism. According to a Harris poll taken in 1979, 65 percent of Americans approved "most of the efforts to strengthen and change women's status in our society," as against only 41 percent in 1970.

THE PHILOSOPHY OF ACTION

The phrasing of the question in the Harris poll obviously obscures the ideological content. Although ideology has been a cause of dissension, action can become a factor toward unity. In particular, action has highlighted a new aspect of union among women, "militant sisterhood," which is, by definition, the dynamic of sisters in movement. In being collective, action has been perceived as an effective way to make sisterhood concrete and to move women out of the often-paralyzing emotionalism of consciousness-raising groups. Union among sisters has had its privileged moments when militants have communed with each other in their rediscovered force, during an exhilarating collective action, and have transformed this effusive experience into a well of fresh energy upon which each one could draw while waiting for a new communion in the feminist faith. The testimony of various participants has consecrated the Houston conference as one of the summits of new feminism, from which the women present emerged radiating with sisterhood and collective energy, after the feminist flame had been literally carried by relays all the way from the symbolic starting point of Seneca Falls, New York. Added to this symbol of continuity with the first wave of feminism, many symbols of unity marked the three days in Houston: the chain of women's hands and the immense choir of women's voices singing the liberation hymn "We Shall Overcome," which greeted the adoption of the amendment presented by the ethnic minority women; or again, the release of balloons upon the adoption of the amendment for sexual preference, which sealed the agreement for new cooperation between heterosexuals and lesbians within the Women's movement. In this general glow of goodwill, even members of the antifeminist minority opposition joined hands in the chain of feminine solidarity, and the "spirit of Houston" flourished while the majority of participants felt conscious of being "vital individual parts of an important collective, interconnected whole."[5]

This last phrase brings up the issue of whether the Women's movement is truly representative of women. Certainly, this is difficult to evaluate because, aside from counting the membership of a few large organizations, there is no effective way to take a census of feminists. However, we can advance the conclusion that, although some feminist ideas have infiltrated many sectors of society, feminism does not yet have a solid base in those sectors. In this sense, we agree with Jo Freeman on her point that the new feminist movement had spread without building a theoretical foundation. Having admitted that, we think the essential thing now is for feminists to recognize this weakness. At times there has been some awareness of this lack, to judge by the insistence with which some feminists have expressed the desire to give sisterhood a populist character by integrating the greatest number of women into the movement and achieving representation from the humblest social origins.

The editors of *Ms.* analyzed the composition of the participants at the Houston conference. They particularly observed the large number of anonymous delegates, such as miners' widows from Kentucky, or individual women speaking out on behalf of housewives. They were also pleased to see that the conference was not dominated by white women nor by prosperous women, who were underrepresented in proportion to their numbers in the national population.[6] At this same conference, Susan Dworkin presented Ellie Smeal, the new president of NOW, as a "popular leader," who defined herself as "an ordinary woman . . . a homemaker." The ideal of a "populist sisterhood" led NOW to support struggling women laborers. For example, NOW supported women textile workers in their bitter dispute with the Stevens firm over sexual discrimination in its policies on promotions and salaries, while feminists in Denver actively sided with women workers in the Coors breweries. It was important for feminism to become "a popular movement . . . feminism with a lower-case 'f.' "[7]

In this last phrase, the new president of NOW was expressing the need to inject new blood into the movement, which had a tendency to waste effort in internal ideological quarrels, and a desire to break away from grand flights of theory. She voiced her conviction that no woman could choose not to be a feminist. The reign of the white, elitist, and bourgeois militant, who had always been seen as the archetype of the American feminist, must give way to "populist sisterhood." In a special issue of *Ms.*, July–August 1982, commemorating the magazine's tenth anniversary, Barbara Ehrenreich and Karin Stallard presented "the feminization of poverty" as the most critical problem American feminists needed to address, if they wanted to avoid a situation in the year 2000 where the poor of the United States would consist entirely of women and children. According to Lindsy Van Gelder, evolution toward this "populist sisterhood" had begun at Houston: "In Houston, I learned in my gut . . . that *feminists* are everywhere; that we are a populist, majority movement . . . and that we *can* work together and succeed on a grand scale."[8]

With this last phrase, a new aspect of militant sisterhood appeared: radical egalitarianism, that is, the conviction that each person is endowed with the same rich potential, and that inequalities in individual performances are due, not to inequalities in natural abilities, but rather to different degrees of education. Hence the golden rule of feminism, "each one teach one," with each woman passing on her own knowledge to others, in the same way as witches, resuscitated by the group WITCH, handed down ancient lore. Therefore, sisterhood, unlike male clan behavior, is antihierarchical. In one way or another, the feminine style of nonpower is perceived as the opposite of the masculine style of coercion. Typical of this spirit was the decision at a monthly meeting of the New York Radical Feminists, in July 1973, to dissolve the coordinating committee, and to open to all members the weekly Tuesday night meeting previously reserved for the committee. There is no question that most advocates of a total absence of structure have been found in the radical feminist faction, but under their influence, egalitarian feminists also came to demand greater flexibility in their organizational structure.

This is the context in which Ellie Smeal recommended the decentralization of NOW through the multiplication of local chapters. On this point, it is interesting to note the emergence of a new style of feminine leader, faithful to the populist and egalitarian philosophy of militant sisterhood, who, having gained confidence from the simple fact of earning a salary,[9] would be capable of effectively assuming responsibility. Evidence of this was shown in October 1976 by the conclusions of a survey conducted jointly by the *Washington Post* and the Harvard University Center for International Affairs. Feminist leaders—of whom 40 percent came from NOW, with the others drawn from reformist associations such as FEW, the Coalition of Labor Women, and the NWPC—distinguished themselves among other leaders by their greater radicalism, their more intense desire to impose arms control, to nationalize oil companies, and to force the government to enact a national policy of fair employment practices. The survey showed that the disenchantment of feminist leaders with the two-party American system was unequaled by any group except young people.

In addition to unity, a second concept that has been central to the feminist philosophy of action is survival. Action is survival in the sense that it provides a way to overcome the existential and cultural death caused by sexism. Women in the movement—women *in* movement—are those who, thanks to feminist consciousness-raising, have survived sexism.

On an individual level, survival through action has meant self-realization for many women. Here we reencounter the theme of the quest for identity, which underlies the entire consciousness-raising process in all the various ideological approaches and feminist literary works. The new recruit who has sought refuge or advice in the movement has undergone an apprentice-ship in self-determination and self-help, enabling her to combat sexist institutions or to use the resources of the law. She has embarked on the first step toward self-realization: autonomy and control of her own life. In this undertaking, she has been aided by all the organizations created within the movement to help single women. Momma and the Sisterhood of Black Mothers, for instance, are examples of groups founded especially for single mothers who did not expect to be married. In no way is this a question of charity work; on the contrary, it is a way of developing pride among women who had refused to take the easy way out. This is achieved by recognizing that these women need to be provided with legal information and job training to arm them for independence and to spare them the humiliation of public welfare. These same principles have inspired the work of the feminist cooperative Women in Transition and the numerous "centers for displaced homemakers," which particularly address the problems of women who are temporarily helpless or distraught during a marital separation or divorce. Innumerable incarnations exist of feminist philosophy in action, with its key concepts of survival, self-help, and sisterhood. Examples even include do-it-yourself divorce groups, such as the Seattle Women's Divorce Cooperative, organized to teach women how to plead their own divorces. The vast multiplication of such experiments must lead, sooner or later, to observable changes in the life-style of both women and men.

For a woman who, through the movement, has been militant in the cause and has taken part in constructive feminist action, self-realization lies in the creative expression of her own perceptions and her aspirations as a free woman, in a labor of personal growth that could only have taken place within a community of women, and which, for this reason, belongs as much to the community as to her.

Joan Cassell points out the possible contradiction between the feminist faith in self-realization and a radical definition of equality that penalizes all superior ability.[10] We believe this objection might apply in the context of individual competition, but not in the context of collective action or inter-action. To say that self-realization can lead to more marked individual differences and thereby threaten the collective character of the group is to ignore the fact that the personal growth work is done in the service of the feminism collective. It is part of a vast undertaking, agreed at the outset, which is the collective, anonymous building of the feminist edifice so that each woman lives by the movement and the movement lives by each woman. "There is no such thing as 'individual action' within a movement."[11]

In this context, each woman who achieves self-realization is contributing her bit to building feminism, since each newcomer who discovers that she can act on her own is a fledgling militant. The very essence of the movement is to work for each woman so that each woman can work for the movement.

Regarding strictly political action, self-realization has taken on two aspects, corresponding to two different concepts of egalitarianism. According to radical feminism, self-realization results from applying the principle of radical egalitarianism to political action within the movement itself. This was done, for example, in the organizational rules of the group known as the Feminists. These rules were based on the conviction that political abilities are universal in human nature; thus, every member had the necessary aptitude, and therefore the right, to make a contribution, and each person's contribution was of equal value with anyone else's. The rotation of tasks and the drawing of lots to decide who should preside over a meeting have been prevalent in radical feminist groups. These practices have expressed a fundamental hostility to power, perceived as a threat to the personal self-realization that each woman is supposed to achieve in exercising new responsibilities.

In contrast, the liberal feminists have considered that self-realization results from applying the egalitarian principle, not to comparisons between feminists, but to comparisons between the two sexes. The two sexes have equal aptitudes; therefore, the notion of equality applies between the average woman and the average man. In this view, it is important for the average woman to realize that, just like the average man, she can manage things on her own, without the help of an expert or a member of the opposite sex. Here we have the survival philosophy in action, as shown by such examples as the do-it-yourself divorce. In either the radical or liberal feminist interpretation, the essential objective of self-realization has been the same, and this is further proof that action is a factor toward unity. The goal has been to give each woman the self-confidence she needs to take charge of her own life.

Survival has also been a guiding principle in the numerous resources created by feminists. These resources include not just groups devoted to improving the status of women, but all sorts of feminist alternative structures that in fact are embryonic institutions. After Women in Transition published *A Survival Manual,* the first attempt at a feminist guide aimed at women experiencing separation or divorce, numerous other guides appeared. *The New Woman's Survival Catalog,* the enormous Bible of new feminism, was followed by *The New Woman's Survival Sourcebook,* whose cover was illustrated by Judy Chicago with a pair of wings of light, symbolizing a new way of living. The purpose of the two latter books was to show the true dimension of feminist action, revealing that the movement was not only a structure for the struggle to improve women's lot, but also a place for experimentation and the development of innovative solutions. Revealing the scope of these innovations was intended to bring women to recognize their own creative potential. These feminist alternative institutions have been necessary, their creators say, because they represent the other side of human experience—until now, only men's side has been shown—and, in keeping with the feminist theory of androgyny, they show what contribution women can make to the culture.

PLURALISM IN ACTION

The creations described above demonstrate that, contrary to the apprehensions expressed by Jo Freeman in 1975, the movement has begun to build something constructive. The pluralism resulting from fragmentation has allowed feminism to explore different forms of action. At first, there was an impression of disorder; hence, the often-stated critique of an absence of strategy. But with time, the situation has settled down, and it is now possible to identify certain main trends within feminist action, certain basic orientations that have remained constant over the years, each one having had its high moments. We call this action pluralist in the sense that it has appeared in a variety of forms, but pluralism of forms has never compromised the unity of aims, since the various forms of action have always been exercised in the same domains.

Within common spheres of activity, feminist action has oscillated between two poles: on one hand, militant intervention for the purpose of politicizing women's issues and demanding changes in the conditions of women's lives; on the other hand, an existential and cultural renaissance, nourished by aspirations for self-liberation and redefinition of women's identity.

Militant action itself has taken two different forms. At the start, shock actions were favored, aimed at awakening public consciousness, with the first declarations denouncing sexist abuses and asserting women's unwillingness to accept the existing system. Later, shock actions gave way to patient, regular work on the legislative level, either to demonstrate that sexism was an integral part of the law, or to lead women to know and claim their rights through specific judicial action.

The existential and cultural renaissance has sometimes appeared to correspond to radical separatism, or survival in self-imposed isolation. Hence the impression that radical feminism has died out since the early 1970s. At least, this is what I wrote to the New York Radical Feminists (NYRF), whom I had found strikingly dynamic in the summer of 1973. I received a reply in the form of a vehement protest from the pen of one of its members, then living underground, who shall remain anonymous out of a concern for her privacy. I cite her testimony here. Doubtless it is subjective, but it is precious evidence that the NYRF, once a prominent organization, was still alive and well a decade after its founding.

Please don't think radical feminism is dead, or has been placated or swallowed up into the jowls of non-descript liberalism. Many of us have feminist businesses, are writing books on feminism, going to law school, working in the media, press, underground radio, and so on. . . . Our lives as women are changing—slowly—but most important, we are stronger together and have gone underground to live our lives and build our own institutions![12]

Are we looking at a form of militant self-segregation? The choice of living underground might make it appear so, but the nature of the actions mentioned in the NYRF letter seems to indicate an eventual desire to leave the underground and work openly to change the system, particularly for those operating feminist businesses or studying law.

One day, when the right time has come, this separatism must end. In any case, this is the direction that liberal feminists, new at this sort of action, have given, perhaps prematurely, to the existential and cultural renaissance. And it is this desire to remake the world for the benefit of all that distinguishes feminist action from the general counterculture movement. Self-liberation and the redefinition of women's identity are preparing the way, in keeping with the great dream of the feminist utopia, for a new humanism. This was also the significance given by the authors of *The New Women's Survival Sourcebook* to the establishment of alternative feminist institutions:

What the material in this book suggests is that feminism is not only a force to secure the liberation of women, but it is a force to enrich and diversify human life.[13]

Women's creation of alternative institutions is part of an effort to reshape and transform culture as a whole.[14]

NINE

Guerrilla Warriors for Consciousness-Raising

Earlier we mentioned the first feminist guerrilla action organized to arouse public consciousness, that is, the burial of traditional femininity at Arlington Cemetery by the New York Radical Women. The decision of Shulamith Firestone and Pam Allen to establish New York as the headquarters of the first radical feminist guerrilla group was a precursor of the concentration of feminist guerrilla action in Manhattan. For a time, Manhattan became the epicenter of the shock waves of feminist consciousness-raising. In 1968–69, within a few months of each other, all the most famous guerrilla groups burst onto the scene: WITCH, the Redstockings, the Feminists, and the New York Radical Feminists. These were all veritable commando forces for consciousness-raising, and in between their commando raids, they developed the radical theoretical framework.

THE SHOCK TROOPS

According to Peggy Kornegger, picking up an expression used by Daniel Guerin, shock action is a matter of "purposeful illegality." It is equivalent to rebellion, like the anarchist action of WITCH.

It is impossible to overstate the difficulties inherent in this type of action. To be successful, it must take the form of a spectacle leaving no room for ambiguity. This was the lesson learned from the earliest guerrilla attempts: the sabotage of the Miss America pageant at Atlantic City by the New York Radical Women in September 1968, and the disruption of the first New York Bridal Fair [1] at Madison Square Garden by WITCH on Saint Valentine's Day, 1969. These actions had a dual purpose: to awaken women to consciousness of their oppression, and to build solidarity among militant sisters. However, in each case, the action was misinterpreted as an attack aimed at a certain category of women, and therefore was damaging to the concept of sisterhood. This was because the slogans were ambiguous and the declarations of intent were fragmentary. The signs carried by demonstrators reading Up Against the Wall, Miss America or Miss America Is a Big Falsie were susceptible to being interpreted as personal attacks against the woman crowned, as well as all those who had hoped to be chosen. The same unclear motivation lay behind the crowning of a sheep as Miss America. Although the intended message was that, in a beauty contest, all women are considered as fair game to be sold at auction and turned into sex objects in the eyes of men, the symbolic action was interpreted as a declaration of war against beauty and an insult to beautiful women. As a result, the action backfired, and attractive women were alienated from feminism. Likewise, in disrupting the Bridal Fair, WITCH's intention had been to expose the greedy exploitation by businessmen of the institution of marriage, as the capitalist basis of women's oppression, but the brides and their mothers attending the fair felt that they personally were being ridiculed and scorned for being, or wanting to be, "nothing but housewives."

The ten-point manifesto issued by the demonstrators at Atlantic City also was unclear and subject to misinterpretation, particularly about the intended meaning of their spectacular "Freedom Trash Can into which we will throw bras, girdles, false eyelashes, wigs . . . bring any such woman's trash you have around the house"[2] and their alleged public burnings of brassieres. For militant feminist guerrillas, these were metaphors for their political rejection of all the restraints imposed on women by the traditional definition of femininity. However, in the absence of clear explanations, opponents immediately seized upon these symbolic acts as childish fixations with articles of clothing, and feminists were ridiculed as "bra burners." Journalists and public opinion had a field day joking about the futility of feminists who could not tell the difference between fashion and politics. The brassiere symbolized sex, and sex was pornography, which surely had nothing to do with politics.

Carol Hanisch, whose idea it was to disrupt the sacrosanct Miss America pageant, afterward wrote a severe, objective critique of the errors committed there. The lesson, it seems, was taken to heart by feminists of all factions, revealing how a shock action, if badly coordinated and not well explained, could alienate not only public opinion, but even worse, a large number of ordinary women. From this time on, indeed, women who were inexperienced in political action, and even some "moderate" feminists, reproached radical feminists for their outrageous actions, precisely because they had misunderstood the point and concentrated on the symbolic object itself and not on the symbolic value of their action. It was essential to avoid any further such misunderstandings, which were so prejudicial to the image of the movement and to building sisterhood. Indeed, the image of feminist "furies," as spread and perpetuated by the media,[3] offered no comfort to ordinary housewives or low-salaried working women, and risked instead isolating them even further.

The demonstrations at Atlantic City and the Bridal Fair were valuable learning experiences for feminists, for from that moment on, either in actions or in writings, they avoided attacks on stereotypes, since these put them in direct confrontation with other women and risked being misinterpreted as personal attacks on them. From then on, feminists turned toward less ambiguous actions which placed them in direct opposition to men, and in particular, to the men responsible for spreading stereotyped images. Beyond raising the consciousness of women about their oppression, beyond building sisterhood, a third objective came into view: raising the consciousness of men about the breadth of their sexism.

THE MEDIA

In 1966, NOW had created a special committee to address the issue of images of women in the media. The media soon became the prime sphere of action for feminists of all tendencies. This development was a logical outgrowth of the demonstrations at Atlantic City and Madison Square Garden, since the media had always been the most effective socialization instrument for spreading the very same false and degrading image that feminists were attacking. The image was false, in that it showed only one aspect of women' activities—domestic life. It was degrading, since the woman was always shown either as a housewife, a consumer of household products and appliances, or as a marketable commodity or sex object, the lure of every kind of advertising. These connotations inspired NOW's first two initiatives in this domain. First, NOW created a Barefoot and Pregnant in the Kitchen award for guilty advertising agencies. NOW also undertook a graffiti campaign, writing "This ad exploits women" across sexist billboards.

More ambitious and radical actions were carried out against the press. These included, two months apart, the takeover of the editorial offices of the radical underground newspaper *Rat* on 26 January 1970, and the detention for eleven hours of the editor-in-chief of the *Ladies' Home Journal,* John

Mack Carter, on 18 March 1970. These two examples provide further proof of how action has always been a unifying factor. While the takeover of *Rat* was essentially the work of the paper's own women staff members, it led to the subsequent founding of *Women's Rat,* the first underground newspaper controlled entirely by women. *Women's Rat* was created by a feminist coalition in which, according to Robin Morgan, most of the New York groups were represented, including the Redstockings, WITCH, the New York Radical Women, and the New York chapter of NOW. Similarly, the sit-in at *The Ladies' Home Journal* was conducted by about a hundred women, representing NOW, the Feminists, the Redstockings, and Media Women, which had not previously been able to agree on a philosophy but did so as a result of this action.

It may seem surprising that a feminist consensus formed around two such different publications as the radical, antiestablishment *Rat* and the ultraestablishment *Ladies' Home Journal.* The point of connection is their common basis in sexism. The staff of *Rat,* according to Robin Morgan, was the perfect example of radical hypocrisy, claiming to be pro-feminist but speaking in paternalistic rhetoric and decorating the pages with pornographic photos and sexist comic strips. Likewise, the press release distributed at the time of the *Ladies' Home Journal* sit-in explained that the attack was directed against the magazine's image of women as limited and passive creatures, with no other interest than domestic concerns. The feminist coalition criticized both publications for their blindness to women's issues, one scorning them in the name of radicalism as concerns of the bourgeoisie, the other, in the name of conservatism, shunning them as revolutionary! Finally, the staffs of both publications exhibited the same sexist hierarchy. According to Robin Morgan, the editors of *Rat* were all men; according to Media Women, the senior editors of the *Ladies' Home Journal* consisted of three men and only one woman.

Ironically, the parallel can be pursued in measuring the results achieved. Both guerrilla actions resulted in only partial victories. For *Rat,* the successful part was the introduction of a new power relationship between men and women in the radical underground press. Women proved that they could respond to the challenge and cooperate in new ways of publishing a paper. They did it for more than a year. The unsuccessful part was that *Rat* never really became a feminist journal, and that the majority of the feminist collective still felt more sympathetic to the New Left than to the Women's movement. The union of sisters never did come about, and *Rat* ceased publication during 1971. As for the *Ladies' Home Journal* action, its successful aspect was the publication, at the magazine's expense, of an eight-page supplement devoted to feminism, written by the feminists themselves.[4] Thus the readers of this traditional women's magazine were treated to a certain amount of exposure to feminist philosophy, and had their first consciousness-raising experience. The unsuccessful aspect was that otherwise nothing changed in the structure and policies of the *Ladies' Home Journal*.

However, it is important not to paint too somber a picture of the journalistic profession. Although the status quo persisted at the *Ladies' Home Journal*, other bastions of the press were shaken to their foundations when women journalists undertook a new type of action: lawsuits. As we shall see in the next chapter, the first collective suit was filed the same week as the sit-in at the staid ladies' magazine. Consciousness-raising had begun among women in the media; from then on, their action would take place in the courtroom. This evolution was further aided by the transformation of their consciousness-raising goal: from action aimed at shocking people into awareness, it became an undertaking of informing and educating the public. The credit for this initiative belongs to certain members of Media Women who, in 1971, after the group's dissolution, published a pamphlet called *Women's Guide to the Media*. The pamphlet judged each sector of the New York media on its quotient of sexism, and reviewed the position of women within the media professions.

ABORTION

On the subject of voluntary interruption of pregnancy, new feminist action had been preceded by the reformist movement that developed in the early sixties in response to the 1962 revelation of the thalidomide drama. That movement had produced such organizations as the Association for the Study of Abortion, founded in 1964, others devoted to family or social counseling, like the Parents' Aid Society of New York, created in 1964 by Bill Baird, and the Association to Repeal Abortion Laws, established in California in 1966 by Patricia Maginnis.

Abortion is the issue that has unleashed the most violent passions and has radicalized the greatest number of women. This is easily explained by the nature of the problem, which typically elicits a gut reaction, in both proponents and opponents. Strong emotions are felt by proponents, whether their refusal of pregnancy is connected with a fear of motherhood, or represents a political and ethical rejection of women's social duty to reproduce. Strong emotions are also felt by opponents of abortion, whether in the name of morality founded on respect for life, or out of fear of feminism, or even from puritanical motives.

The second reason that explains why feminist action crystallized around this issue is the existence of specific, particularly oppressive laws against the voluntary interruption of pregnancy. In the late 1960s, many states still were applying old statutes drafted in the nineteenth century to replace common law; while common law had been liberal in this matter, these old statutes made abortion a crime in all cases unless the mother's life was in danger. Between 1967 and 1970, twelve states[5] reformed their abortion laws, in keeping with the recommendations made in 1959 by the American Law Institute. These recommendations proposed that the old restrictive laws should continue to apply, but several new exceptions were allowed: risk to the mother, the possibility that the child would be born "with grave physical or mental defects," and pregnancy following rape or incest.

The feminist position had been clearly defined in 1967 by Article VIII of the NOW Bill of Rights: existing abortion laws should not be reformed, they should be repealed. For most liberal feminists, this repeal could still be accompanied by some restrictions: the obligation to be a resident of the state where the abortion took place, the requirement of parental consent in the case of a minor, the requirement that the operation should be performed by a qualified surgeon in a recognized medical facility, and the refusal of abortion beyond a certain stage of pregnancy. However, the philosophy of a minority of liberal feminists and most radical feminists, as expressed by the group New Yorkers for Abortion Law Repeal,[6] was that repeal should be total and without exception. Their reasoning was that as long as any legislative restrictions remained, the voluntary interruption of pregnancy would be placed in a different legal category from any other surgical procedure, and would appear to be an exception, an evil that needed to be controlled by law, instead of being a matter between the patient and the doctor.

The original Redstockings were the ones who precipitated the awakening of consciousness among women and the general public about this delicate issue. On 13 February 1969, the New York state legislature was holding hearings on reform of the New York abortion laws. While most partisans of reform were demonstrating in the street, the women who were about to found the Redstockings left the ranks of the marchers and broke into the hearing room, denouncing the hypocrisy of the hearings where the assembled witnesses consisted of fourteen men and only one woman—and she a nun! When the militants were refused the right to testify, they formed the Redstockings and organized their own counterhearing, on 21 March 1969, in the Washington Square Methodist Church in Manhattan. The hearing attracted three hundred people, both men and women, who listened to twelve Redstockings speak in an atmosphere charged with drama. Here again, shock action had yielded to an activity of public education.

The adroit combination of shock action with an informational process, as modeled by the Redstockings, bore witness to a real sense of strategy, and did more service than disservice to the cause of repeal. To test the truth of this, one only has to measure the Redstockings' impact in starting a chain reaction: by 1970, a number of decidedly respectable nonfeminist organizations[7] had pronounced themselves in favor of abortion law repeal, while the state legislatures of New York, Hawaii, and Alaska voted for such repeal by rejecting the more conservative approach of the American Law Institute. Even more, in May 1971, the United States Supreme Court agreed to review the cases of *Roe v. Wade* and *Doe v. Bolton*. The Court's judgment, rendered on 22 January 1973, declared the abortion laws of Texas and Georgia unconstitutional, specifying that during the first trimester of pregnancy, the abortion decision was a matter between the woman and her doctor.

RAPE

Even more than abortion, rape is the issue that transformed action from shock tactics to the more patient work of fostering public awareness and understanding. It is true that spectacular rallies occurred, like the one organized by the Feminists on 28 September 1971 in response to a grand jury decision acquitting a man who had raped two little girls; but this type of action gradually gave way to an effort at broad public education and information. Taking up the Redstockings' tactic of public debate, the New York Radical Feminists (NYRF) organized a day of rape testimony on 24 January 1971. For hours at a time, in one of the first such public discussions of rape, women who had been raped described their experiences and debated society's prejudices against the rape victim, which they had internalized psychologically. This debate was followed on 17 April 1971 by the

NYRF Rape Workshop, devoted to political, sociological, and psychological aspects of the issue. Other groups organized similar action, such as the conference on rape organized in 1974 by the National Black Feminist Organization in cooperation with New York Women Against Rape.

At first, the chief aim of all these actions was to educate women. It was important to give them a political view of rape, as an act of vile domination and aggression that scoffed at the victim's right to control her own body and implied a threat of death. Feminist action was intended to shake women out of their resignation and silence by making them perceive rape as an act of mass terrorism, of which anyone can be a victim, even though the patriarchal society has always encouraged a feeling that the guilt lies in the rape victim herself. As a political act, rape must be seen as one of the most primitive expressions of the arbitrary subjection of women, according to the thesis of Susan Brownmiller's book *Against Our Will,* which remains one of the most complete studies of rape, and is the perfect culmination of the rape consciousness-raising efforts begun in 1971.

Refusing to see women obliged to stay home behind triple-locked doors every night after dark, the activists naturally extended their rape education activities to practical matters. These included confrontation through self-defense (which we will study below under survival tactics), as well as policelike methods of investigation and exposure. Accusing the police and judicial authorities of laxity in this field, New York militants decided to organize their own investigative efforts, and published lists of habitual rapists. In March 1973, the group known as the Feminists launched a graffiti campaign against New York rapists, publicly displaying their full names and home addresses. This was done less to incite vigilante actions of summary justice than to end the anonymity which had allowed repeated offenders to molest women with impunity. The idea was further developed by the Kitty Genovese Women's Project, named in memory of Kitty Genovese, a 28-year-old waitress who was murdered in front of her home in 1964 after having been subjected to sexual violence for thirty minutes while the neighbors closed their blinds and ignored her screams.

Action against rape was the occasion for a new feminist coalition among the NYRF, the New York chapter of NOW, the Manhattan Women's Political Caucus, and New York Women Against Rape. August 1973 was declared Rape Prevention Month. In a solemn fourteen-point declaration, the various New York feminist groups announced that they were participating in separate and joint informational actions, this time aimed at the general public, and therefore, at men. The message was that men should support women in their struggle against rapists since rapists lower all humanity, in the same way as racists or torturers of any kind. Rape consciousness-raising had thus reached a new second level. A third level was attained—addressing rapists themselves—when Santa Cruz Women Against Rape had the idea of arranging confrontations between rapists and their victims, in which the raped woman would play the role of an active educator, in contrast to her typically passive role in the judicial process.

RITUALS

Consciousness-raising action took on yet another aspect with the ritual celebration of landmark events in the American struggle for women's rights, which have become red-letter days in the feminist calendar.

Ritual celebration has a dual function. As seen by outside observers, it demonstrates the strength and solidarity of the Women's movement, so as to persuade the public that feminism has a broad base. As experienced by those in the movement, it reaffirms and renews the union among sisters, spiritually and emotionally nourishing their feelings of "sisterhood" and enabling them to become more deeply rooted in women's history.

This is the dual meaning, for example, of the commemoration of the famous march of 4 March 1913, when 5,000 suffragists, braving masses of hecklers, fought their way up Pennsylvania Avenue in Washington proclaiming women's right to vote. In August 1977, 5,000 feminists, dressed in white in imitation of the suffragists, joined hands with the past and followed the same route to demand ratification of the Equal Rights Amendment. On 9 July 1978, more than two hundred organizations assembled a throng of more than 100,000 people (in the estimate of Mildred Jeffrey, president of the NWPC)—feminists again dressed in white along with male supporters of their cause—who marched to the Capitol Building to demand extension of the ERA ratification deadline.

The twenty-sixth of August, anniversary of the date when the women's voting rights amendment came into effect, inspired another ritual celebration. In 1973, it was proclaimed Women's Equality Day by President Nixon, after Congress had voted approval of a measure to this effect introduced by Bella Abzug. From then on, perhaps so as to avoid any attempt at official coopting, and also because of a certain demobilization in the wake of the achievements already accomplished, the mass marches that had marked 26 August since 1970 were replaced by a variety of events spread out over a week. I was a witness to the Feminist Days of August 1973 in Manhattan. If I concentrate here on the festivities of 25 August 1973, that is because it seems to me a summation of all the consciousness-raising activities organized during the crucial years 1969–73, which cannot possibly all be mentioned here because of the necessary limits of length.

The week preceding 25 August (the date chosen because that year the twenty-sixth fell on a Sunday) had seen shock actions against symbolic targets. Prominent among these was the New York Stock Exchange on Wall Street with its satellites, the brokerage firms, which in spite of the ritual incantations uttered there by WITCH in 1968, remained "the epitome of the male-dominated institutions of the Wall Street empire."[8]

The Biltmore Bar, with its men-only sign, on the corner of Madison Avenue and 43rd Street, had been the object of an attempt at sexual desegregation, as had been Clancy's Bar in Washington in 1971. At Rockefeller Center, the statue of Atlas had been rigged out in a banner reading "Atlas, you've held us up long enough."

On the big day, 25 August, a feminist fair was held at Battery Park, a symbolic site facing the Statue of Liberty. It began in a spirit of gloom, with the impending threat of the return of clandestine abortion, in an emotional uproar over the decision of Senator James L. Buckley to introduce a constitutional amendment banning the voluntary interruption of pregnancy to counteract the liberal ruling handed down by the Supreme Court the preceding January. The ritual commemoration had its own rites of procedure, starting with the simulated burial of all women who have died of illegal abortions, "murdered by back-alley abortionists." In the funeral procession was a tombstone dedicated "to the memory of the unknown woman," in bitter plagiarism of the usual masculine official military commemorations, along with a coat hanger and a knitting needle, which, in feminist attacks, are identified as the typical tools of the illegal abortionist.

With the speeches, the celebration changed spirit and was placed under the sign of unity. Now the question of unity arose not so much between radical and liberal feminists, but rather with those women who had previously had the greatest difficulties in merging their interests with the Women's movement: ethnic minority women, represented here by the National Black Feminist Organization and the lawyer Brenda Fasteau, who denounced forced sterilizations; members of Lesbian Feminist Liberation, whose president, Jean O'Leary, with a young entourage, delivered an ideological speech; and older women, whose situation was mentioned in the address by the national president of NOW, Wilma Scott Heide. She broadened the debate even further by recalling that the liberation of women meant the liberation of men as well. In the crowd, members of a group called the Men's Liberation Movement showed their approval with signs reading Men Are Not Just Success Objects (echoing the familiar feminist slogan, Women Are Not Just Sex Objects). To all the speakers, the listeners were attentive, sometimes serious, never disrespectful.

After the speeches, the atmosphere became more relaxed and a festive spirit took over, as the crowd broke up to wander among the stands or form small groups at random. Improvised exchanges of views took place in a sort of consciousness-raising fair; then, an audience gathered around a picturesque group, three women of various ages and a young man performing a sketch about age discrimination against women in hiring. The script had been written by Anne Kainen, who played the role of the older woman and was a member of the Older Woman's Task Force of NOW. When she learned of my research, she spontaneously, in a spirit of "sisterhood," offered me the original script of her play.[9]

The feminist fair ended in a spirit of history. At the end of her address, Judy Wenning, president of the New York chapter of NOW, had already provided a link with the past by introducing Mabel Rees, aged ninety-three, a former suffragist. The pilgrimage to the sources continued with a picturesque ferry trip to Staten Island, a symbolic reenactment of the 1848 walk in the countryside at Senaca Falls. Dressed in period costumes, the modern militants gaily paraded through the quiet streets under the indulgent and bemused gaze of the passersby.

The reason for including this anecdotal account is to convey the atmosphere that reigned in the Women's movement during its heyday in the years 1970–73, when its successes were coming easily and the counterrevolutionary backlash had not yet been organized. In those days, the struggle was joyful. There was joy in action and communication, joy in experiencing unity among all the various feminist factions, which, as we have seen, were able to form coalitions around the major issues of the media, abortion, and rape.

However, in any political movement, the reign of the consciousness-raising phase is always short-lived. This type of action usually ends as soon as the problems have been raised and stated clearly enough; or else it evolves toward trying to harness shifting opinions to move in a constructive direction—which is evidence of the movement's political maturity. In the new feminist movement, the year 1973 was a turning point; it climaxed the long period of the great offensive, and opened an era of counterattack, when the movement often found itself having to adopt a defensive stance. The first sign of this change was the publication, in that year, of a book by Marabel Morgan consecrating a new "feminine mystique": *Total Woman*.

TEN

Feminism and the Law

THE PROGRAM

About 1973, the liberal branch of the Women's movement began trying to establish a detailed program. This new orientation seems to us to have been a realistic adjustment to take account of two factors. First, some basis for action appeared necessary in order to enable the movement to move forward coherently and to use its energy constructively toward external goals instead of wasting it in internal quarrels. Second, it was essential to build as broad a base as possible to unify women, particularly so as to make available to the struggle the resources of nonfeminist women's organizations that had been alienated from the movement by shock actions or outrageous declarations, and that could weigh heavily in determining the outcome of the battle. The development of a platform for reform would reveal how much common interest there was between feminist and nonfeminist women's organizations. Moreover, the inclusion of a wide range of proposals in this platform would have another advantage: every woman, from radical militant to nonfeminist, and every organization, from political caucus to labor union, could find something in it to support.

The first formal program platform developed by the new feminist movement in the United States was the *National Women's Agenda*, presented on 2 December 1975 to President Gerald Ford, the governors of the fifty states, and members of Congress. It had been signed by ninety women's organizations, who recognized in the preamble the priority of their common interest in every sector and at every level of American society, while affirming their continuing desire for pluralism in their purposes and points of view. The platform covered eleven headings for bold and substantial reforms.

The second platform was developed at the National Women's Conference held in Houston in November 1977. It, too, corresponded to a pragmatic spirit of coalition: "We must agree when we can, disagree when we have to, but never lose sight of our overall objectives."[1]

Adopted within the framework of a conference financed by federal funds, the Houston action plan was duly made official on 17 August 1978 by the publication of a 308-page report, *The Spirit of Houston,* and the nomination of a National Advisory Committee for Women, cochaired by Bella Abzug and Carmen Delgado Votaw. The committee's assignment under the Department of Labor was to advise the president and Congress with a view toward gradual execution of the plan. This official recognition corresponded to the will of the Houston delegates, as expressed in Resolution 26 of the platform, and translated their desire to make the government face up to its responsibilities and recognize women's issues as a national concern.

The Houston action plan contains twenty-six resolutions, three of which have been widely publicized because of the bitter divisions they have provoked among women and the doubt that has reigned over their adoption. We are speaking of the Equal Rights Amendment, the right to the voluntary interruption of pregnancy, and freedom of choice in sexual preference. With deliberate regularity, each of the twenty-six resolutions is introduced in the platform by a time-honored phrase placing the issue in the hands of legislators at the federal or state level, either demanding the establishment of permanent structures (as in the case of all the resolutions on violence), recommending new legislation (supporting child care centers and opposing discrimination against pregnant working women), or demanding enforcement of existing laws.

POLITICAL POWER

Relations with the Power Structure

Having obtained official recognition of their demands, the feminists who believed in reforming the existing system particularly favored one method of action over others: political pressure on government agencies, the president, or Congress. A powerful feminist lobby developed, of which the leading voices were the National Women's Political Caucus (NWPC), the Women's Lobby, Inc., founded by Carol Burris and Flora Crater, and the National Organization for Women (NOW).

Political pressure from liberal feminists was considerably increased in the 1976 presidential election campaign. The NWPC had formed a Democratic Task Force in 1974 and a Republican Task Force in 1975, which participated in the state party caucuses and the national party conventions. In 1976, Republican women had obtained their party's support for the Equal Rights Amendment, although not a declaration in favor of the 1973

Supreme Court decision legalizing abortion; however, they suffered a dual setback in 1980 when President-elect Ronald Reagan and the New Right vowed firm opposition to both abortion and the ERA. Democratic feminists, who were much more numerous in the NWPC than Republicans, no doubt because most women in Congress were Democrats, had no difficulty in persuading their party to support the ERA. More delicate were their negotiations that led the Democratic party to approve the Supreme Court decision allowing the voluntary interruption of pregnancy. Needless to say, the sexual preference plank of the feminist platform was rejected out of hand by both Democrats and Republicans.

Although the women of the NWPC were close to the traditional parties and had entrée to the inner circles of national politics, the same could not be said of NOW. Some of its officers, Karen de Crow and Artie Scott, were asked by the NWPC Republican Task Force to leave Kansas City, where the 1976 Republican party convention was being held, for fear that their mere presence might suffice to jeopardize the negotiations for adoption of the ERA in the party platform. Similarly, the evening reception to which NOW invited delegates to the Democratic convention was ostentatiously snubbed by many of them, while the one given by the NWPC was a huge success. In the eyes of politicians, NOW was a frighteningly militant organization, incarnating their worst nightmares of feminism. We see this factor as both positive and necessary, in that NOW's independence from traditional politics enabled it to retain its uniqueness as a feminist organization, and was the only way to guarantee the support of the radical minority of feminists, whose presence in the ranks was, we believe, the best guarantee against the movement's being co-opted. By the end of the 1970s, NOW had lost its aura of middle-class respectability, and was even perceived as belonging to the radical Left, as Elinor Langer[2] points out. In any case, it was a force to be reckoned with; if we can take the word of Gloria Steinem, it was collecting more money than even the Democratic party.

The 1976 presidential campaign also saw the appearance in the liberal feminist press of political profiles of the candidates according to their positions on women's issues. Ms., for instance, measured the views of five presidential hopefuls and forty congressional candidates. The NWPC, after having passed feminist judgment in 1976 on the respective positions of presidential candidates Ford and Carter, came back to the charge in the 1978 congressional elections and devoted five pages of the Women's Political

Times to the voting records of all the members of the House of Representatives on sixteen feminist bills submitted in the intervening two years, scoring them from 0 to 100. The practice was continued in subsequent elections.

In the lead-up to Ronald Reagan's election, it appears, therefore, that liberal feminists were gambling on the strength of the women's vote, counting feminists and nonfeminists. However, this would not be a block vote resulting from any specifically feminine characteristic, but rather would be a reflection of women's new political awareness and participation, inspired by feminists of the androgynous approach. Militants were cheered in this gamble by the results of a 1980 Harris poll showing that significantly more women intended to vote, as well as a twenty-point difference between male and female voters among supporters of Ronald Reagan in the 1980 presidential campaign. The gender gap was born, and it continued to make headlines in all the publications of the Women's movement. Gloria Steinem and her staff at *Ms.* even devoted the magazine's cover to it in March 1984, inviting readers to participate in a new Harris poll on their intention to vote and their views for or against the reelection of Ronald Reagan. As another publication subsequently reported, "the 1984 election results showed the same gender gap that had first appeared in 1980. Women were still 8% more likely to vote Democratic than men. But because the gap did not increase, the press coverage gave the impression that it had disappeared."[3]

Only time will tell whether the new factor of the women's vote will have a durable existence as such in a still sexually polarized society, or whether it is a temporary phenomenon, as a personally directed reaction against a president who, after campaigning on his opposition to the ERA, blamed rising unemployment on the increased number of women in the labor market and did everything possible to overturn the 1973 Supreme Court ruling permitting abortion. In August 1983, American women's antipathy for Ronald Reagan was intensified when Barbara Honnegger resigned from her position in charge of women's affairs at the Department of Justice, denouncing the hypocrisy of the "demagogue" in the White House who publicly claimed to oppose sexual discrimination but privately had blocked Honnegger's report on a hundred discriminatory statutes.

Getting Involved in the Political Power Structure

The Ninety-eighth Congress of the United States, elected in November 1982, counted only twenty-four women. Granted, thanks to a theatrical gesture from President Reagan, a woman, Sandra Day O'Connor, had finally been appointed to the Supreme Court; granted, the U.S. ambassador to the United Nations (Jeanne Kirkpatrick) and the secretary of transportation (Elizabeth Dole) were women; but, important though they were, these promotions remained exceptions to the rule and ought not to mask the dramatic underrepresentation of women in American politics.

In 1976, according to figures gathered in the bicentennial year by the National Women's Education Fund, in the course of two centuries of American history, the Senate had seated only 11 women in contrast to 1,715 men, and the House of Representatives, 87 women against 9,521 men. In the same period, only 5 women had held cabinet posts, and none had ever sat on the Supreme Court.

These statistics were scrupulously published by the *Women's Political Times*, demonstrating that the NWPC was actively aware of this underrepresentation of women. Faced with the reluctance of lawmakers to enact legislation responding to feminist demands, the NWPC, in keeping with the philosophy of liberal feminists, presented itself as a lobbying organization whose purpose was to build a "national feminist network." This expression used by Mildred Jeffrey, then president of the NWPC, seems to have been calling for a counterpart to the "old boy network." Congresswoman Barbara Nikulski (Democrat from Maryland) parodied the way in which key posts were assigned: "You know," she said, "Pete Preppy looks through his yearbook, calls up Mike Macho and says 'Got anyone good for State?' 'Sure,' answers Mike, 'try Tom Terrifico.' "[4]

Clearly, the NWPC's main concern has been effectiveness. A program of feminist demands already has existed for more than a decade; its execution depends upon bringing more women into political life. The introduction of women, in the NWPC's view, should be done according to the traditional rules of the political game, and within the two-party system. The NWPC has never foreseen a third-party effort; this stance was reiterated in 1989 when the NWPC resisted NOW's call for one. Therefore, the first level of action by NWPC militants has been to gain more representation by women at the national Democratic and Republican party conventions. Their work has met with partial success, since in 1980, the goal of equal sexual representation among delegates was attained among Democrats, but not among Republicans.[5]

The NWPC itself also has held national conventions. The one held in San Antonio in July 1983 attracted a number of candidates for the Democratic nomination. "I am a feminist," Walter Mondale was not afraid to declare, but his proposals on women's issues, like those of the other candidates, were rather vague. The NWPC strengthened its efforts to promote the election of more women by making financial contributions to their campaigns, knowing full well that money is the overriding problem of all candidates.

But what precisely has become of feminism among women candidates and women elected to office? In the light of ten sample candidacies followed by the NWPC in 1976, it appeared that even if the candidates were known to hold feminist views, they never campaigned solely on feminist issues. Some even restrained their ardor when appearing in heartland areas. The position of those already elected is obviously more comfortable. Several interesting initiatives and successes can be signaled here. First, there are the results obtained in the Ninety-third and Ninety-fourth Congresses. The passage of the landmark Equal Credit Opportunity Act, forbidding sexual discrimination in the granting of credit, was due to the work of Margaret Heckler, Leonor Sullivan, and Bella Abzug. Minimum wage legislation was extended to domestic workers thanks to the initiative of Shirley Chisholm, and the military academies were opened to women on a bill introduced by Patricia Schroeder. The honors, again, are due to a woman, Martha Keys, for the measure granting a 20 percent tax deduction to low-income families for expenses related to child care. During the Ninety-fifth Congress, for the first time in the history of the United States, fifteen of the eighteen congresswomen formed a bipartisan women's committee to transcend party differences and to join forces, whenever possible, on issues concerning women. The committee agreed to meet every Tuesday and invite various cabinet members to discuss their policies, particularly regarding the hiring and promotion of women.

The NWPC congratulated itself for another initiative, presenting it as a good illustration of the feminist network in operation, as a chain of solidarity linking elected women to their women constituents. In one of the first examples of this networking, the NWPC president Mildred Jeffrey testified, in January 1978, before the congressional committee charged with studying proposed amendments to the Humphrey-Hawkins Full Employment Act, and made several suggestions for modifying the bill. Some days later, Barbara Mikulski took up the relay, and introduced in Congress a number of measures proposed by the NWPC. On 9 March 1978, two of these measures were enacted by the legislators: increased child care facilities for single mothers, and greater representation of women and ethnic minorities on the consulting committees proposed by the Full Employment and Balanced Growth Act, in proportion to their members in the labor force.

Again, the rule of equal representation, dear to liberal feminists, has been at work in the ultimate illustration of how feminist networking has enabled women to gain access to power. According to the NWPC, the federal agencies which, under President Jimmy Carter, were directed by women—Patricia Robert Harris at Housing and Urban Development, Juanita Kreps at Commerce, Eleanor Holmes Norton at the EEOC, and Grace Olivarez at the Community Services Administration—recruited as many women staff members as men.

The picture darkened considerably under President Ronald Reagan. Sandra Day O'Connor appeared little disposed to support feminist claims, as witness her dissenting vote in June 1983 when the Supreme Court reasserted the right of American women to the voluntary interruption of pregnancy. As for Elizabeth Dole, in an interview granted to Judith Mann soon after taking office as secretary of transportation, she was content to repeat President Reagan's statements on sexual discrimination, without lending any support to the Equal Rights Amendment.

THE CONSTITUTIONAL BATTLE AND THE STRUGGLE AGAINST THE ANTIFEMINIST BACKLASH

The Equal Rights Amendment

At the start of the 1980s the liberal forces of the Women's movement were still fighting for the same cause that the National Women's party had been championing since the end of World War I: the Equal Rights Amendment. This had become the primary objective of the egalitarian feminists, and they threw all their resources into this battle. This factor contributed to the general impression that the liberal wing had taken over the Women's movement at the expense of the radical influence, an impression that was reinforced by the forming of coalitions around the egalitarian battle plan.

The reasons for such crystallizations are obvious. Although militants recognized that the Equal Rights Amendment alone could not eradicate sexist prejudices from individuals or the society, they nevertheless believed that an amendment to the Constitution was the only possible remedy to destroy the underlying prejudice of the fundamental law of the land. The soundness of their argument cannot be denied, if we recall the government interpretation, in the case of women army doctors in World War II claiming equal pay, that the accepted constitutional meaning of the term *person* did not include the female sex. It was all the more frustrating and humiliating for American feminists, in the best-organized women's rights movement in the world, to be facing defeat, after more than half a century of combat, for lack of three ratifying votes. In 1980, in fact, thirty-five states had ratified the amendment, thirty-three having done so in the three years following the historic vote of Congress in 1972 passing the ERA. But after 1975, only two further ratifications had been scored, and in three states, legislatures that had already voted ratification now voted in favor of rescinding their previous votes, although the constitutionality of this rescission was doubtful. Not surprisingly, the strongest opposition came from the South. The same nine southern states that had earlier refused to ratify the amendment granting women the vote now refused to ratify the one granting sexual equality. The taste of defeat was all the more bitter in that numerous surveys had shown that, with little variation, there was a constant majority of public support for the ERA. When President Reagan took office, this majority even rose sharply from 58 to 63 percent.

How, then, can we explain the ERA's successive failures to be ratified, either through legislative votes, as in North Carolina and Florida, or by local referendum for the adoption of a home-grown ERA modifying the state constitution, as in New Jersey and New York? Feminist analysts have decided that the main reason lies in their previous underestimation of the opposition. It had been naive of them to believe that their only opponents were sincere but misguided housewives. In the analysis of the NWPC, NOW, and the editors of *Ms.*, the ERA's real adversaries have been the organized political forces of the extreme Right. Of the women who have made careers out of urging other women not to have careers but to stay home and vote against sexual equality, the most notorious include the following: Phyllis Schlafly, an outspoken ultraconservative and head of the National Stop ERA Movement; Helen Andelin, author of *The Secret Power of Femininity* and founder of the Femininity Forum, under whose banner the California anti-ERA forces were assembled; Maureen Startup, also from California, who organized a convention for that state's annulment of its previous ratification of the ERA; Annette Stern, a "home executive" in her own preferred term, leader of the New York group most hostile to the ERA, Operation Wake Up, and founder of WUNDER.[6] According to feminist sources, the funding for these groups has come, partially or entirely, from openly racist organizations like the John Birch Society, from anti-Communist groups like the Cardinal Mindszenty Foundation, or from bastions of traditionalism like the American Legion and the Daughters of the American Revolution. Powerful opposition has also come from the direction of organized religion, led by the Baptist, Mormon, and Catholic churches. Last but far from least, the economic implications of equality must not be overlooked. As the NOW leaders observed, big business has been visible by its absence from the coalitions supporting passage of the Equal Rights Amendment. The hostility of the world of high finance is definitive proof of early feminist successes. Court-ordered retroactive correction of sexual discrimination has cost big companies a lot of money: $100 million for AT&T, for example, and $75 million for Sears. But these sums are minuscule in comparison with the real amounts involved, according to the estimate of a private economist consulted by Elinor Langer:

If, in 1970, women who worked had earned the same amount per hour as men who worked, it would have cost employers an additional $96 billion in payroll alone. . . . If women had earned the same as men and worked the same number of hours, the addition to the payroll would have been $303 billion.[7]

More recent figures from the Labor Department show that in 1988, women made up 44.8 percent of the U.S. labor force, and that in the 1990s, they will fill 60 percent of new jobs, so that by the year 2000, women will account for about half of the work force.

It is understandable what worry this can cause in powerful and recalcitrant business sectors, such as insurance companies, for example, which furthermore are well represented in state legislatures, according to a NOW study of the Illinois state senate.

In state legislatures called to vote for or against the federal amendment, therefore, it has been easy for multinational companies to defend their special interests. The ERA has become a political hot potato, and this, say the feminist analysts, is the second reason for its defeat. The vote of Florida legislators on the ERA, for example, as the local press objectively reports, was not really for or against sexual equality; instead, the ERA vote was used by them as a bargaining chip for unrelated political transactions, some negotiating to retain their chairmanship of a committee, others wanting to put an obstacle in the path of a political adversary favorable to the amendment. As the editorial writer of the *Women's Political Times* bluntly put it, "They're playing political football with our issue."[8]

Naturally, this sport has been concealed behind a smokescreen. When speaking publicly, opponents of the ERA have found pretexts in the language of the amendment itself, with scare talk about the institutionalization of public toilets in common to both sexes, homosexual marriages, and the military draft for women, all scaremongering images which they evoked as representative of the Women's movement itself, and as the logical outcome of passage of the ERA. Now we confront the third reason for the ERA's failure, in the view of feminist analysts: the negative image that many women have of feminists, stereotyped as ruthlessly ambitious career women with hearts of steel under their elegant business suits, or else as bare-breasted, bisexual flaming revolutionaries. Trying to understand the crushing defeat suffered by the ERA in New York, Lindsy Van Gelder interviewed four women whose interests and opinions coincided with the spirit of the ERA, but who nonetheless had voted against it in a referendum simply because they had wanted to censure the Women's movement for the image it gave of itself, and had refused to give the movement their vote of confidence.[9]

Here we reencounter the same old problem of credibility, which has always undermined feminist efforts. The problem is all the more serious in that it creates opposition to feminism in certain categories of women themselves, particularly housewives and low-income wage earners. While some opposition comes from groups that defend their special interests by pretending to believe that the concept of a politically organized women's rights movement is fundamentally unsound and unnecessary, housewives and low-income women are sincere in rejecting the ERA out of fear for their own security. Feminists engaged in reform face a double challenge: on the one hand, to convince women that their action is worthwhile and that the stereotypes are false; on the other hand, to expose the intrigues of power and money interests hiding behind the skirts of Phyllis Schlafly and her troops.

To meet this challenge, feminists recognized early the need to come out of isolation and form alliances. They saw that well-chosen allies could bring much-needed credibility to their image; this would signify the creation of a united front, as opponents had done in the National Stop ERA Movement. For this reason, as soon as the anti-ERA backlash effect began to appear, a policy of coalition emerged among feminists, beginning in about 1975, of which the first fruit was the *US National Women's Agenda*. A broad coalition for the ERA was created in the following year: ERAmerica, which, from its founding, brought together more than a hundred diverse organizations, including women's clubs, religious groups, labor unions, and civic bodies, all denouncing the sexual discrimination that afflicted American women and proclaiming the legitimacy of the amendment through which they were seeking their place in the Constitution. This coalition, which opened a new era in feminist militancy, did not come about solely through the will of feminists; it seems to have resulted from a growing awareness among all sorts of liberal organizations of the real implications of opposition to the ERA, thus confirming what feminists had been alleging about the true identity of the special interest groups opposing it. In fact, it began to appear more and more evident that the extreme Right was using the ERA as a political "litmus test," as a victory on this issue could be the prelude to other conservative offensives against, for example, arms reduction, consumer protection, and labor union demands. According to the *Women's Political Times,* key liberal leaders held an important strategy meeting in Washington from 17 to 19 April 1978 to devise common ways of countering the new upsurge of strength on the extreme Right.[10] They decided to establish a permanent regional structure to facilitate communication with each other. But even more important, it seems to me, was the dialogue opened in the late 1970s between feminists and labor union leaders, ending more than a century of mutual suspicion. New relationships of reciprocity developed: in exchange for labor union support for the ERA, the NWPC committed itself to support labor and social legislation such as the Humphrey-Hawkins Full Employment Act and the Labor Law Reform Bill. I think it is important to mention this agreement, since it rested on a basis of equality and mutual respect. By this I mean that there was no trace of paternalism in this labor union support, and this fact, expressing united struggle for a common cause, is the great advance achieved by the new feminism of the 1960s and 1970s over the protofeminism of the postwar years.

This cooperation with others seems to us to have opened a new era for militant feminism in more than one way. It has not only brought feminism out of isolation, but also drawn it out of a defensive posture. Too often, in fact, feminists have been content to spend their time denying the half-truths spread by Phyllis Schlafly about public toilets, homosexual marriages, and the draft. Regarding public toilets common to both sexes, for example, feminists have recalled that the Supreme Court has already recognized a constitutional right to personal privacy in intimate matters in the

1965 case *Griswold v. Connecticut*. The legalization of homosexual marriages would not be discriminatory if it applied to both sexes. On the draft, feminists have proposed that both men and women should be exempt if they have children under eighteen years of age. But in the new era of cooperation, starting in the late 1970s, feminists began a positive approach to demonstrate the benefits of the Equal Rights Amendment to those most frightened by it: housewives. In the case of divorce, they began emphasizing, the elimination of inequality before the law would mean that housewives would be guaranteed the right to compensation for services rendered, instead of uncertain and humiliating alimony payments. Widows whose husbands had died without leaving a will would automatically be entitled to receive their husbands' pensions, instead of having to fight a costly legal battle to do so. The ERA would eliminate an existing tax inequality, in which the estates of widows but not widowers were subject to inheritance taxes. Every housewife would have the same access to credit as her husband, which was not yet the case, in spite of the Equal Opportunity Credit Act.

This return to the offensive was marked by renewed vigor in NOW, 100,000 members strong after gaining new adherents at the Houston conference. The oldest organization in new feminism started off on a new footing in February 1978, with a solemn proclamation of a state of emergency for the Equal Rights Amendment, excluding any possibility of failure. "We have passed the point of no return,"[11] they said, in announcing a new, two-level strategy: state and federal. At the state level, they would mount a campaign in every state that had not yet ratified the ERA. At the federal level, they would lobby Congress to obtain an extension of the deadline for ratification, originally set at 30 March 1979.

The boldest scheme devised by NOW was a boycott of the states whose legislatures had voted against ratification. All liberal organizations were urged not to hold any meetings or conventions in the fifteen recalcitrant states.[12] The boycott results were encouraging for feminists, since 380 organizations of all types heard the appeal. The NOW initiative cost many cities dearly, hitting where it hurt. Miami Beach lost $9 million following the cancellation of convention reservations by the American Library Association, the National Organization of Religious Women, and the National Education Association. Chicago lost $15 million in similar circumstances. The attorney general of the state of Missouri, estimating the lost business to Kansas City and Saint Louis at $18 million, filed a suit against NOW for violation of the antitrust laws. Similar legal action was brought by the state of Nevada and by a travel agency in New Orleans. Recalling that the antitrust laws were aimed at business activities in restraint of trade, NOW retorted that a boycott was not a business activity, and that in any case, independent organizations were free to opt for or against the boycott. Further, NOW filed a countersuit for defamation, claiming $20 million from each of the accusing states. An initial success was gained when a federal district court in Missouri recognized that a boycott is a legitimate form of political expression.

The National Organization for Women outshone itself with another initiative: the demand for extension of the original seven-year deadline for ratification of the ERA. Credit is due to NOW for the legal research regarding the constitutionality of the extension measure. Investigations revealed that no clause in the Constitution imposes a time limit for ratification; this practice began only with the Eighteenth Amendment. They also argued that although a time limit was mentioned in the preamble to the ERA, there was none in the text of the amendment itself; furthermore, since this time limit had been set by Congress, then Congress had the authority to modify it. Having done its homework, the feminist lobby threw all its weight into the battle and carried off a new success, since the extension of the deadline was voted in by a comfortable majority of 233 to 189 in the House of Representatives, and by 60 to 39 in the Senate. As recalled by the countdown kept by the *National NOW Times,* a new date was set for sexual equality: 30 June 1982.

This proved to be a vain effort, alas, because under fire from the New Right, the new deadline expired without the Equal Rights Amendment being ratified by any other state. With regard to the Constitution, the new feminist militants had suffered the same setback as the post–World War II ERA activists; that is, although they were uncontestably better organized and better supported, with a majority in numerous public opinion polls, they were still far from escaping from the trap of combat by proxy. In July 1982, immediately after expiration of the deadline, the Equal Rights Amendment was introduced anew to Congress, but American women would have to await the pleasure of the chairmen of the House and Senate Judiciary Committees for the ERA to be inscribed again on the legislative calendar. A vote did take place in the House of Representatives in November 1983, but the amendment failed, six votes short of the required two-thirds majority, with the Democrats dividing 225–38 in favor and the Republicans opposing it 109–53.[13]

Voluntary Interruption of Pregnancy

On 22 January 1973, in the case of *Roe v. Wade,* the Supreme Court, ruling for the first time on the issue of abortion, rendered a decision in favor of its legality in the United States. This historic decision immediately aroused an army of dissenters. The forces opposing a woman's right to choose the voluntary interruption of pregnancy have been, by and large, the same as those fighting the Equal Rights Amendment. On each anniversary of the Supreme Court ruling, in contrast to the symbolic funeral rites feminists used to hold for women who had died from the butchery of illegal backstreet abortions, now the antichoice forces, calling themselves partisans of the "right to life," began organizing emotional demonstrations in front of the Capitol Building and elsewhere. Thousands of children from Catholic and fundamentalist Protestant schools, let out of lessons for the occasion, were paraded, waving red roses symbolizing the children who will never be born. The Catholic church is believed to have invested huge sums annually in the campaign to overturn the Supreme Court decision, and there has also been a faction of resistance in the medical professions. Opposition has been focused in the National Right-to-Life Committee, established in the 1970s. The most fanatical foes of abortion have frequently had recourse to violence against family planning centers and feminist clinics. A more insidious and more dangerous strategy, from the feminist point of view, has been the attempt to outlaw abortion entirely through a constitutional amendment. In spring 1977, only four years after *Roe v. Wade,* the *Women's Political Times* announced that seventy members of Congress had already offered such constitutional amendments. Feminist ranks were worried, recognizing that there was a serious risk of returning to the days of dangerous illegal abortions that existed before 1973; in 1977, with those days still fresh in mind, the journalist Roberta Brandes Gratz summarized the case in a thought-provoking article entitled "Never Again! Never Again?" She cited Koryne Horbal, a member of the National Abortion Rights Action League (NARAL), who reproached feminists for being too soft and yielding on this question: "women's groups have not made it clear to liberal Congressmen and state legislators that abortion is a non-negotiable issue."[14]

It was essential to communicate to liberal male politicians that they could not dodge an uncomfortable situation by giving their support to women on other controversial issues in exchange for defection on the thornier question of abortion.

In early 1983, after Senator Jesse Helms had tried in vain to push through a constitutional amendment asserting that human life begins at conception, his colleague Orrin Hatch attempted to open debate on another amendment that would give state legislatures or Congress the right to outlaw abortion. In 1983, and again in 1986, the Supreme Court reaffirmed the right of American women to voluntary interruption of pregnancy, but opposition only increased. Just before the end of President Reagan's second term, his administration filled a friend-of-the court brief with the Supreme Court, asking it to overturn its 1973 *Roe v. Wade* decision. The Court, fortified by conservative members named by President Reagan, agreed to review the case of *Webster v. Reproductive Health Services,* in what many viewed as the most serious challenge to the legality of abortion since 1973. The case came before the Supreme Court in April 1989, and to show their support for *Roe v. Wade,* feminists rallied in one of the largest political demonstrations ever held in Washington, rivaling others that have marked historic turning points, such as the 1963 march for civil rights. Working together through the coordination of the Fund for the Feminist Majority under President Ellie Smeal, feminists drew an estimated 300,000 women from all over the United States, in contrast to only a few hundred antichoice advocates who marched in opposition. "It's a turning point," said Ellie Smeal. "It's a totally new ball game. It's given us the confidence that we are the majority."

The Supreme Court's decision, in July 1989, considerably reduced American women's abortion rights, confirming several essential clauses of a restrictive Missouri law. By five votes to four, the Court held constitutional the provision forbidding public funding for the voluntary interruption of pregnancy. Therefore, the decision left the states free not to finance abortions. Also, contrary to the 1973 ruling in *Roe v. Wade,* the July 1989 decision allowed tests on the viability of the foetus at twenty weeks after conception. In addition, the Court under Chief Justice Rehnquist judged constitutional the preamble to the Missouri law which declared that "life begins at conception." Admittedly, the justices said that this declaration did not necessarily have concrete applications on the right to abortion; nevertheless, they let stand Missouri's definition of conception as the moment of fertilization. Finally, the Court reversed itself on one of the fundamental bases of its 1973 ruling, which gave women an absolute right to abortion during the first trimester (three months) of pregnancy without state intervention in their privacy; henceforth, following *Webster*, the states can intervene from the first trimester.

Consequently, the abortion debate now will be focused at the state level. Instead of a uniform law for the whole country, each state will have its own abortion laws. American women who have the means to pay for an abortion will travel to the so-called liberal states, but the new restrictions will dramatically strike poor women, as well as the youngest and those least informed. Pro-choice advocates fear a return to risky illegal abortions.

In the three months following the *Webster* decision, the Supreme Court agreed to review other abortion-related cases: Ohio and Minnesota laws involving the constitutionality of parental-notification rules for minors, and an Illinois statute requiring abortions to be performed in strictly licensed clinics. The Pennsylvania legislature was about to pass new severely restrictive legislation that appeared destined to be challenged in the Supreme Court, and other collisions seemed likely.

The decision in *Webster v. Reproductive Health Services* galvanized American public opinion and political attention. It not only gave a jolt to the Women's movement, but seemed to arouse pro-choice advocates far beyond the ranks of already convinced feminists. In a story headed, "Can Pro-Choicers Prevail?," *Time* magazine reported on 14 August 1989 that since the Court had agreed to review the case, NOW and NARAL had each gained 50,000 new members. Three months after the decision, when President George Bush vetoed legislation that would have provided federal funding of abortions for women who were the victims of rape or incest, the House only failed by a narrow margin to override the veto. The president's stance, which was seen as allowing abortion rights to women of means and denying them to all others, was widely criticized by members of his own party as politically damaging. Representative Bill Green, Republican, of New York, said, "Mr. Bush may have stumbled on the one issue that could cost him the election in 1992."

THE FEMINIST STRUGGLE AND WOMEN AT WORK

In keeping with Resolution 10 of the Houston platform, and in keeping with the importance assigned by egalitarian feminists to women's rights in the workplace and their systematic attacks on sexual discrimination, numerous initiatives have aimed at combating sexually discriminatory practices and at improving women's lot in employment. The observer could even conclude that the fierce fighting for the Equal Rights Amendment is primarily motivated by the desire to obtain equality for women in hiring, salaries and job responsibilities. This is the basis on which all the previously mentioned professional associations operate, considering that women are not "stealing men's jobs," but that an enormous majority of them are working out of economic necessity. In 1981, they represented 43 percent of the total national active labor force (including full-time and part-time work), and of these, roughly 45 percent were single, widowed, separated, or divorced, while about 25 percent were married to men earning less than $10,000 per year. In 1988, the figure for working women in the national active labor force had risen to 44.8 percent, and among young women, it was much higher. The Labor Department estimated two-thirds of married women aged 20 to 34 were working, and that by the end of the century, women would represent roughly half the American labor force. According to the feminist philosophy of survival, work, for a great many women, is a necessity, the only way to escape social determinism.

Legal Action

The preferred form of legal action has been to file a court suit pleading for application of existing legislation, specifically, the legislation known as Title VII of the 1964 Civil Rights Act. It must be said that the author of the sexual clause of this act had considerably underestimated its importance. Feminists and women plaintiffs influenced by feminism have, in fact, invoked Title VII not only regarding injustices in hiring, salary, or promotion, but also for any matter concerned with sexual harassment. Numerous feminist advice centers[15] were set up in the 1970s to provide information about the legal procedures to follow in such cases. Numerous such suits have been filed and won under Title VII; in one of the first examples, Diane Williams, an employee at the Department of Justice, received $16,000 in back pay for having been fired after refusing to give in to the sexual advances of her boss.

Feminist militancy in the workplace has favored court action, and particularly, class action suits. As a new embodiment of "sisterhood," this form of protest appears above all as the collective response of women to their common oppression. It was born, in the most spontaneous way, among women in journalism. On 16 March 1970, forty-six women employed by Newsweek filed a suit with the Equal Employment Opportunity Commission (EEOC) claiming that the magazine was practicing sexual discrimination by restricting them to tasks of research and compilation; Newsweek at that time had only one female editor for fifty-one male editors, twelve female reporters for sixty-four male reporters and thirty-four female researchers for only one male researcher. An agreement was signed, on the symbolic date of 26 August 1970, stating a declaration of good intentions on the part of the employer and establishing a women's committee charged with seeing that the management carried out its promises. Two months after the Newsweek initiative, 147 women employees of Time Incorporated undertook similar action, for the same reasons. The accord reached in the Time suit stipulated that all jobs in the company should be henceforth open to all qualified persons, regardless of sex, and that compliance would be supervised by the Human Rights Division of the State of New York.

The class action suit for sexual discrimination took on a new dimension when filed by a group whose common interests were outside the job field. It became a collective summons to a class of officials issued by an organized class of feminists. This was the interesting procedure followed by the Women's Equity Action League (WEAL) regarding discrimination in higher education.

Before it is possible to enter battle in the name of the law, there has to be a law covering the issue; in this case, the law concerned private or public institutions of higher education receiving federal funds. Now, although Title VII of the 1964 Civil Rights Act included sexual discrimination, this title does not mention education. However, Title VI of the same act applies to all institutions receiving federal funds, therefore including teaching institutions, but does not include the clause on sexual discrimination. Thus, a gap existed in the law as it stood, and it needed to be remedied. WEAL did research to dig up an appropriate precedent, and found executive order 11246 of 24 September 1965, amended by executive order 11375 of 13 October 1967, which forbade sexual discrimination in federal employment and applied to all contractors and subcontractors with the federal government.

On 31 January 1970, WEAL filed its first class action suit, summoning the federal administration to apply this executive order to all university establishments bound by contracts with the federal government. Several hundred suits were filed by the same and other organizations within the Women's movement against institutions of higher learning, the first target being the University of Maryland. Feminist pressure was also exercised on Congress, through Edith Green, Democratic congresswoman from Oregon, who in February 1970 submitted four bills aimed at eliminating all sexual discrimination in teaching institutions. Under pressure from two directions, in the euphoric year of 1972, which also saw the passage by Congress of the Equal Rights Amendment, the Ninety-Second Congress adopted Title IX of the Amendments to the Federal Education Act stipulating that:

No person in the United States shall, on the basis of sex, be excluded from participation in, be denied the benefits of, or be subjected to discrimination under any educational program or activity receiving Federal financial assistance.[16]

Now it was a matter of getting the law enforced. This was the second grand offensive of WEAL, launched when the Department of Health, Education, and Welfare published some alarming statistics: HEW revealed, in fact, that of 3,472 university-level institutions, nearly two-thirds had either not returned the proper forms certifying their conformance with the antidiscriminatory legislation, or had falsified their declarations. In spite of this, no institution had been penalized. WEAL's response was immediate and dramatic. The group filed suit against the secretary of health, education, and welfare for administrative negligence in the matter of sexual discrimination. The suit was granted a favorable outcome by the courts, which ordered further investigations in seventeen states. A settlement was reached in 1978 between the parties, in which the secretary undertook to investigate respect for civil rights in schools and universities, and to recruit 898 staff members, to be assigned to an HEW subagency, the Office of Civil Rights; by this recruitment, HEW was to make up for its delay in examining 3,000 discrimination complaints that had been lying unattended, and to do so by 30 September 1979.

These figures belied a new myth circulating in the 1970s on university campuses alleging reverse sexual discrimination; rumors were heard of women being hired and promoted just because they were women. In 1978, representation of women on the faculties of America's ten most prestigious universities was stagnating at 15 percent, after having declined between 1971 and 1974, and overall, only 8 percent of these women had reached the peak of the academic pyramid. However, by 1981, according to data presented by Catharine Stimpson at a colloquium in Toulouse, France,[17] 35 percent of all U.S. college and university teachers were women.

Another major initiative undertaken by WEAL in this second offensive concerned sexual discrimination in the retirement schemes that applied in most universities. Until 1978, in fact, it was customary in the United States for women to pay higher retirement contributions than men for an equal or lower pension, on the theory that women live longer than men. However, 84 percent of men and women have equal longevity. In other words, all women were penalized because a minority of them live longer. This was the basis of a class action suit filed by WEAL against more than 2,000 university establishments whose retirement funds were administered by the Teacher's Insurance and Annuity Association. In July 1983, the Supreme Court affirmed the lower court's 1978 decision which ended the regime of higher retirement contributions for women, proclaiming the principle of equal retirement pensions for equal contributions. However, this decision had no retroactive effect.

From Feminist Law Student to Feminist Lawyer

Feminists' interest in legal action has been shown by a massive influx of women enrolling in law schools. In 1970, for example, women represented only 10 percent of first-year law students; in 1980, they made up a quarter of the beginning enrollment. By 1989, 40 percent of the law students in the United States were women. Pursuing law studies has been seen as a political act in the cause of women's rights, and figured among the militant activities listed by one of my radical feminist correspondents. As early as 1973, Judith Hole and Ellen Levine reported the words of a woman jurist who said that every law school in the country was harboring a group of militant feminists. If anyone wonders about the political motivation that might drive an increasing number of young women toward this sector of the university, it seems obvious that their choice is the result of a primary commitment to the feminist movement and their awareness that women need to know how to use the laws or reform them for their own benefit. In any case, the Women's Liberation movement has always needed lawyers.

The first action by feminist law students consisted of transforming women' rights issues into a new branch of legal studies. Their objective was to gain acceptance in the law schools of an emerging academic discipline, to be called women's rights law. Their argument was that numerous sexist laws remained on the books in many states, and that lawsuits for sexual discrimination were on the increase; these factors provided substantial material for debate and for fascinating research. Furthermore, it was important that graduating classes of women lawyers should be trained in these areas to prevent this lucrative market being entirely taken over by men. The mission of eradicating sexism from the patriarchal legal system could only be incumbent upon women of goodwill.

The first success in this matter was the appearance of specific courses on women and the law, such as the one taught by the feminist jurist Diane Schulder at the University of Pennsylvania, beginning in 1969. The following year, similar courses were started at Yale, Georgetown, and George Washington University, focusing on sexism in state laws and analyzing Supreme court decisions concerning the status of women. The year 1971 saw the birth of the first periodical aimed at jurists specializing in women's rights law: the *Women's Rights Law Reporter*.

Actions by women law students had early echoes in the legal professions. The Law Women's Caucus of the faculty of the University of Chicago Law School filed a suit with the EEOC in February 1970 against the university's placement office, which offered its services to notoriously sexist law firms. Under pressure from the EEOC, the law school promised to ostracize any firm guilty of sexual discrimination. Similar decisions were taken by the law schools of the University of California at Berkeley and the University of Michigan.

At the professional level, feminist lawyers naturally took up the relay. Here again, they resorted to class action suits. In March 1971, the Legal Task Force of the Professional Women's Caucus filed a class suit against all law schools receiving federal funds, for sexual discrimination in the recruitment of law students. The action was based on statistics published by the Committee on Women in Legal Education formed by the Association of American Law Schools, indicating that between 1966 and 1970, the number of women law students had only increased by an average of 3 percent, and in the same period, a third of the law schools had seen their percentage of women students decline.

Following the same reasoning that inspired women to study law, feminist lawyers have put their skills at the service of the cause of women's rights. Nonprofit groups and associations were formed. Human Rights for Women, for example, was born in 1968. This tax-exempt foundation, created with a generous donation from Alice Paul, one of the leading suffragists, specialized in the documentation or even financing of sexual discrimination lawsuits. Landmark suits aided by this foundation include the 1969 cases of *Bowe et al. v. Colgate Palmolive* and *Mengelhock v. State of California*.[18] In the same spirit, but on a larger scale, radical feminists of the Chicago Women's Liberation Union established a legal clinic where, every Wednesday night, legal advisers came to give counseling to women wishing to pursue legal action to defend their rights.

By 1989, women lawyers made up 20 percent of their profession and were boldly challenging the status quo. From 30 March to 2 April 1989, over 1,300 women attended the Twentieth Women and the Law Conference held in Oakland, California, on the theme "In the Courtroom and in the Community: Twenty Years of Feminist Struggle." There were more than a hundred workshops, covering a broad range of issues in criminal law, education, economic empowerment, employment, feminist jurisprudence, family law, housing, health, immigration, international law, sex, violence, and women in prison. The workshop called Unpacking Violence against Women focused on a feminist theoretical basis for activism against violence against women; its closing speaker was Catharine A. MacKinnon, one of the leading feminist scholars of jurisprudence, best-known for pioneering the theoretical work behind establishing sexual harassment as a form of sex discrimination and for drafting an antipornography ordinance with Andrea Dworkin.

From Support Group to Union?

Feminist legal action has also been undertaken by office workers, and this is interesting from another point of view: it shows the emergence of permanent workers' defense structures in an employment sector that is overwhelmingly female (80.1 percent of office workers are women). By 1984, a grid of mutual-interest groups covering this enormous force of working women was well established. In the feminist surge of the 1970s, some twenty or more such associations were organized, usually at the city level. The most well known have been Union WAGE in Berkeley, Women Organized for Employment (WOE) in San Francisco, Women Employed

(WE) in Chicago, Women Office Workers (WOW) in New York, and 9 to 5 in Boston. The financial resources of these groups have come from dues paid by the members, grants given by various nonprofit organizations, conferences, lectures, and other initiatives. On the morning of 16 July 1977, when I met members of the group 9 to 5, they were busily engaged in a book sale, selling such feminist works as Jean Tepperman's *Not Servants, Not Machines: Office Workers Speak Out*, at the foot of Massachusetts Avenue in Cambridge.

For the day of the national secretaries' strike in 1974, Women Employed and 9 to 5 jointly published a Secretary's Bill of Rights, which first proclaimed the human dignity of secretaries, and went on to address the social legislation covering them. As a member of 9 to 5 told us, clerical workers were asking not only for their rights on the job, but also wanted the consideration of being treated as human beings. To achieve this goal, different groups have pursued two types of strategy. One consists of putting pressure on government agencies to enforce the law; thus, the group 9 to 5 filed lawsuits against banks, insurance companies, and publishing firms in Boston, in order that the official order for "affirmative action" should not be just vain words. The second strategy consists of organizing workers at the workplace. In this case, the aim is to make them aware of the political dimension of their position as workers in relation to management, and to train them in activist techniques enabling them to use their power, organize meetings, and manage protest activities.

Although these groups have won some legal battles against an insurance company here or there, their successes remain fragmentary. According to a pamphlet published in 1979 by the Women's Work Project,[19] the condition of office workers had even deteriorated in the previous twenty or thirty years, particularly in the matter of salaries. A woman office worker who, in 1956, received 72 percent of the salary of her male colleagues, only received 60 percent of a man's salary in 1975. Inevitably the question arose, as asked by Jean Tepperman in 1976 and repeated by Wendy Stevens in 1979:[20] don't we need a union of women office workers? The idea quickly spread among those concerned. The group 9 to 5, which formerly had viewed the idea unfavorably, now began to think that women were ready to try this. In fact, thanks to the activities of the organization mentioned above, many women office workers have acquired experience in activism and public speaking, enabling them to play a role at the highest levels of labor unions, and perhaps to amend existing unions so that feminism is not entirely absorbed by unionism. It seems certain that only a national organization, bringing together women office workers in a united front, would permit these new talents to have sufficient impact to make a real change in the working conditions for women in this employment sector and to protect their jobs. A new menace is cited by the Women's Work Project pamphlet, that is, the accelerated pace of office automation, which they claim is being used by big banking corporations as a convenient way of ridding themselves of the growing demands of their employees.

In the employment sector, as in the civil rights field, a policy of unity is needed. We have seen the first fruits of the struggle, and we can say that this experimentation with a strategy of coalition is the most significant evolution in feminism in recent years. This new orientation recalls that followed by nineteenth-century feminism in its earliest phase, when the cause of women was linked with that of the black slaves in a common struggle for rights. Do twentieth-century feminists run the risk of being the big losers in this policy of coalition, as their sisters were in 1865? I think a negative answer can be given to this question, since the political contexts appear to me to be quite different. In the 1860s, the black question was the crucial issue, and the women's question had been raised, in some ways, as a side issue. In contrast, if we consider the virulence of the antifeminist backlash in the 1980s, it appears that the women's question, even if it does not make the headlines every day, has been perceived as the primordial issue today in the field of civil rights. Nevertheless, this assessment does not imply a relaxation of vigilance.

ELEVEN

Alternative Institutions

It is in the proliferation of alternative institutions that the philosophy of sisterhood and survival has found its fullest expression, since it is the collective work of women who, while redefining themselves and their own lives, contribute to the reshaping of society.

Although many feminists devote themselves to working within the system, through women's studies programs of art, history, and literature, and through reform-oriented activism, a majority of radical feminists have preferred to develop alternative institutions, and to make a complete break with the existing system instead of trying to reform it. They are not satisfied with what they consider to be stopgap measures, such as the Equal Rights Amendment.[1] In both cases, however, politics are closely intertwined with existential reasoning. Peggy Kornegger, for example, sees the development of alternative institutions as "women's intuitive anarchism," the "existential courage" prescribed by Mary Daly, or even Laurel's "womanvision". And in both cases, there is faith in the importance of "small changes,"[2] which together add up to mass action and a collective challenge to the patriarchy. Such a convergence cannot occur without the existence of an effective communication network enabling various groups to benefit from each other's experiences and so to progress.

AN AUTONOMOUS COMMUNICATIONS NETWORK

The Women's Liberation movement was able to spread quickly in its early months by using the already-existing communication network established by the black civil rights and student protest movements. The first feminist publication I have found, *Voice of the Women's Liberation Movement,* launched in March 1968 by Jo Freeman, served to unite radical feminists during the twelve months it lasted and to inspire the creation of other publications, through well-known channels among activists. Very soon, in fact, through the derision of television and the press, feminist militants became aware of the necessity of using the media to their advantage, and particularly, the need for a feminist press that could correct sexist images of women's liberation and cement the movement politically.

The Feminist Media

The flourishing of feminist media is unquestionably best represented in the printed press. According to Judith Hole and Ellen Levine, more than a hundred feminist periodicals existed in 1971. Their number alone is an indication of their diversity. Some, such as the *Amazon Quarterly, Quest,* or *Heresies,* focused on ideological debate. Others primarily reported on successes or failures on the legal battlefield; this was the case with *The Spokeswoman, Changing Woman,* and the *Women's Political Times.* Still others were devoted to literary and sociological research, with each issue being devoted to a particular subject area; these included *Aphra,* which ceased publication in 1976, and *Signs,* originally run by Catharine Stimpson and her colleagues at Barnard College, then published at Stanford, and since 1985, at Duke University. Certain preferred themes reoccur, depending on the ideological orientation of the periodical: *The Second Wave,* of the radical feminist persuasion, favored the theme of anarchism, while *Ms.,* the liberal monthly fostering interfeminist reconciliation, granted extensive space, among other topics, to profiles of prominent women and news of the constitutional battle.

These examples excepted, the average feminist publication gave an esthetic impression of hodgepodge. The layout of *Big Mama Rag,* for example, or *Off Our Backs,* seems intended to preserve a general impression of confusion. This planned disorder obviously carries a political message. It is the trademark of a journalistic style in which each publication aims to give individual expression to the views of as many women as there are on its staff. The feminist press mirrors the kaleidoscopic image of diversity that makes up the Women's movement. Its pluralistic expression faithfully reflects the pluralistic action of Women in Movements, to use one of the French feminists' slogans. A microcosm of this pluralism is the journalism collective.

The collective, in fact, is the soul of these publications. Decisions are made collectively; the self-criticism meetings of *Big Mama Rag* were open even to women not on the staff of the publication. There is no specialized division of labor, but instead, following the rule of radical egalitarianism, task assignments are made on the basis of rotation; each woman knows how to do everything connected with the publication. The title of *editor,* which still appears in the hierarchical listing of credits for *Ms.,* the *Feminist Art Journal, Lilith,* or *Signs,* no longer exists in the average feminist periodical. It has been replaced by such terms as *The Collective* or *Us* in the case of *Big Mama Rag, Off Our Backs,* and *The Second Wave. Off Our Backs* still continues its custom of inviting its women readers to join the staff on weekends to help in the layout and production work, even seeing this as a better means of staff recruitment than the traditional interview. Numerous early feminist publications depended on the efforts of volunteers; for six years, from 1971 to 1977, *The Second Wave* appeared regularly thanks to the devotion of a collective in which no member ever received a salary. Later, the rhythm flagged and publication became irregular for lack of available staff time, as the members of the collective all had to earn their living elsewhere. There were also financial difficulties, since donations and subscriptions did not suffice to cover the costs of publication.[3] It is true that most feminist publications contain little or no advertising; what there is relates mostly to other feminist publications, with a few exceptions seen in *Off Our Backs* and the *Women's Political Times.*

On the other hand, advertising abounds in the pages of *Ms.,* which, in contrast to the publications previously mentioned, is operated as a business. All the products of the "feminist mystique" are represented: l'Oréal hair-coloring products, Crêpe de Chine perfume, Fabergé lipstick; only the content of the message has changed subtly.

"I want to be noticed because I'm worth it,"[4] says the woman in the l'Oréal ad. And why choose Crêpe de Chine perfume? "Because I like to be mysterious,"[5] answers the seductive model. In both cases, the accent is placed on the woman's choice, on the woman's choosing of her own free will to seduce the Other, the great absent man. The thirty winning colors of Fabergé lipstick have supposedly just been discovered by Laure Connelly, the youngest woman horse trainer in the United States, a woman who knows which horse to bet on and likewise is betting on Fabergé. In this way, the products of the "feminine mystique" follow a woman from her confinement in a gilded cage to her incursion and victory in a traditionally-masculine profession. The message does not end there: "You don't have to be a licensed trainer to wear Fabergé's Lip colors. You just have to want to look like a winner."[6]

As to what sort of winning is meant, all interpretations are possible, but winning there is, and the feminist code is respected. The advertising pages of *Ms.* provide us with a fine illustration of what feminism can become in the hands of a press agent.

However, far be it from us to criticize the intentions of *Ms.* For its thorough coverage, the debate in its Forum pages, its Gazette section, and its special issues, it was essential to keep *Ms.* alive, by whatever ruses necessary—even though shocking to purists, so long as it could be said that feminism was living off of advertising more than advertisers were living off of feminism. Many American feminists have recognized the value of *Ms.* and have lent it their support, starting with Onka Dekkers of *Off Our Backs,* and continuing with Lindsy Van Gelder, who participated in the *Ladies' Home Journal* sit-in, and the radical feminist Robin Morgan. In its attractive format, the magazine found its way into many homes and did an excellent job of reaching the broad public, initiating many more women to feminism than the average fringe-group feminist publication could ever have done. Once and for all, *Ms.* removed the scare image from feminism, and in the service of the Women's movement, it introduced professional journalism skills, which were not necessarily in contradiction with feminism.

From the richest glossy magazine to the most modest monthly newssheet, feminist publications have woven the bonds necessary for the daily life and cohesion of the movement. Each of them has a department particularly devoted to this mission: the "Gazette" of *Ms.*,[7] the "Forum" of the *Women's Political Times* and *The Second Wave,* the "NWSA" News of the *Women's Studies Newsletter,* the celebrated "Droppings" of *Off Our Backs,* the "Letters Home to Mama" of *Big Mama Rag,* or the heading "Kol Ishah" (literally, the voice of a woman) in *Lilith,* where Jewish women speak out. In these columns, readers have found news of the movement, ranging from events within the organization whose organ it is, to the appearance of new ramifications in the movement, to political demonstrations and cultural events. These publications have also served as an open mailbox. For example, in a typical issue, a health center in Cleveland wants to contact other similar groups through the intermediary of *Off Our Backs,* and the owner of an art gallery in Berkeley uses the *Newsletter* of the Women's Art Center in San Francisco to communicate with women artists. Let us also remember the women who have chosen to live underground and who have used feminist publications to correspond with their sisters in the Women's Liberation movement.[8]

The feminist network in the 1970s often included speaker's bureaus, which acted either as specialized feminist talent scouts, for example the New Feminist Talent Agency, or as an annex to the regular activities of a feminist association or journal. NOW, the National Women's Political Caucus, the New York Radical Feminists, the *Feminist Art Journal,* and *Big Mama Rag* all have had their own speaker's service bureaus, furnishing a feminist speaker, free of charge or for a modest fee, to local low-budget organizations. They had a dual purpose: to enable feminists to develop their public-speaking skills, and to enable other women to discover feminism.

From about 1969, many local FM radio stations began offering time to feminists to spread their message. One of the more well-known examples is "Womankind: Discussion and Commentary from the Feminist Community," a half-hour program dealing with feminist theory and action, produced by station WBAI-FM, the New York outlet of the Pacifica Foundation. The same station organized consciousness-raising session, first presenting a prerecorded tape of a group discussion, then opening the telephone lines for live calls from male and female listeners for an improvised on-the-air consciousness-raising session. Another example is the weekly broadcast "All Together Now" on station WDET-FM in Detroit. It was organized by the Women's Radio Workshop in Detroit, and devoted to debates over the major issues of feminism.

To help women's groups who were involved in radio broadcasting, Radio Free Women of Washington organized a centralized, updated repository and distribution service for the tapes of such broadcasts, which constituted an invaluable sound archive of the Women's movement.

Women's Centers

At the height of the feminist surge of the 1970s, every city had them. The feminist newly arrived in a city, or any woman wanting to make her first contact with the movement, usually to join a consciousness-raising group, could go straight to a women's center whose address she had found through the feminist media. Women's centers, like women's art centers, were often located in older buildings in unfashionable neighborhoods, which offered the advantage of cheap rents. Sometimes a friendly institution provided them with space, for example, the YWCA in Berkeley, California.

Functioning as clearinghouses within the feminist network, they offered a variety of services. First, they acted as meeting places, opening their facilities to use by different feminist groups, whether or not they were organizationally related. For instance, in 1973, the New York Radical Women held their weekly Wednesday night meetings at the "Women's Barracks" on West 20th Street in Manhattan, paying a monthly rent of twenty-five dollars. When I visited the premises, the run-down building sheltered an improvised second-hand clothes exchange on the ground floor, with garments on hangers or piled in baskets, free for the taking, while the office was on the first floor, and on the second floor, a karate class was in progress.

Some presented themselves as feminist cultural centers. The Woman-to-Woman Feminist Center in Denver, for example, opened a "woman-to-woman library" in 1977 with 600 volumes already cataloged and 100 more being entered.

More spectacular is the development of the Los Angeles Woman's Building, which originally planned to house only women artists, but expanded its horizons to accommodate the prestigious Feminist Studio Workshop, a feminist bookshop, a psychology research group, a summer arts program, and a "women's switchboard." Two floors formerly occupied by the Feminist Studio Workshop were subsequently rented to women artists, and the Women's Graphic Center, founded at the end of the 1970s, has achieved considerable success.

All these centers have acted as switchboards for the Women's movement, recording the names of women wishing to join consciousness-raising groups and assigning them to various existing groups. But the "grand central station" of women's switchboards was unquestionably the Women's Action Alliance, founded in 1971 on an idea of Gloria Steinem and Brenda Feigen Fasteau as an apolitical annex of the National Women's Political Caucus. With an initial endowment of $300,000 from the Stern Foundation, the Women's Action Alliance was organized to respond to public requests for information, publish information packets about women's centers and other feminist organizations, and try to coordinate the efforts of the radical feminist branch of the Women's movement.

"SELF-HEALTH" INSTITUTIONS

Alongside women's centers, there developed feminist health centers. A new notion was born, "self-health," which referred to a reconquest by women of their own bodies and a feminist approach to health care. This idea was consecrated by the First National Women's Health Conference, organized at Harvard in 1975 by the collective that produced *Our Bodies, Ourselves*, together with a couple of dozen other groups. Here we are witnessing the first phase of the sexual revolution as prescribed by radical feminist theorists, notably Robin Morgan.

Reconquering your own body, as feminists continually proclaimed, means first unlearning all the distorted truths you have been taught by patriarchal science. Next, it means learning to know your own body through self-examination and self-exploration. The pioneering work in this matter is *Our Bodies, Ourselves*, by the Boston Women's Health Collective, hastily compiled from an abundance of diverse material they had assembled for a course they were giving on women's bodies and health. The themes addressed in this book — women's anatomy and sexuality, pregnancy, abortion, and contraception — and the accusations they raised against conventional medical institutions, prefigured the main orientations of the emerging feminist health movement. Images occupied an important place in the book and continued to do so in the movement. The huge illustration on the discovery of the clitoris that introduces the section "The Body" in *The New Woman's Survival Catalog* validates not only the erectile organ of the woman featured in the center of the composition, but also the "politically correct" attitude of observation and exploration shown by the three women spectators. But printed images proved far too static. Films have been the preferred method of getting across the militant message. *Self-Health*,[9] for example, shows women teaching other women about their bodies. In *Healthcaring, From Our End of the Speculum*, a mother introduces a speculum into her own vagina while her daughter holds a light and speaks of the importance of knowing one's own body.[10]

The speculum therefore became the symbol of the feminist health movement. The July 1973 cover of *Sister* showed Wonder Woman in her familiar star-spangled costume, slashing the air with her speculum and leaving prostrate the worthy dignitaries of the American Medical Association, Right-to-Life supporters, Freudian psychiatrists, traditional family planning advisers, and "zero population growth" advocates. "With my speculum, I am strong! I can fight!"[11]

In the feminist caduceus, the traditional serpent of Asclepius representing the healing art is entwining itself around the mirror of Venus, in which is reflected the clenched fist of "sisterhood" holding a speculum.[12]

The feminist "self-health" movement takes its inspiration from the thesis put forth by Barbara Ehrenreich and Deirdre English in *Witches, Midwives and Nurses:* that is, the male monopoly on the medical profession has developed as a consequence of the fact that doctors have always treated the rich, while women healers have always been entrusted with the ailments of the common people and the poor. Thus, class interests and financial interests have coalesced to expel women from the medical profession. Women's reconquest of health care means recovering lost ancient wisdom as well as lost professional power.

To achieve these goals, feminist health centers have proliferated. The movement began in California, with centers in Los Angeles, Santa Ana, Oakland, and Chico, following by similar experiences in Salt Lake City (Utah), Detroit (Michigan), Ames (Iowa), and Tallahassee (Florida). In 1975, the list compiled by *The New Woman's Survival Sourcebook* contained some fifty addresses.

The services offered by feminist health centers are varied. Above all, they provide health information in keeping with the philosophy of self-health. Many, following the path traced in California, organize free courses where women can learn to use the precious speculum and perform pelvic and breast examinations on themselves. More generally, women can obtain answers to particular health questions and have access to related services of family planning or social counseling.

Numerous centers include a clinic for the voluntary interruption of pregnancy. Some, such as the Delta Women's Clinic in New Orleans or the Emma Goldman Clinic in Iowa City, have specialized in this domain. In all cases, the important thing is to humanize the abortion operation and to avoid the unseemly profit-making opportunities it might otherwise offer. Abortion in these clinics is performed by qualified, recognized surgeons, either men or women, but the paramedical personnel are usually all women. In addition, the woman patient benefits from the constant support of a counselor. On this point, I would like to mention the laudable initiative of a women's health group in Philadelphia that founded an organization called CHOICE,[13] for the purpose of training and placing counselors in abortion clinics. In 1975, the basic price for an abortion by aspiration performed in a feminist health clinic was about 165 dollars, including postoperative care, a modest sum compared with the same procedure in a hospital. Such clinics have complained that they are obliged to pay high or even exorbitant salaries to qualified surgeons and extremely low salaries to their staff members, a paradoxical situation for institutions that are trying to offer an alternative to the conventional medical system.

The medical practitioners in feminist health centers are not merely abortionists (or "angel-makers," to use a colorful old French expression). Concerned with all aspects of a woman's life cycle, they are also involved with birth, and among them are midwives who attend women giving birth at home. In this regard, the experience of the Santa Cruz center provides figures that the feminist health movement can be proud of. Out of 287 births attended by its practitioners during the two-year period of 1971–73, 286 occurred without incident. There was only one stillbirth, and there were no maternal deaths in childbirth. These results, the feminists point out, are better than those obtained by the obstetricians in Santa Cruz hospitals, which, for the period reported, had a childbirth infant mortality rate of 15.4 per thousand.[14] The feminist health practitioners explained these successful figures by the excellence of the prenatal education offered by the center and the absence of any drugs or techniques used to hasten labor. Life was allowed to proceed at its natural pace, instead of being hurried along by considerations of efficiency or cost. In the feminist health movement, home childbirth, attended by midwives, has a double significance. First, it grants the mother the right to participate fully in her own experience of giving birth, putting her back in contact with the forces of nature from which she is usually separated by obstetrical techniques. Secondly, it reaffirms the valid return of midwives to normal childbirth, and with them, the rejection of the overuse of invasive techniques for reasons of expediency, such as caesarean delivery, anaesthesia, and the episiotomy.[15] This return of midwives is presented as a welcome benefit, taking childbirth out of the realm of a monopoly by doctors, in whose hands the United States has a scandalous infantile mortality rate, behind that of most other developed countries. (In 1973, it was 18.5 per thousand, placing the United States fourteenth in the world.[16] In 1988, it was still 10.5 per thousand, seventeenth out of twenty-two developed nations measured.)[17]

In the matters of home childbirth and voluntary interruption of pregnancy, it is clear that the feminist health care movement is in strong opposition to the medical profession. The roots of the conflict are power and money. Certainly the modest sums charged by feminist health clinics threaten what feminists see as a monopoly motivated by special interests. The midwives in the Santa Cruz study, for example, had no fixed rate, but set their fees in accordance with the patient's ability to pay. The challenge from the medical profession was not long in coming, and reached a climax in 1974 with the arrest of three midwives, Kate Bowland, Linda Bennett, and Janine Walker, who were accused of illegally practicing medicine. The trial achieved even more notoriety when the defense was assumed by two feminist lawyers, Anne Flower Cummings and Susan Jordan, members of an exclusively female law firm, and helped achieve legalization of licensed midwives in California and other states. Ten years after the Santa Cruz midwives case, there were about 125 birth centers nationwide. Some were staffed solely by midwives, with doctors on call at hospitals for backup; many others were adding their own staff doctors. Many women preferred the alternative birth center as a more humane, nonviolent way to give birth, in contrast to what they saw as an excessive tendency by hospitals to use invasive techniques routinely to hasten childbirth. In making this choice, they were reacting against a form of violence.

FEMINIST RESPONSES TO VIOLENCE

Feminists have also fought other types of violence to women's bodies, in the form of the rapist's deadly aggression and the brutality some women suffer from their own husbands.

The Anti-Rape Movement

The first constructive response by feminists to the problem of rape has been the establishment of rape crisis centers, whose existence only serves to underline the lack of existing facilities under the patriarchal system to respond to this need. Particularly signaled out for criticism are the attitudes of suspicion and scorn for the victim, shown by the police and the forces of justice, and it is in relation to them that the crisis centers have been set up as alternative institutions.

A typical rape center operates with a dozen or so staff members and runs a telephone hot line. The first ones set up in the early 1970s already were receiving an average of 175 calls a month, of which a third were distress calls from rape victims or their families. From a psychological point of view, these first calls are critical, because the feminist responding to the call knows how to help the victim recover her sense of self-worth after the humiliation and defilement of the rape. Some centers, such as that in

Washington, have also organized encounters between recent rape victims and those who have managed to get over the trauma. In the case of persisting grave psychological problems, rape centers provide access to counseling by qualified psychiatrists and psychologists.

The second type of service offered by the emergency centers is mainly information about what to do in case of rape. The first step is to take the victim to the nearest hospital; next come the steps to follow if the victim decides to file a complaint. With time, better relations and a form of cooperation have developed between rape centers and the police and judicial authorities. Martha Shelley recalls, for example, how a rape commission was created in Los Angeles, composed of police officers, doctors, psychiatrists, and professors of psychology. The Roanoke (Virginia) center, in 1973, was proud of its good relations with the local sheriff and county prosecutor.

Such collaboration provoked an emotional reaction from the socialist feminists of Santa Cruz Women Against Rape (Santa Cruz WAR), who felt that the anti-rape movement was being coopted by the police and judicial authorities so as to convince the public that they were capable of handling the problem. On the contrary, in the views of the WAR group, the problem is aggravated by the entrenched sexism and racism in the police and judicial systems, since often, the victim herself is put on trial in the courtroom, while the only rapists condemned are members of racial minorities. WAR expressed the view that the solution is not so much incarceration of rapists, but community education to attack the symptoms and causes of sexism and violence in society. In society as presently constituted, these socialist feminists proposed mutual vigilance between women, the publication of rapists' photos so as to make rape a public issue, and educational confrontations between rapists and raped women, in which the victims would take the active role that is denied them in the traditional judicial process.

Legitimate doubts may be expressed about the realistic effectiveness of such proposals. It may also be observed that there is no suggestion of administering similar medicine to perpetrators of other forms of violence, who are not necessarily downtrodden minorities. Indeed, such a loophole would make rape the only crime without any possible recompense for the victim, and we would be tempted to see there a new blow struck by socialism against feminism, a "secondary" struggle, out of socialist generosity for the underdog and a primary focus on the class struggle.

More understandable is the position of the women of the Feminist Karate

Union in Seattle. This institution was created in 1971 by Py Bateman, under the auspices of the Women's Commission at the University of Washington, with a first class of fifteen women who had each been raped by a man. Combat techniques were gradually introduced, leading up to combats with members of the opposite sex, each new phase of initiation being preceded by a consciousness-raising session so as to avoid any tendency toward defeatism. For some courses, the group registered as many as 130 students. This success must be interpreted to mean that the formula responded to genuine needs felt by struggling women, in keeping with the feminist philosophy of survival. The theory was, "Rape will only stop when it becomes dangerous for a man to attack a woman."[18]

There, finally, we have a statement that clarifies a certain confusion. There has been a temptation until now, in viewing feminist martial-arts training, to speak of women's copying the violence of men. But a counter-theory exists, according to which feminist violence only aims to destroy masculine violence so as to end all violence whatsoever. In this case, women's martial-arts training has the potential of being simply a dissuasion, which could also operate in the case of battered women.

Shelters for Battered Women

The problem of battered women is presented by the women of *The New Woman's Survival Sourcebook* as the patriarchy's "dirtiest little secret." The conspiracy of silence surrounding the issue of domestic violence explains why the new feminist movement delayed approaching the problem. According to statistics cited by Betsy Warrior,[19] domestic violence is nevertheless reported to police, since it represents, for example, 60 percent of the night calls received by the police force in Atlanta, and 45 percent of the day calls officially reported in Boston. But neither the police nor social welfare agencies have ever taken domestic quarrels and blows seriously, considering the matter as dirty linen that ought to be washed in private, and pointing, besides, to the fact that victims frequently make an about-face when it comes to filing a complaint. Neither the police nor social welfare agencies have ever investigated the reasons for this about-face: the victim's fear, the aggressor's almost-certain release after a reprimand about the limits of his marital authority, the lack of any organizations offering refuge, and especially the economic dependence of women. This attitude of derision and even connivance of the authorities began to be challenged by feminists, as in a suit filed in 1976 before the Supreme Court of the state of New York by twelve battered women. It is against this same background of derision and connivance that American feminists, from 1973, began organizing shelters for battered women.

In this domain, they recognized that they lagged behind their British sisters, who by 1973 had already set up thirty such shelters, including one in Chiswick which, in its first three years of operation, had harbored over five thousand women and children. The first American feminist shelter of this type was in Phoenix, Arizona. Initially intended only for the victims of alcoholic husbands, it provided a refuge for a thousand women in its first year of existence, from November 1973 to November 1974, when the first study of the problem was published: *The Battered Wives of America*, by Del Martin. In August 1975, the staff of *Ms.*, which devoted a special issue to battered women, counted about ten shelters, which aimed to reconcile government financial aid with a certain freedom of maneuver enabling them to fulfill their missions as alternative institutions. By 1982, there were three hundred shelters all around the country, according to Elizabeth Pleck in her book, *Domestic Tyranny: The Making of American Social Policy against Family Violence from Colonial Times to the Present.*

Setting themselves up, in fact, in counterpoint to existing police and social welfare institutions, feminist shelters did not merely try to provide an emergency remedy. The women who ran them also tried to help battered women escape from the vicious circle in which they were locked by the public welfare authorities, who, after caring for them in hospitals, sent them back home to their husbands, where they were likely to be subjected to new assaults. After administering first aid, the shelters for battered women conform to the "militant sisterhood" philosophy of autonomy and survival. They help battered women believe in their own worth and take charge of their own lives, assisting them to get job training and find work. It is essential to break the fatalistic ties of physical and psychological dependence which, until now, have made these women accept everything because they have thought they were nothing. The painful situation of battered women brings up, more than any other, the issue of nonsexist education and the elimination of sexual stereotypes.

FEMINIST TEACHING AND RESEARCH

Feminist Child Care Centers and Play Groups

For radical feminists and androgyny theorists, as we have seen, the issue of education must be addressed from the earliest age in order to achieve the cultural revolution. The model of what not to do, said the first feminists who addressed this issue, was provided by child care centers that were financed and controlled by the state or by private enterprise, and therefore served the sole interests of their sponsors by socializing the children into stereotyped behavior and releasing the mothers as a supply of cheap labor. The radical feminists, in particular, denounced the sudden renewed interest of big companies in this matter as politically motivated. The WIN[20] program and the Nixon administration's family assistance plan freed welfare mothers from child care duties, but only to enlist them in low-level job training schemes that would condemn them to low-paying jobs and further aggravate the concentration of women at the bottom end of the professional scale.

Faced with this counterfeit generosity, feminists alternatively proposed to tackle the challenge of "human liberation," seeing this as "a chance to educate children in an atmosphere that encourages human development."[21]

The equal participation of men and women in the adventure of educating children would not only end sexual polarization in adult roles but is also seen as beneficial to the children, emotionally, socially, and politically. Girls and boys should be given creative, nonalienating work that is not sexually stereotyped. Numerous feminist organizations have attempted to promote this type of teaching, such as the Action Committee for Decent Child Care, under the umbrella of the Chicago Women's Liberation Union; the Child Care Resource Center at Cambridge; and on a national scale, the Women's Action Alliance, which made nonsexist child development one of its priority objectives, and which proposed as a logical consequence, but without pursuing the full implications, the idea of reeducation for parents and teachers.

It is difficult to estimate the number of unlicensed child care centers, all the more so since this alternative network includes not only feminist nurseries but also cooperative play groups organized by parents, such as the one I visited at the Berkeley-Oakland Women's Union, where I was received, to be precise, by one of the fathers.

Feminists place the accent on the originality rather than the quantity of attempted experiments. Judith Hole and Ellen Levine cite, for example, the financial sacrifice made by the staff members of a feminist child care center to acquire a "Petit Frère"[22] (Little Brother) doll, endowed with male genitalia, so that the children would not be restricted to the notion of the female doll. Another interesting initiative is shown by a Los Angeles nursery school which organized play groups in two city garages, and which, faced with hostility from city officialdom, stated its credo: "We want quality education childcare—not custodial, not institutional, but care that offers a protected, stimulating, creative and loving environment."[23]

It is not a question of just "watching" children—for feminists, this word is charged with coercive connotations—but of organizing creative games that will help children discover themselves and develop autonomy and self-assurance. This is why, more and more, the term *play group* has come into use. This idea is also behind one of the most singular experiments tried in this domain, the Artemis Child Experience Center with an all-male staff, conceived by nonsexist men in Tucson, Arizona, who belonged to the Double-F Movement.[24] That such an experiment should be tried in early childhood education shows the reach of the feminist concept that men should share child rearing responsibilities with women. This, of course, is an extreme example, intended more for consciousness-raising purposes than as a model for general emulation, since the feminist ideal is a staff composed of both sexes.

Nonsexist Children's Books

The problem of education arises not only in terms of educators but also in terms of teaching materials. Very early, feminists became interested in the children's book market. In June 1970, Feminists on Children's Media was founded, a collective composed of mothers, teachers, and women editors of children's literature who were resolved to combat sexism in children's books. Their actions took the form of a study, *Sexism in Children's Books*, which was presented to the Writers' Guild and the Children's Book Council on 15 October 1970.

For the part of the study consisting of selected extracts from textbooks, Feminists on Children's Media collaborated with Women on Words and Images, a study commission formed by the New Jersey chapter of NOW. This team analyzed 144 school textbooks, put out by 15 different publishers, and later published their findings under the title *Dick and Jane as Victims*. The figures disclosed revealed that sexual discrimination was deeply embedded in educational material: stories about boys outnumbered stories about girls by five to two; adult male characters were three times more numerous than adult female characters; in biographies, there were six male subjects for every female subject. *Dick and Jane as Victims* was sent to all the school textbook purchasing committees in the state of New Jersey for their use.

Another part of *Sexism in Children's Books* dealt with general trade books that had received some award or official recognition. Of one thousand books studied, Feminists on Children's Media found only two hundred that presented a positive image of women's intellectual, emotional, and physical potential. These feminists particularly criticized situations where little girls were forced to choose between traditional alternatives, femininity or physical strength, love or a professional career. Such expressions as *tomboy, wet hen,* or *hero* were also banned as vehicles for sexual stereotypes, as was discriminatory use of the masculine pronoun *he* when referring generally to children. On the other hand, the two hundred books chosen were recommended in a well-annotated bibliography, *Little Miss Muffet Fights Back,* which responded to a real market need, to judge by the four thousand orders received for the list even before its publication. From the young Indian girl who spent the first eighteen years of her life alone on an island in *Island of the Blue Dolphin* to the insatiably curious Alice in *Alice in Wonderland,* the two hundred selected books illustrate the blossoming of a female individual without any concern for conformity.

This essential criterion, which also characterizes adult feminist literary expression, guided militants in a new phase of their activities: the production of nonsexist children's books. This work was undertaken jointly on a nonprofit basis by two collectives, both founded in 1970, Lollipop Power and the Feminist Press, which agreed to divide their efforts by age groups. The first specialized in books for the two-to-eight bracket, while the second concentrated on books for children over eight.

Lollipop Power was a venture of a small group composed of mothers, teachers, and two sociologists who, at first, only intended to put their work into the service of the Women's movement. Their books were so successful that they soon found themselves in charge of an operation selling to the general public. Between 1970 and 1973, this handful of women, in their spare time, managed to compose, publish, and sell 20,000 copies of their first six nonsexist books.[25] The first book was entirely produced by the group, from the writing to the printing and binding. Later, the group no longer printed its own books but continued to function on the same principle of task rotation and collective decisions. Because each woman had other commitments, the rate of publishing slowed down after 1973 and it was an open question whether Lollipop Power would remain a small, handicraft-scale operation or would become more formal and centralized, with the advantage of reaching more children, but with the risk of becoming less personal, like some other feminist businesses. In spring 1979 the group was still remaining faithful to its ideals.

As for the Feminist Press, whose staff is still carrying on its work now at the City University of New York in New York City, it identifies itself as "a tax-exempt non-profit educational and publishing corporation founded [in 1970] to produce some of the new literature needed most for educational change."[26]

Among the nonsexist titles offered, there appears a certain predilection for great women figures in American history: Amelia Earhart, the aviator, or Elizabeth Blackwell, one of the first women doctors in the United States. Five criteria are proposed for nonsexist literature:

1. Girls as active protagonists
2. Boys expressing a wide range of emotions
3. Boys and girls in noncompetitive friendships
4. Children relating to adults
5. A large category including various patterns of living and unusual themes such as single parenthood, divorce, extended family, multiracial family, adoption, handicaps, death, and nontraditional careers.[27]

On the basis of these five criteria, the research team of the Feminist Press drew up a balance sheet in 1978 evaluating the impact the Women's movement had had so far on current children's literature and arrived at the conclusion that the change was more symbolic than real. Of the five nonsexist criteria, only the first was respected, and this was often by making the young girl protagonist stand out as eccentric against a stereotyped background, where she was loved in spite of, and not because of, her personality. To these critics, editors responded that they were concerned with quality and not with messages, but the feminists persevered in suggesting that the two are not necessarily incompatible.

More cooperative were the administrators of the Carnegie Foundation and the Ford Foundation, which in 1977 awarded the Old Westbury group grants totaling $340,000 to produce thirteen books and pamphlets on diverse subjects, to be used in high school teaching. It is difficult to overstate the potential power of such an initiative in an educational sector that previously had been a privileged hunting ground for publishers more concerned with book sales than with the sexual discrimination clauses of Title IX. In executing this mission, the Feminist Press has carried on the work started by university feminists in women's studies programs, and has been a very effective instrument of such work.[28]

Women's Studies

Women's studies first appeared as counterculture courses in the "free universities" of the student protest movement between 1965 and 1968. In reality, at that time, such courses were small, impromptu reading and discussion groups organized for mutual consciousness-raising. The first women's studies course to be officially integrated into a university curriculum was, I believe, the one organized by Sheila Tobias, in spring 1969, at Cornell University. Her initiative had been inspired by the existence of similar courses aimed at a different American minority group: blacks. Benefiting from the experience of previous black studies programs, university feminists soon managed to cover the distance separating an isolated course from a structured program. In fall 1970, the first full women's studies program was born at the University of California at San Diego.

The advantage of a structured program is that it is interdisciplinary, enabling women's issues to be studied through research in several fields, and also thereby bringing together many women faculty members who would otherwise remain scattered in different teaching or research departments. In this sense, Florence Howe likened women's studies programs to "political units," and said "their existence usually means some institutional recognition, at least in the form of office space, equipment, staff, and a minimal budget, or, more generously, the power to hire faculty, control curriculum, and grant degrees."[29] In fall 1978, less than a decade after the first one, 301 university women's studies programs were in existence, of which 54 percent led to a diploma. At that time, two women had earned doctorates in women's studies: Sally Wagner and Karen Rofkin, both at the University of California.[30] However, warned Hester Eisenstein,[31] women students hesitated to major in this field, often because of pressure from their families: how can you make a living with a degree in women's studies?

We might wonder why feminists in higher education have chosen to pursue their action within the bounds of conventional university institutions. Indeed, this question has been asked by radical feminists. Florence Howe responded that, since women's studies reflected both the strength and the educational character of the Women's movement, it was natural that the movement should spread to university campuses, "not simply to proselytize, but to investigate and rediscover its history; not only to pose problems, but to know how to solve them."[32]

Women's studies programs generally were assigned three missions. The first was a mission of compensation, making up for past lacks; this was most evident in the teaching of history, filling in the gaps left by historians' inevitably arbitrary selection of events. The second mission was consciousness-raising; it was most apparent in the teaching of literature, whether analyzing the female stereotypes conceived by misogynous authors, or exploring women's particular experience and awareness by rediscovering such authors as Christina Stead, Zora Neale Hurston, Rebecca Harding Davis, or Mary Wilkins Freeman. The third mission of women's studies programs, a synthesis of the other two, would be to create feminist history and culture, which had previously been lacking, and which are necessary for the dignity of women. The feminist battle being fought by women's studies, therefore, takes place on two fronts: teaching and research, particularly in history and literature.

Activism in teaching involves changes for both students and teachers. For students, it operates as a new dynamic between them in the feminist classroom, and proposes a mode contrary to traditional academic behavior, since the main purpose is to change the way in which women think and act. Certainly, reading remains the principal teaching tool; but as we have seen in literary criticism, every subject is approached by relating it to the personal life of each participant. For example, it is difficult to study the family without considering how children are raised and educated, including your own experience, and weighing the effects of this experience on your own life. Here we reencounter two of the basic principles of consciousness-raising: what's personal is political, and personal experiences should be compared so as to achieve cooperation in sisterhood. Consequently, the women's studies class typically has two constants: the personal introspective journal, which is an effort to analyze readings and theories in relation to the student's own experience, and collectively written articles, which provide practice in working together as feminists. The women's studies program animators at Goddard College in Vermont stated that they wanted their students to have "a strong sense of an inner core of self that most women never develop. We want them to be able to act on the world, and in the world."[33]

Women's studies programs are also oriented toward the liberation of children and adolescents, in elementary and secondary education. However, in 1978, only two programs existed in these sectors, including one at the University of California at Berkeley which was threatened with closure by budgetary problems. Created in 1972, in response to pressure from the local chapter of NOW, this program's main purpose was to develop teaching material that would introduce objectivity into teaching methods by creating new educational activities free from sexual or racial stereotypes. Feminists were cooperating with ethnic studies groups to produce original material that was both feminist and multiethnic. Two photos published by the *Women's Studies Newsletter*[34] illustrate the experiment, one showing a young black girl repairing a bicycle, the other a little blond boy learning to knit.

The Berkeley experiment was not only aimed at introducing equality into teaching programs, but also sought to teach the teachers. This same goal inspired two basic reference works published by the Feminist Press: *Nonsexist Curricular Materials for Elementary Schools* and *Feminist Resources for Schools and Colleges,* together covering all levels from the primary grades through university. This same intention lay behind the summer courses for high school teachers, such as those organized at Sarah Lawrence College and Stanford University, to inform them of recent discoveries by university researchers on the history of women, as well as new ways to teach and interpret this history. As an encouraging sign, forty-one out of the forty-three participants in the 1976 Sarah Lawrence program reported having integrated women's history into their courses.

Twelve questions were asked these teachers by Gerda Lerner, seeking to explore how, in the past, motherhood and sexuality had affected women's lives, how they had reacted to their subordination, or how individual feminist consciousness had developed into collective consciousness. These questions illustrate a feminist approach to history, as do the efforts of Linda Gordon, historian at the Cambridge-Goddard Graduate School, to develop a variety of historical approaches dealing with cultural, political, and economic development from a feminist point of view.

History thus inspires the women engaged in the adventure of women's studies, particularly the pioneering research done by feminist historians, which other women take up and pursue. It is revealing that here we rediscover the names of two historians who have contributed writings to the Women's movement. Likewise, university research groups have formed in the domain of literary criticism. Among the most well known of these is the one at Barnard College, of which the leaders have included Mirra Komarovsky, the pioneer in feminine sociology, Carolyn Heilbrun, whose contribution we have seen toward the androgynous perspective, and Catharine Stimpson, the first editor of *Signs*. And we must certainly not omit the annual conference organized by the Barnard College Women's Center, whose theme in 1979 was "The Future of Difference," a concept that originated in contemporary French feminism but had been previously neglected by American feminists.

As Florence Howe expressed it, women's studies programs are not building "separate empires" but have established a network, which took concrete form in 1977 with the founding of the National Women's Studies Association (NWSA). It is evident that the future of women's studies, in the search to create feminist teaching in the service of a free society, is linked to the development of this association, whose purpose is to meet the needs of women engaged in this field and to ensure representation of their views and application of their research and discoveries in the context of ideological and institutional struggles. To fulfill these objectives, the NWSA has a national office and coordinating committee. It also has several large regional consortiums; the one in the Great Lakes region appears the most active, with a collective program covering a dozen colleges and universities in three states. Under its first president Florence Howe, the NWSA aligned itself strategically to make women's studies an international phenomenon, and welcomed in its ranks any women of foreign nationality doing research about women. One of the best illustrations of this internationalization is the visit by three American members in December 1982 to Toulouse (France), attending the French national colloquium entitled "Femmes, féminisme, recherches," and the mailing to a hundred French researchers of the report presented on this occasion by Catharine Stimpson.

Given this orientation and the diversity of initiatives undertaken, it seems that the future of women's studies is assured. These programs have consolidated the position of the Women's movement on university campuses and have made it penetrate, although timidly, into high schools and elementary schools. On this point, Amy Swerdlow expresses the widespread feminist wish that the Women's movement should militate for more integration of women's history in school curriculums, in keeping with the Houston resolution. Likewise, it would be desirable, if we recall the statement of purpose of the Goddard College program and the radicalization of women students by women's rights law studies, that the professors of women's studies participate in training the feminist militants of tomorrow.

All the same, we cannot deny that a danger exists of women's studies being co-opted. Admittedly, as Sheila Tobias and Alice Rossi wrote in 1970, women's studies have a transitional character and are expected eventually to blend into an ideal, humanist, nonsexist culture, but this is not going to happen overnight. Hence, the warning by Berenice A. Caroll and Melanie Kaye,[35] which incarnates the feeling of radical feminists within women's studies programs: before envisaging the possibility of integrating men in the teaching of these subjects, before being concerned about their own careers, women teachers and researchers must look outside university campuses and aim at reaching all women, whether or not they are militant feminists. Caroll saw the gap widening between campus feminists and nonuniversity militants, who reproach the former for trying to enlist women in masculine structures. Definitely, the feminists of academia have innovated little in terms of ideology; university women have only applied feminist theory previously developed by militant groups whose theorists had fled from ivory towers. Therefore, it would be only fair for the activists in women's studies programs to pay their debts to the Women's movement. In Melanie Kaye's view, they ought to introduce more political analysis into their courses, so as to really train women for militant action and wrench them out of the old vicious circle of self-destruction. She is therefore prescribing a sort of rejuvenation of the movement. Another orientation appears here, with the participation on campus of women from the larger feminist movement in the community. An example is a seven-week course on sexism in sports, offered at the women's studies center of Rutgers University by a member of the New York Radical Feminists in 1979.[36] Berenice A. Caroll stresses that it is important to help nonuniversity women succeed in their objectives with the broad mass of women. To do so, contact must be established on the basis of mutual sharing, and women's studies must be directed not inward, toward academia, but outward, toward women in the community.

How, precisely, can this populist conception of women's studies be achieved? The question is not raised. However, Berenice A. Caroll's idea can be put into practice through the parallel participation of university women in the alternative schools set up by radical feminists, known as women's liberation schools or schools of feminism. University women can thus find ways to participate in community-oriented feminist activities without jeopardizing their job security.

Schools of Feminism

Women's liberation schools are the work of the radical feminist branch of the movement. Their philosophy is summed up in the motto: "What we don't know, we must learn; what we do know, we should teach each other."[37]

Once again, independence and sisterhood should prevail, so that militant women collectively gain knowledge. When the Chicago Women's Liberation Union (CWLU) was organized in 1971, the founders named three fundamental needs they intended to meet: to explain feminist ideas to women through a means other than the patriarchal media; to provide political education to CWLU militants and other members of the Women's movement; to offer all women a chance to learn survival techniques. These reasons, in fact, are the basis of all schools of feminism. The pioneers of the Chicago plan even envisaged the possibility of using the school "to train cadres and organizers of rap groups," cherishing hopes of recruiting women for the "self-health" movement from among those who had participated in courses on female anatomy and childbirth preparation.

From the start, it was apparent that these types of schools, dedicated to women and feminism, were a challenge to existing institutions, and particularly, to traditional teaching under the patriarchal system. This is shown by their names, such as the Free You, in San Diego, or Breakaway, in Berkeley, clearly signaling a rupture with conventional university structures (and by extension, a rejection of official women's studies programs). The rupture is equally clear with other counterculture institutions which, being generally dominated by men, have been axiomatically considered sexist.

Experience with women's liberation schools convinced radical feminists that for a project to function smoothly, it needed structure. The Chicago school, for example, had an executive board of fifteen members, subdivided into five committees. In contrast, Breakaway's founders, haunted by the fear of seeing an elite develop within their free-spirited antiinstitution, decided to resign at the end of the first semester, which they did, to the detriment of the school's continuity. Later, a more flexible management plan was developed in which the board was elected half at a time, with inclusion of student representatives.

The courses offered focused mainly on such issues as women's liberation, female anatomy, the family, the law, and women's studies; but an important innovation was the teaching of techniques previously considered men's territory. The Chicago Women's Liberation School taught car repairs; the New York Womanschool responded to a heavy demand for courses in business management; Breakaway in Berkeley and the Women's Community School of Ann Arbor offered carpentry classes. Karate was another popular subject at Breakaway and elsewhere.

The low entry fees—three dollars for a ten-week course, for example—were meant to attract large numbers of women. In 1972, a year after its opening, the school in Chicago had recruited 220 students. However, most of them were white, middle-class, young mothers, who could leave their children in cooperative child care run by the school itself. This is probably a reflection on the character of the community in Chicago, a city with bitter racial divisions; in Berkeley, in contrast, Breakaway did not have this problem, but attracted women from all sorts of ethnic and social backgrounds, especially with its mobile class formula.[38] It is easy to see how such a school could be instrumental in spreading the new feminist movement among all walks of society. Nevertheless, the number of experiments of this type remains limited; in 1975, in the peak period of feminist activism, *The New Woman's Survival Sourcebook* only listed sixteen. The great advantage of such schools could be to convince university feminists to leave the campus sometimes and participate in feminist organizations in the community, as we suggested earlier. This, in a way, is what Miriam Schapiro and Judy Chicago did, after having vainly tried, in 1971, to institute feminist art programs within the conventional bounds of Cal Arts in Los Angeles.

THE FEMINIST MOVEMENT IN THE ARTS

The enthusiasm with which women have turned toward artistic and literary expression seems a response to a sort of compensatory instinct to make up for what Adrienne Rich called "our deprivation of the power to name."[39]

Some militants have tried their hands at a number of forms of expression. Kate Millett, for example, after writing *Sexual Politics* and her autobiographical work, *Flying,* went on to codirect a film, *Three Lives,*[40] on the complex reality of modern women's lives, and has occasionally shown her sculptures, remaining faithful to her original training. Her *Naked Ladies,* exhibited at the Los Angeles Women's Building in May 1977, gave artistic expression to the message of the feminist movement. The contrast between the huge stature of the women and the paltry size of the common household objects surrounding them—frying pan, refrigerator, supermarket cart, television set—symbolizes the discordance between women's potential and the insignificant tasks to which they have been confined. The towering size of Millett's figures and their nudity represent the potential strength and untouched nature of women's ability. This ability is the message passed, in style and content, by Millett's sculpture and the works of other feminist artists. The main fields in which women have given particularly free rein to their creative energies are film and the graphic and plastic arts. For example, the women's film festival "Women Picture Women," held in Denver in spring 1977, showed four persistent themes: art, women's bodies and "self-health," sex roles, and survival techniques. In art, more so than in literature, perhaps because of the later arrival of the feminist art movement, survival got the most attention, with women's evolution toward autonomy and the ability to make decisions. The level-headedness and serenity of Nell Cox's heroine in *Liza's Pioneer Diary* are an antidote to the tics and behavioral problems of the leading character in John Cassavetes's film *A Woman under the Influence,* whose unhealthy, ambiguous complacency is castigated by Nell Cox, who says "romanticizing crippled women is disgusting."[41]

Even more interesting from a feminist point of view is Isabel Castellano's film, *El Conflicto de Ruth.* Not only do we see a positive female role, but in this case, the heroine reasserting her existential priorities is a Puerto Rican. The film was produced by a team of Hispanic women working in a feminist collective: the film workshop of the New York group, Women Make Movies.[42]

The women's collective, an incarnation of sisterhood, is organized so as to bring women out of their isolation within the patriarchal art world and break down the inhibitions that have been born out of the scorn that masters of the cinematic art have always shown for women's work. Because of this conditioning, say the women of the Feminist Studio Workshop, women do not try to change the world, but accept it as it is. Therefore, they must be given a new context—new space, new atmosphere—in which they can freely create. This is the motivation on which women artists have joined together on a cooperative basis to found galleries, such as AIR[43] in New York, which bring women artists out of obscurity or isolation to show their work and share their artistic explorations with each other. The Women's Interart Center of New York, on the top floor of an old building on the West Side, could accommodate seventy-five artists; the Women's Art Center of San Francisco was open to men as well as women when I visited it in 1975. Along with exhibitions, most feminist art centers organize workshops where women teach other women art and craft techniques such as basketweaving, photography, or working in wood, metal, or stone.

The motto of the Chicago Women's Graphic Collective, specializing in poster design, was a hymn to sisterhood and its power to combine individual energies to produce an explosive effect and liberate talent: "Sisterhood is blooming; springtime will never be the same."[44]

In this collective, each poster began as an idea of one individual, and was then discussed, developed, and produced by the collective. This, said the militants, was the first break with establishment art. The second was the implication that everyone is, or can become, an artist. This collective was responsible for some of the best posters in the Women's movement. From the one on medical care[45] showing a winged woman trying to escape from the serpents on the patriarchal caduceus, to the gigantic teeth of "Frustration,"[46] they are all explosions of splendid anger, emphasized by vivid slogans and colors.

The method used by the Feminist Studio Workshop, founded in Los Angeles in 1973 by Sheila de Bretteville, Judy Chicago, and Arlene Raven, was another effort to lead novices to rediscover their own anger. In this method, the conflictual relationship between teacher and pupil was used to challenge the pupil to create. The aspiring artist's anger was not buried self-destructively, as was usually the case in a patriarchal teaching establishment, according to Judy Chicago; instead, it was directed outward in an original work of art.

The feminist movement in the arts has thus encouraged a combative sense of feminism; whether on film, or in the graphic or plastic arts, this is the figurative version of the same outcry being expressed in feminist literature. But because of the audience's need to come on site to view the artwork, feminist artists, more so than writers, succeeded in inciting the woman viewer to direct confrontation with her own life experience. Mary Beth Edelson, for example, when her work was exhibited at the AIR

Gallery in New York in 1973, invited women visitors to write their own "blood stories" on index cards she had placed in boxes here and there for the purpose.

This simple anecdote on the rehabilitation of women's blood—whether menstrual flow or uterine hemorrhage—suffices to reveal the extent to which the feminist art movement was an affront to conventional art. The new value given to women's blood also indicates that feminist artists, like feminist authors, have turned toward new frameworks for the imagination. This evolution particularly occurred under the influence of Miriam Schapiro and Judy Chicago, who conceived the feminist art movement as an expression of the sense every woman ought to have of her own power, her own beauty, her own past as a woman. Everything that makes up a woman's life experience ought to be reevaluated: this is the meaning of the dialogue between Miriam and Judy jointly exploring hexagons, circles, and holes. Miriam Schapiro and Judy Chicago proposed to rehabilitate not only holes but also fabric, ribbons, and lace, in a sort of turning inside out of the traditional symbols of femininity. The artist's intention was clear: these materials are charged with negative connotations because they are handled mainly by women. They have come to be symbols of women's experience, and therefore, symbols of insignificance. Consequently, women must reaffirm the value of their experience, and so, of these symbols.

It is easy to see what an uproar this theory provoked among feminists, both artists and others. I myself raise two objections. First, might not this theory be simply an artistic application of the "pro-woman" line, glorifying the symbols of women's experience in the patriarchal universe, thereby concealing a justification of reverse sexual bias in socialization? Besides, we might wonder if, in rehabilitating the symbols of femininity, Miriam Schapiro and Judy Chicago were not carrying to extremes the very sexual polarization that was already carried so far by men, and falling into female sexual fetishism.

Certainly, in the beginning, their ideas produced some very interesting and surprising experiments. One of the most famous was conducted in 1972 in Los Angeles, when participants in the Feminist Art Program directed by Miriam and Judy at Cal Arts at UCLA were invited to follow their fantasies in decorating the rooms of a house slated for demolition. The result was "Womanhouse," an exhibition consisting of the house itself, inside which every room abounded with female images, objects, and situational art constructions. The kitchen, the very center of woman's nurturing functions, bristled with breasts and ovoid forms. In the bedroom, a mannequin figure called Lea, enslaved by the alienating mirror which turns woman's external image into her only identity, sat continuously at her dressing table, perpetually applying makeup. From the linen cupboard, in a literal interpretation of women's "coming out of the closet" of their confinement, Sandy Osgel showed another mannequin figure of a woman emerging, her body neatly sliced interstitially with the shelves between two piles of clean sheets.

The great success of "Womanhouse" was its power as an environment, and its appearance as the site of women's creativity. Its temporary character underlined the lack of a permanent structure for these purposes. This need was met by the founding of "Womanspace" in the Los Angeles Woman's Building, which in its first year, in 1973, already had one thousand members. The feminist movement in the arts was well under way.

FEMINIST BUSINESSES

The ultimate field in which feminist alternative institutions have developed is business. The Women's movement early found that it needed particular services, and women who had some commercial sense took the opportunity to combine their talents with their own liberation. Often, their prior experiences had led them to feel this was impossible within the patriarchal system, and their only solution was to set up businesses entirely controlled by women.

Three major difficulties were encountered by early feminist firms, as outlined by Anne Pride in her article, "Getting the Business."[47] First was the absence of qualified personnel and the lack of capital; the consequence was a lag in production and the inability to be competitive in prices. The second was women's own socialization, which had led them to believe the myths and be convinced of their own lack of real value; undervaluing themselves, they also undervalued their products, and did not sell them at a high enough price. Finally—and this is presented as the most painful problem—women in feminist businesses often ran into hostility from their militant sisters, who saw their activities as collusion with capitalism. For this reason, feminist entrepreneurs felt a need to justify themselves by defining a convincing business ethic.

What, then, they asked themselves, is a feminist business? First, it is any commercial enterprise in which a woman undertakes to control her own economic future; here we recognize the familiar feminist principles of autonomy and survival. Next, it is not enough for the company to produce feminist goods or services; the company's philosophy itself must be different from that of the patriarchal business system. Like other feminist alternative institutions, the feminist firm is often a collective in which the workers control their own labor and share the decisions. Here we see autonomy and survival leading to independent businesses and worker-managed firms. For a woman, controlling her own working conditions means, for example, being able to set flexible hours, in keeping with children's school schedules. Self-discipline is the rule in worker self-management, with each women needing to understand that demanding too many personal privileges will create tensions within the group. Typically, to avoid the development of conflicts, frequent meetings were organized to discuss not only the company's market and business plans but also the feelings of its staff and managers. Close bonds were forged through mutual cooperation and devotion to the same objectives, which, just as much as the artistic creativity discussed earlier, made work an expression of "sisterhood."

Another criterion was that, in the name of sisterhood, feminist businesses should not compete with other initiatives of the same allegiance. A good illustration of this was provided by feminist publishers. With exceptions such as the Diana Press, which appeared to be a cross between a traditional commercial business and a feminist firm, we can observe a certain specialization to avoid competition between feminist publishers: Know, Inc. and the Times Change Press centered on political publications, while Daughters, Inc., United Sisters, and the Women's Press Collective concentrated on literature.

Some publishing collectives also operate a nearby bookstore. This is the case in Oakland, California, where the spacious shop, A Woman's Place, is an outgrowth of the Women's Press Collective. At A Woman's Place, chairs and reading desks are scattered between the bookshelves, and a corner of the shop is set up as a library. The collective was founded in 1972 by a half-dozen women, and is still going strong. The visitor can discuss feminism with the members of the collective. In contrast, the very efficient Womanbooks, in New York, which lasted until the late 1980s, did not belong to any particular branch of the movement; the bookstore was purely a commercial operation, but run on collective principles. One of the managers would gladly advise you about your choice of books and a lively conversation soon developed with other women customers. Five times a year the shop published the *Womanbooks Review,* offering commentaries on recently published works by women and announcing the calendar of authors' readings and other events organized by the collective. Such bookstores thus have become part of the feminist communication network. The same goes for restaurants, exemplified by Mother Courage in New York or Bread and Roses in Cambridge. The latter was so popular with students that one had to wait for a table; in the meantime, one could take the opportunity to appreciate the works by women artists. Bread and Roses forbade tips, but customers were invited to leave contributions to the feminist cause of the week. Feminist restaurants have generally offered the option of at least some vegetarian dishes.

Many feminist law firms have also been formed. We have already mentioned Anne Flower Cummings and Susan Jordan, in connection with the Santa Cruz midwife trial; another well-known firm was the partnership of Sarah Bales and Sandra Edhlund in Milwaukee. These lawyers have specialized in issues likely to provide test cases concerning all women, and some have refused to represent men in cases of divorce or rape.

The great difficulty for all these businesses, as Anne Pride said earlier, has been financial, since they often suffered discrimination, especially before the Equal Credit Act of 1974, from credit institutions. "Our capital is ourselves," as one of the members of A Woman's Place in Oakland told me. Following the principles of autonomy and survival, a feminist credit movement started, which was easier than starting a banking network; women's banks came later.[48]

A credit institution is a legal entity covered by federal law. Its shareholders can agree to pool their savings to form the initial capital. Feminist credit institutions thus appeared in the 1970s like other alternative institutions, functioning in accordance with feminist principles. The boards of directors were women, periodically elected by the women shareholders and responsible to them. The profits were distributed among the shareholding members of the firm. The directors emphasized that theirs were practically the only financial institutions willing to lend to poor or ethnic minority women, and in this sense, they were financing the feminist revolution, since they only made loans to feminist individuals or businesses. In order to be considered for assistance, loan applicants had to show that they belonged to a feminist organization.

A great controversy broke out between militant troops and feminist credit institutions over the Feminist Economic Network (FEN), a union of feminist credit companies founded in 1975. Against an attack led by Martha

Shelley, FEN was defended by the feminist record company, Olivia Records, and by the Oakland Feminist Women's Health Center and Diana Press. Martha Shelley accused FEN of fascism and despotism on the part of its directors, criticizing them for designating themselves for their positions because of the financial contributions they had made to the company's capital, and for having established a "coercive" system of inspecting the finances of FEN's branches. To this, the women of Olivia Records answered that, for feminist enterprises to survive, two sorts of organization were needed: one, internal, within the movement, where feminists collectively grouped around the same work could equally share resources so as to help the cause of women; the other, external, conforming to the law the better to circumvent it and ensure the survival of organizations of the first type. Survival thereby became identified with profit.

The debate has remained open, but from the start, a general view was that since profit in feminist businesses had been made possible by the very existence of the new feminist movement, it could only be legitimate if a part of it came back to help the movement. This did not mean that it ought to come back to individuals—authors or other feminists—but rather to collective feminist activities, untainted by commercialism, anywhere where such activity encountered financial difficulties. One thinks in particular, of educational programs and publications, such as *Aphra* and *The Second Wave*, which have now disappeared precisely for this reason. Such a return is not only fair, it seems to me to be prudent, since, all things considered, feminism is the leading customer of any business claiming to mix feminism with commercial activity. In other words, the extinction of the Women's movement would threaten the existence of the business.

A happy precedent for this type of return was created by Robin Morgan, who turned over her royalties from her anthology *Sisterhood Is Powerful* to a foundation she established, the Sisterhood Is Powerful Fund, for the purpose of aiding feminist institutions in danger. The fund was able, for example, to help the feminist health centers of Los Angeles and Santa Cruz with their legal costs in entanglements with the law. Refusing to find a way to give such aid to feminist institutions would seem to betray a greater allegiance to commercialism than to feminism. Accepting this obligation would enable feminist institutions to have greater freedom of action and avoid the trap of being co-opted by official programs.

Being co-opted is not the only danger lying in wait for feminist enterprises; there is also the risk of being locked in self-centered concerns. the slow, patient work of building alternative institutions will acquire meaning only if, not content with allowing women to recreate themselves, it eventually subverts existing institutions by catering for hitherto unmet needs of women in the general public. To exclude the openness to feminism would be to succumb to personal temptation, and this time, "what's personal is NOT political!"

Overall, in judging the results achieved, we can only observe the slow rate of social and political progress attained by liberal feminism. On the asset side, there is primarily the way in which women have learned new techniques of organization, and their use of collective legal action. They have attained much success through these means, and all business firms now must be much more circumspect in the matter of sexual discrimination. This learning process is also the main benefit gained from alternative institutions. The militants who have undertaken these ventures have sought new ways of learning, of creating and of being, in the freedom of feminist self-management, breaking with the ignorance to which they had previously been confined by their upbringing in the patriarchal system. That they have been able to carry out such a diversity of projects with such limited financial resources is testimony not only to their enthusiasm but also to the death-blow finally dealt to the old stereotype of women's incapacity, which so long impeded any initiative by women. From the success of the Santa Cruz midwives to the profits of feminist businesses, the intrepidness and self-determination of feminists have demonstrated that the art of creating, producing, and succeeding is not the sole privilege of men. The essential result of this is to demystify the act of creation, whose overrated reputation has done so much to inhibit women.

Conclusion

As mentioned in the Introduction, the path followed by American feminists in the last fifty years has been that of a minority in rebellion, conscious of its exclusion from mainstream society and in search of its own identity. Except for certain shock actions in the early 1970s, this process has never been deliberately intended to unify women, and each of the major steps forward in the new feminist movement in America has provoked polarization within the movement around two or more different axes of thought or action, in keeping with ideological choices not foreign to traditional political currents: on one hand, classic liberalism or Americanism, and on the other, leftist radicalism modified to suit nonsexist tastes.

Such polarization seems to me to have been necessary during the first ten years following the official birth of the new feminist movement. It allowed time to fill in the ideological gaps left by the first wave of American feminism. This mission was accomplished far beyond all hopes: never, in fact, had such a noble company of females thought and written so much about the cause of women. This feminine intelligentsia enabled many American women to find their roots in the broad timescape of American history. It also offered women in other Western countries methods and models of critical analysis and action that have played, and continue to play, an undeniable role in changing society. Denouncing the relegation of women to emotional domains, aware of the universality of sexism and their powerlessness to struggle against the patriarchal ideology—the "glue" binding together all national and political "isms"—except by offering their own ideological alternatives, American women have patiently reexamined accepted concepts in order to better master and mold them, weighing words and peeling away their layers of meaning in order to reinterpret them and to create others more appropriate to the universal cause of women. The result is a mosaic of abstractions, which we have attempted to reconstruct in this kaleidoscopic view of new feminism in America, and an unprecedented richness of original thinking about the eternal war between the sexes, which contemporary philosophy must reckon with.

The high degree of ideological awareness attained by American feminist theorists has produced not only the pluralism needed for recruiting the largest possible number of converts, but also has deflected other traditional "isms" toward feminist goals, influencing them to recognize women's autonomy and give greater priority to the cause of women in general. It is particularly thanks to American radical feminists that feminism everywhere has come of age and has come out from under the wing of socialism, where it was when Simone de Beauvoir wrote *The Second Sex*. Simone de Beauvoir herself recognized the soundness and significance of this long-overdue emancipation.

Within the American context, it is possible to state that, by 1975, feminists had laid the groundwork that one day might permit American women to escape from the trap of combat by proxy: a host of independent alternative institutions in all sectors of society, and a diversity of currents of feminist thought, with enough nuances between them to allow them to speak to the condition of every woman, whatever her main concerns, from the job issues affecting the career woman, to the threefold complex of sexual, racial, and economic issues oppressing the minority woman.

However, more than a decade has passed since then, and it seems that American women may not have known how to play these two major cards they were holding in their hand. To start with, there is the unfinished work of theoretical analysis. If the first wave of American feminism ebbed because of a lack of ideology beyond the suffrage issue, the second wave may be in danger of squandering its force in a deluge of ideology. Now, polarization has become fragmentation, since no philosophical synthesis yet seems to have been achieved that would provide a framework for unity. We have tried to demonstrate that such a synthesis is possible; there are numerous elements of coherence, and a strong will toward concerted effort exists, from feminist historians and egalitarian feminists, through the radicals and on to the Socialist Workers party. Only such a synthesis will give the movement the credibility it needs to attract the allegiance of women who, aware of the urgency of their own particular struggle, still hesitate to enlist in militant feminism, and will thus facilitate the creation of a third force challenging the traditional two-party system. The National Women's Political Caucus seemed, at first, to offer hope for such a third force, but it quickly aligned itself with the two major parties, especially leaning toward the Democrats. To the degree that women remain in the minority within the two traditional party structures, it is predictable that the party majority line, given tacit support by feminist adhesion, will influence feminism more than feminism will influence party policies, and that when it comes to votes in Congress and the state legislatures, women's issues will continue to be used as a political football.

Between the egalitarian current of collaboration within the system and the radical current of revolutionary separatism, happily, there is a third way, a middle ground. NOW, retaining its most left-leaning wing and its fierce independence of the two major parties, bears witness to the possibility of blends between the reformist and radical currents, and prefigures, although somewhat timidly, what could be an autonomous panfeminist federation practicing a policy of coalition. Such panfeminism would be the realization of the old dream militants have always cherished and would be the concrete manifestation of sisterhood, which, ever since 1968, when the war cry was Sisterhood Is Powerful, has always been the underlying theme of the Women's Liberation movement.

At the NOW convention in July 1989, the same month as the Supreme Court decision in *Webster v. Reproductive Health Services,* President Molly Yard and former President Ellie Smeal called for the creation of a third party to fight for abortion rights and other women's issues. In the climate of the abortion defeat, NOW delegates unanimously approved, but the announcement immediately drew fire from NWPC and NARAL, whose activists attacked the third-party idea as "counterproductive," distancing themselves from NOW's tactics and complaining of the group's "stridency." However, it is the conclusion of this book that only a third force, a panfeminist movement, can guarantee change and progress, not because women have acquired any superiority whatsoever, but rather because the battle for each given issue must be fought with a specific struggle on its own ground, and the greatest chance to win lies with those who have first thoroughly studied the particular fundamental questions involved. Refusing the third way would be tantamount to remaining forever mired in the impasse of combat by proxy and sacrificing feminism to other political ideologies, whether in the name of liberalism, radicalism, or socialism. This would be definitive proof that feminism, even for its adherents, is relegated to second place after traditional political choices.

An ideological synthesis is not only possible; it is necessary. Above all, it is time for radical feminists, even if the true sexual revolution has not yet occurred, to come out in greater numbers from their splendid isolation, so that the American feminist movement, given into the custody of the egalitarians and still influenced by the old pre-1960s' women's associations, does not become taken for granted as just another pressure group. It is urgent for a unified feminist party to be born in America, whose first task would be to make people forget the old elitist image of feminism and to represent itself with convincing credibility. Although the movement has succeeded in spreading and has begun to infiltrate new sectors—ethnic minorities and the working class—the majority of its recruits nonetheless still come from the white middle class. In a further paradox, in spite of having been partly inspired by the Housewife's Syndrome that afflicted middle-class women in the 1950s, it has not managed to enlist the loyalty of most middle-class housewives.

Here we encounter the second problem of the new feminist movement: the issue of its representativeness, which explains why feminism has not managed to escape from the trap of combat by proxy, in spite of the diversity of independent feminist organizations. The difficulty arises from a fact that is both a strength and a weakness: that American feminist ideology aims to be universal, covering all women. While this universality has enabled it to receive favorable echos from women all over the world, wherever it has been able to get across its message, this same universality has prevented the movement from establishing a practical foothold in the daily affairs of American women who do not belong to the elite intelligentsia. In the eyes of many of these women, feminism is a luxury they cannot afford, since they believe it will do nothing to resolve their immediate problems. Many housewives feel threatened by the Equal Rights Amendment, and this is because feminists waited too long to reach out and explain its benefits to them, preaching only to the already-convinced. Working-class women, in the types of workplaces where feminism is most frequently lacking, do not always see the relevance of the theories which feminists have developed in closed circles among themselves; neither do ethnic minority women who, in addition to the sexual and economic discrimination affecting all women, are also struggling against racism.

The problem of representativeness will not be resolved simply by forming committees and special organizations, nor by membership campaigns and high-sounding declarations of purpose. This problem will only be resolved when a philosophical synthesis is developed into a program for action, which then needs to be translated into reality by the broad mass of women themselves, acting in their own interests, and not by fancy words and faraway lobbying. With the range of independent feminist structures already in existence, the Women's movement can intervene at all levels and in all sectors of society. We do not believe that the family will be a priority sector, contrary to what Betty Friedan says; saying so only encourages feminism to remain behind the closed doors of domestic life and to get stuck in discussion, which it already has too great a tendency to do. The new frontiers of American feminism are in women's workplaces and in areas of poverty. Thirty years after John Kennedy's well-remembered speech about the New Frontier, and nearly as long since Lyndon Johnson's War on Poverty, poverty still remains largely the sad privilege of women in America. According to a report published in 1980 by the President's National Advisory Council, by the year 2000, all the poor people in America will be women and their dependent children.[1] A 1988 report bears out this trend:

> The eroding economic situation of minority youths is eclipsed by that of mother-only families. Whereas the per-capita income of white mother-only families was nearly two-thirds that of two-parent families in 1960, by 1985 it had fallen to 57 percent. Among blacks, the decrease was from 61 percent to 48 percent. The deterioration in the status of these families has accompanied a radical increase in their numbers. In 1967, only about 10 percent of all families were headed by a single mother; by 1984, the figure was over 21 percent. In 1984, over half of all black families were headed by a woman.[2]

The "feminization of poverty," further aggravated by the restrictions on abortion rights, which fall most heavily on poor women, is the issue offering the best chance for united action among American feminists and American women. Because of this, and the magnitude of the work to be accomplished, it is also their greatest challenge.

The "feminization of poverty" is a logical consequence of the status of second-class citizen which, in spite of myths about American wealth, is reserved also for the women of the United States and not only for those in other countries. According to 1982 statistics from the Department of Labor, 34.7 percent of working women were still doing clerical work, constituting 80.1 percent of this employment sector; 19.4 percent were employed in service industries, where they made up 96.5 percent of domestic workers and 59.3 percent of other job categories in this sector; lastly, only 7.4 percent of working American women held management-level positions.

In 1986, with funding from the Ford and Rockefeller Foundations, the Pay Equity panel of the National Research Council sponsored eleven studies on the wage gap. The results were released in April 1989. Several studies reveal that the predominance of women in a job category lowered its median wage. For instance, Elaine Sorensen of the Urban Institute found that when the number of women in an occupation increased by 10 percent, the median wage decreased by 2 percent, this trend being more noticeable in government than in manufacturing and service jobs. Likewise, Alice and Masao Nakamura found correlation clusters among working women who are black, have children, and relatively little education. Nationally, they report, black women get only sixty cents for every dollar paid white men, and Hispanic women, at fifty-five cents, get even less. It is indisputable that working women in the United States continue to earn less then men, for reasons that include race and sex discrimination. The latest Department of Labor statistics as this book goes to press show that among full-time, year-round workers, American women on the whole earn 70 percent of the average men's wage. This looks like an improvement, compared with 1982. Still, we must not forget that in the meantime, the average male wage has decreased with the decline in unionized manufacturing jobs, and that twice as many women as men earn only the minimum wage.

Though acknowledging that class and race may be more significant factors than gender in black and Hispanic women's impoverishment, we persist in thinking that the "feminization of poverty" in the United States flows from a fundamental constitutional inequality between the sexes, existing since the very origin of the American republic, since a discriminatory interpretation has been applied to the term *person* as it is used in the Constitution, the basic law of the land. It is for this reason that the Equal Rights Amendment, with all its symbolic value, is a necessity. Radical feminists are wrong to snub it as merely a stopgap measure and to disdain the fight for it as unworthy collaboration with the capitalist and sexist system. For them to remain stubbornly apart in comfortable separatism, safely on the fringes of a society that is not threatened, is to commit an even greater sin of collaboration and laissez-faire. As worthy and remarkable as their alternative institutions may be, they will not suffice to subvert the patriarchy of Uncle Sam! Instead, a program for united action, including economic issues as well as the fight for the ERA, would give American feminism the second wind it has so obviously lacked in the 1980s, especially since the defeat of the ERA. This appears to us to be the essential condition to prevent this last failure from inaugurating a postfeminist era which some people are in such a hurry to enter, but instead, opening an era of panfeminism. Panfeminism would mean not only the union of liberal and radical feminists on the same front line of action, but also the union of feminists and the left-out women in American society. Ultimately, the ERA defeat could prove to be a valuable lesson. It gives American feminism a new lease on life, since it prolongs the struggle, as did the successive defeats in the long-drawn-out fight for the Nineteenth Amendment giving women the vote. It is a well-known fact that many politicians hostile to the woman's suffrage amendment ended up voting for it simply because doing so (i.e., giving the activists what they wanted) seemed to them the only way to put an end to the Women's movement. For several decades, the facts seemed to bear them out.

If, thanks to the vigilant presence of radical feminists, American women do not fall into the earlier error made by some suffragists[3] of compromising feminist principles to get their amendment at any price, the eventual passage of the ERA (needless to say, without crippling amendments to it) should not be the end of the line. It should be only a rite of passage, a means and not an end, enabling the new second-wave American feminist movement, on the strength of the law and the experience it has acquired in collective legal action, to deliver a new battle to inscribe sexual equality in the socioeconomic facts and end the "feminization of poverty."

In so doing, it will have become a truly credible representative movement of American women organized for action; and having armed itself effectively, can and should pursue the battle for cultural androgyny, which is both a reinforcement and an extension of the battle for economic and political equality, and which, by dealing with the fundamental questions touching all human beings, liberates everyone universally.

Chronology

1946

Congress, called upon to vote for the first time on the Equal Rights Amendment (ERA), voted against it.

1950, 1953

The ERA suffered two more defeats in Congress.

1961

President John F. Kennedy established the first Presidential Commission on the Status of Women.

1963

Publication of *The Feminine Mystique* by Betty Friedan.

Passage by Congress of the Equal Pay Act. The act applies to all employees who are entitled to the benefits of the minimum wage provisions of the Fair Labor Standards Act (1938), and prohibits employers from discriminating on the basis of sex in the payment of wages for equal work.

Publication of *American Women*, the report of the Presidential Commission on the Status of Women.

1964

Title VII of the Civil Rights Act forbade sexual discrimination in the private sector.

Ruby Doris Smith Robinson raised the issue of the position of black women within the Students' Nonviolent Coordinating Committee (SNCC).

1965

A group of women activists raised the issue of womens' rights at the conference of Students for a Democratic Society (SDS).

1966

Founding of the National Organization for Women (NOW).

1967

President Lyndon B. Johnson signed Executive Order 11375, which forbade sexual discrimination in the public sector.

Birth of the first radical feminist group, the New York Radical Women (NYRW).

Publication of the SCUM Manifesto, by Valerie Solanas.

1968

Burial ceremony for traditional femininity enacted by NYRW.

Publication of the first radical feminist newsletter, *Voice of the Women's Liberation Movement.*

Birth of the first radical feminist journal, *Notes from the First Year.*

Sabotage of the Miss America pageant at Atlantic City by a group of radical feminists.

Birth of the Women's International Terrorist Conspiracy from Hell (WITCH).

First national conference of the Women's Liberation Movement.

Creation of the Women's Equity Action League (WEAL).

1969

Formation of three New York radical feminist groups: the Redstockings, the Feminists, and the New York Radical Feminists (NYRF).

Sabotage by radical feminists of bridal fairs in New York and San Francisco.

The Redstockings in New York organized a day of public debate on abortion.

Establishment of the first university-level women's studies program, at Cornell University (New York).

Publication of the *Redstockings Manifesto.*

1970

Takeover by women of the radical underground newspaper *Rat.*

WEAL filed lawsuits for sexual discrimination against several universities.

46 women journalists from *Newsweek* sued their magazine for sexual discrimination.

A hundred feminists held a sit-in at the *Ladies' Home Journal* to protest the image of women presented by women's magazines.

Publication of *The 1969 Handbook on Women Workers* by the Women's Bureau of the federal government.

Opening of the New York Women's Center.

The United Auto Workers became the first major labor union to declare its support for the ERA.

147 women journalists filed suit against *Time, Life, Fortune,* and *Sports Illustrated* for sexual discrimination.

Hawaii, Alaska, and New York became the first states to liberalize their abortion laws.

The Women's Bureau, on its fiftieth anniversary and the fiftieth anniversary of the effective date of women's right to vote, declared its support for the ERA.

National strike by women held on 26 August (fiftieth anniversary of women's right to vote).

Publication of *Sexual Politics* by Kate Millett.

Creation of the North American Indian Women's Association.

Founding by Chicana feminists of the Comisión Feminil Mexicana Nacional (California).

Birth of the organization Radicalesbians.

First appearance of the feminist periodicals: *Off Our Backs, Ain't I A Woman?* and *It Ain't Me, Babe.*

1971

Rape speakout day organized by NYRF.

Women's studies introduced in the public high school curriculum in Berkeley, California.

The University of Michigan became the first university to launch an affirmative action program for the hiring and promotion of women.

Founding of the National Women's Political Caucus for the purpose of promoting women's participation in politics.

Creation of the first feminist foundation, the Sisterhood Is Powerful Fund.

Founding by Gloria Steinem and Brenda Feigen Fasteau of the Women's Action Alliance, the first national coordinating center for the various programs of the Women's movement.

1972

The ERA passed the House of Representatives and the Senate, 49 years after its first introduction in Congress. However, the deadline of 1979 was imposed for its required ratification by two-thirds of the states before it could become law.

The Equal Employment Opportunity Act gave the Equal Employment Opportunity Commission (EEOC) the right to undertake legal proceedings against sexual discrimination offenders.

Title IX of Education Amendments to the Civil Rights Act forbade sexual discrimination in educational programs receiving federal funds.

National conference of Puerto Rican Women (Washington, D.C.)

Launching of the *Women's Studies Newsletter* by the Feminist Press.

Founding of *Ms.* magazine.

Creation of the Women's Lobby, Inc., a pressure group specializing in women's issues.

Shirley Chisholm ran as a candidate for the Democratic party's nomination for the presidency of the United States.

Prostitutes organized themselves into a union, COYOTE (Cut Out Your Old Tired Ethics).

The *Womanhouse* exhibition organized by the Cal Arts Feminist Art Program (Los Angeles).

Creation of the *Ms.* Foundation to support women's initiatives.

The League of Women Voters declared its support for the ERA.

First conference of Older Women's Liberation (OWL) (New York).

1973

The United States Supreme Court recognized American women's constitutional right to abortion, in its decision in the case of *Roe v. Wade*.

Formation of the National Black Feminist Organization.

Sexual categorizing in employment advertisements was held unconstitutional by the Supreme Court.

The AFL-CIO declared its support for the ERA.

Opening of the Los Angeles Woman's Building.

Founding of the first feminist publishing firms: Daughters, Inc. and Diana Press.

AT&T (American Telephone and Telegraph) agreed to devote $35 million to retro-active correction of discriminatory practices in women's salaries.

Creation of the first organizations of women office workers: Women Employed (Chicago), Women Office Workers (New York), 9 to 5 (Boston).

August 1973 declared Rape Prevention Month.

Establishment of the first feminist credit union (Detroit).

First national conference of feminist lesbians (Los Angeles).

Founding of the National Abortion Rights Action League (NARAL).

1974

Founding of the Coalition of Labor Union Women (CLUW).

Creation of the Association of Mexican-American Women.

Ella Grasso became the first woman to be elected as a state governor (Connecticut) in her own right (without depending on the name of a late husband, etc.).

The Equal Credit Opportunity Act forbade sexual discrimination in credit matters.

Conference on rape sponsored by the National Black Feminist Organization.

Formation of the National Congress of Neighborhood Women for the promotion of blue-collar women.

The Women's Educational Equity Act provided for financial aid to nonsexist educational programs.

1975

First meeting of the American Indian Women's Leadership Conference (New York).

Opening of the first women's bank (New York).

Formation of the Women's Ordination Conference to promote the cause of the ordination of women priests in the Catholic church.

Founding of *Signs*, feminist studies review.

First feminist conference on health organized by the collective Our Bodies, Ourselves (Harvard).

1976

Formation of ERAmerica to work toward ratification of the Equal Rights Amendment.

The General Convention of the Episcopalian church pronounced itself in favor of the ordination of women.

NASA accepted the principle of the training of women astronauts.

Founding in Chicago of the National Alliance of Black Feminists.

National campaign against the pornographic film *Snuff* organized by Women Against Violence Against Women.

1977

The National Women's Conference held in Houston.

NBC agreed to devote $1.7 million to retroactive correction of discriminatory practices in women's salaries.

March of Five Thousand for the ERA (Washington, D.C.) (in commemoration of the 1913 suffragist March of Five Thousand up Pennsylvania Avenue).

Formation of the first women's caucus in Congress, composed of 15 women representatives and 1 woman senator.

The *Reader's Digest* agreed to pay 1.5 million dollars in retroactive salary adjustments to women employees.

The Kitty Genovese Women's Project (Texas) published the names of 150 men convicted for sexual violence.

Creation of the National Women's Studies Association.

1978

NOW organized a boycott of the states that had not yet ratified the ERA.

Congress extended the ERA ratification deadline to 30 June 1982.

March of 100,000 demonstrators in Washington, D.C., in favor of ratification of the ERA.

Creation of the National Lesbian Feminist Organization.

First national feminist conference on pornography.

1979

Twelve office employee groups joined to form Working Women, a national organization of office workers.

Participation of about 50 organizations in National Abortion Rights Week.

A commemorative conference on feminist theory was held in New York on the thirtieth anniversary of the publication of *The Second Sex* by Simone de Beauvoir.

For the first time in the history of the United States, the presidents of the most prestigious women's colleges, the "seven sisters," were all women (Barnard, Bryn Mawr, Mount Holyoke, Smith, Wellesley, Radcliffe, and Vassar).

Sister Theresa Kane addressed a demand to Pope John Paul II calling for the ordination of women priests in the Catholic church.

March of 5,000 feminists against pornography (New York).

1980

Feminist Hispanic conference (San Jose, California).

March of 90,000 demonstrators organized by NOW in favor of ratification of the ERA (Chicago).

Equal representation of both sexes at the Democratic party national convention.

Joyce Miller became the first woman to hold office in the AFL-CIO.

1981

For the first time in the history of the United States, a woman (Sandra Day O'Connor) was appointed to a seat on the Supreme Court.

Barbara Hutchinson became the first black woman to hold office in the AFL-CIO.

1982

ERA reintroduced into Congress, after expiration of the ratification deadline extension.

1983

The Supreme Court reaffirmed American women's constitutional right to abortion.

Sally Ride became the first American woman to participate in a space mission.

The Supreme Court ruled to forbid sexual discrimination in retirement schemes.

The National Council of Churches published a collection of biblical texts rewritten to eliminate sexism.

1984

Under feminist pressure, for the first time in the history of the United States, a presidential candidate, Walter Mondale, chose a woman running mate: Geraldine Ferraro, representative from the state of New York.

The choice was ratified by the Democratic party convention in San Francisco.

The ERA was again reintroduced into Congress.

1988

President Ronald Reagan, in one of his last acts before leaving office, filed a "friend of the court" brief urging the Supreme Court to review a Missouri case challenging *Roe v. Wade,* thus reexamining the abortion issue. The Court, dominated by conservative judges appointed by President Reagan, agreed to do so.

1989

When the Supreme Court began hearings in the abortion challenge (*Webster v. Reproductive Health Services*), more than 300,000 pro-choice advocates marched in Washington in favor of keeping abortion legal.

In July, the Supreme Court rendered its judgment in *Webster v. Reproductive Health Services,* upholding the constitutionality of Missouri's prohibition of the use of public funds, facilities, or employees to perform abortions not necessary to save the life of the mother. Both pro-choice and pro-life groups agreed this decision was an open invitation for state legislatures to pass increasingly restrictive abortion laws.

NOW reacted to the Supreme Court decision by calling for starting a third political party to fight for abortion rights and other issues. The announcement provoked new controversy in the Women's movement, as some feminists disagreed with this strategy.

In October, President George Bush vetoed legislation that would have provided federal funding of abortions for victims of rape or incest. Congress failed to muster the required two-thirds majority to override the veto, but the vote of 231–191 suggested that pro-choice support was growing.

Notes

CHAPTER 1: POWER STRUGGLES: A PLAY IN FOUR ACTS

1. This government agency was founded by an act of Congress on 5 June 1920 for the purpose of overseeing the welfare of women workers, and defined itself as a department of factual research.
2. Ferdinand Lundberg and Marynia Farnham, *Modern Woman: The Lost Sex* (New York: Universal Library, 1947).
3. Ibid., 143 and 269.
4. Not Mary Wollstonecraft Shelley, author of *Frankenstein*, but her mother, author of *A Vindication of the Rights of Woman* (1792).
5. Herschberger, *Adam's Rib* (1948). Reprint, 1970.
6. Friedan, *The Feminine Mystique* (1963). Reprint, 1971, 57.
7. Ibid., 57–58 (1971 edition).
8. The word *sex* was added to the various discrimination factors cited in Title VII on a motion by Congressman Howard Smith, a Democrat, who thought this would ensure defeat of the Civil Rights Act. His maneuver turned out not to have the effect he intended, and the entire text was adopted by both houses of Congress.
9. Sudsoffloppen, San Francisco's first women's group, was formed in September 1968 by women so disenchanted with New Left politics that they resisted defining themselves as a political entity, but they continued to meet, and after several months of talking and writing, they took this name. "One of our members had used the name in her paper and we all felt that the concept of a nonsensical name was good because it would leave us plenty of room to grow and develop. No notion of who or what we were could be derived from the name separate from the work and ideas we produced." Pam Allen, "Free Space," in Hole and Levine, *Rebirth of Feminism* (1971). Reprint, 1973, 121.

CHAPTER 2: THE GLORY AND THE OPPRESSION

1. Beard, *Women as Force in History*.
2. Davis, *The First Sex*, 188.
3. Lerner, *The Grimké Sisters*.
4. Flexner, *Century of Struggle*.

5. Daly, *Beyond God the Father: Toward a Philosophy of Women's Liberation.*
6. Firestone, *The Dialectic of Sex.*
7. Millett, *Sexual Politics.*
8. Brownmiller, *Against Our Will.*

CHAPTER 3: EGALITARIAN FEMINISM

1. Daly, *The Church and the Second Sex,* 77.
2. Friedan, *It Changed My Life.*
3. *NOW Statement of Purpose,* ibid., 87.
4. Wilma Scott Heide, "Women and the Law," in *Women's Role in Contemporary Society,* The Report of the New York City Commission on Human Rights, Foreword by Mayor John Lindsay, Introduction by Eleanor Holmes Norton (New York: Avon, 1972).
5. Elected officeholders and members of the Democratic Party, Bella Abzug and Shirley Chisholm have both served in the House of Representatives for several terms. Shirley Chisholm even ran for the Democratic presidential nomination in 1972, the first black woman (indeed, one of the first women) to be taken seriously as a candidate for the nation's highest office.
6. Publishing informational brochures about electoral issues is one of the main activities of the League of Women Voters. The reference is to a set of brochures published in 1972 and packaged in a single envelope under the title *Public Action Kit.*
7. Marijean Suelzle, "Women in the Academic Marketplace," Berkeley, University of California, May 1971. Author's prepublication copy, received directly from Suelzle.
8. Jessie Bernard, *Academic Women* (University Park, Pa.: Pennsylvania State University, 1964).
9. Bird, *Born Female,* iv.
10. Friedan, *It Changed My Life,* 161.
11. Colette Price, "New Ways of Keeping Women Out of Paid Labor," in Redstockings, *Feminist Revolution,* 81.
12. The Women's Bureau, *The Myth and the Reality* (Washington, D.C.: U.S. Department of Labor, Women's Bureau, Advance Copy, 1974).
13. Gloria Steinem, "If We're So Smart, Why Ain't We Rich?" *Ms.* 12 (June 1973): 38.
14. Ibid., 125.
15. Bird, *Born Female,* chap. 6, 146.
16. Friedan, *It Changed My Life,* 111.
17. "Gloria Steinem and Elizabeth Reid Talk about Revolution," *Ms.* 4, no. 7 (January 1976): 76.
18. Friedan, *It Changed My Life,* 117.
19. *NOW Statement of Purpose,* cited in Friedan, *It Changed My Life,* 90.
20. "Gloria Steinem and Elizabeth Reid," 88.

21. Letty Cottin Pogrebin, "Can Women Have It All?" *Ms.* 6, no. 9 (March 1978): 47.
22. Friedan, *It Changed My Life,* 328.
23. Bird, *Born Female,* xiii–xiv.
24. Florynce Kennedy, in New York City Commission on Human Rights, *Women's Role in Contemporary Society,* 86.
25. Friedan, *It Changed My Life,* 315.
26. Jane J. Mansbridge, *Why We Lost the ERA* (Chicago: University of Chicago Press, 1986), 207.
27. Lady Bird Johnson, Betty Ford, and Rosalyn Carter.

CHAPTER 4: RADICALISM

1. WITCH was variously said to stand for the following:
   Women's International Terrorist Conspiracy from Hell, when the group first surfaced on Wall Street in 1968.
   Women Incensed at Telephone Company Harassment, when telephone company employees protested against their working conditions.
   Women Infuriated at Taking Care of Hoodlums, for a protest on Mother's Day.
   Women Independent Taxpayers, Consumers, and Homemakers, for a consumer protest against rising prices.
   Women Inspired to Commit Herstory, according to the interpretation suggested by Robin Morgan in *Going Too Far,* 121.
2. The Daughters of Bilitis was the first lesbian organization, founded in 1956 by Del Martin and Phyllis Lyon. Its journal is *The Ladder.*
3. Colette Price, "New Ways of Keeping Women Out of Paid Labor," in Redstockings, *Feminist Revolution,* 82.
4. Bunch-Weeks, Charlotte, "A Broom of One's Own: Notes on the Women's Liberation Movement," in Cooke and Bunch-Weeks, *The New Women,* 168.
5. *Redstockings Manifesto,* in Morgan, *Sisterhood Is Powerful,* 534.
6. Morgan, *Going Too Far,* 178.
7. *Redstockings Manifesto,* in Morgan, *Sisterhood Is Powerful,* 534.
8. Atkinson, *Amazon Odyssey,* 59.
9. Ibid., 49.
10. Ibid., 55.
11. Densmore, Dana, "Who Is Saying Men Are the Enemy?" *The Female State* 4 (April 1970): 4.
12. Valerie Solanas, *SCUM Manifesto* (copyright by Valerie Solanas, 1967), 1. SCUM was said to stand for "Society for Cutting Up Men."
13. Sherfey, *The Nature and Evolution of Female Sexuality,* 144.
14. Susan Lydon, "The Politics of Orgasm," in Morgan, *Sisterhood Is Powerful,* 197.
15. Atkinson, *Amazon Odyssey,* 53.
16. Sullerot, *Le fait féminin,* 18.

17. Coletta Reid and Charlotte Bunch, "Revolution Begins at Home", in Charlotte Bunch and Nancy Myron, eds., *Class and Feminism* (Baltimore: Diana Press, 1974), 70–81.
18. Millett, *Sexual Politics,* 33.
19. Marilyn Salzman Webb, "Woman as Secretary, Sexpot, Spender, Sow, Civic Actor, Sickie," in Cooke and Bunch-Weeks, *The New Women,* 109.
20. Woman identified as "J." in Kate Millett, "Prostitution: A Quartet for Female Voices," in Vivian Gormick and Barbara K. Moran, eds., *Woman in Sexist Society* (New York: New American Library, 1971), 92.
21. Ellen Strong, "The Hooker," in Morgan, *Sisterhood Is Powerful,* 292.
22. Atkinson, *Amazon Odyssey,* 124.
23. Ibid., 44.
24. Firestone, *Dialectic of Sex,* 127.
25. Joyce O'Brien, "In Favor of True Love over Settling," in Redstockings, *Feminist Revolution,* 111–12.
26. Mainardi, Patricia, "The Marriage Question," in Redstockings, *Feminist Revolution,* 107.
27. Firestone, *Dialectic of Sex,* 142.
28. Ibid., 144.
29. Daly, *The Church and the Second Sex,* Feminist Postchristian Introduction, 17.
30. Densmore, "Who Is Saying Men Are the Enemy?" 7–8.
31. Solanas, *SCUM Manifesto,* 4.
32. Densmore, *Sex Roles and Female Oppression,* 19.
33. Hite, *The Hite Report,* 371.
34. Atkinson, *Amazon Odyssey,* 23.
35. Linda Seese, "You've Come a Long Way, Baby," in Cooke and Bunch-Weeks, *The New Women,* 162–63.
36. Atkinson, *Amazon Odyssey,* 80.
37. Firestone, *Dialectic of Sex,* 187, 195.
38. Ibid., 195.
39. Ibid., 217.
40. Carol Hanisch, "The Liberal Takeover of Women's Liberation," in Redstockings, *Feminist Revolution,* 127.
41. Solanas, *SCUM Manifesto,* 4.
42. "*Ms.,* Politics and Editing: An Interview," in Redstockings, *Feminist Revolution,* 171–72.
43. Ellen Willis, "The Conservatism of *Ms.,*" in Redstockings, *Feminist Revolution,* 174.
44. *Redstockings Manifesto,* in Morgan, *Sisterhood Is Powerful,* 535.
45. Redstockings, "Agents, Opportunists and Fools," in Redstockings, *Feminist Revolution,* 149.
46. Martha Shelley, "Gay Is Good" (1970), in Women's Press Collective, *Lesbians Speak Out,* 65.
47. New York Radicalesbians, "Woman Identified Woman" (1970), in Women's Press Collective, *Lesbians Speak Out,* 87.

48. Jean O'Leary, "Lesbian Feminism—The Building of a New Society," speech delivered at Battery Park, New York, on the occasion of the Feminist Fair of 25 August 1973. Author's personal copy, 2.

49. New York Radicalesbians, "Woman Identified Woman," 87.

50. Shelley, "Gay Is Good," 65.

51. Jean O'Leary of the group known as Lesbian Feminist Liberation went so far as to reclaim the Freudian slogan Anatomy Is Destiny in order to assert that women are predestined by nature to a matriarchal lesbian body. "Lesbian Feminism," 2.

52. Anne Koedt, "Lesbianism and Feminism," *Women: A Journal of Liberation*, 3, no. 1 (1972): 36.

53. Atkinson, *Amazon Odyssey*, 83.

54. Ibid., 132.

55. Caroline Lund, "Female Liberation and Socialism, An Interview," in Jenness, *Feminism and Socialism*, 13.

56. Frances Beal, "Double Jeopardy: To Be Black and Female," in Cooke and Bunch-Weeks, *The New Women*, 55.

57. Francesca Flores, quoted by Mirta Vidal, in her essay "Chicanas Speak Out—New Voices of La Raza," in Jenness, *Feminism and Socialism*, 57.

58. Evelyn Reed, "In Defense of Engels on the Matriarchy," in Jenness, *Feminism and Socialism*, 110.

59. Evelyn Reed, *The Myth of Women's Inferiority* (Boston: New England Free Press, n.d.), 66.

60. Friedrich Engels proposed this theory in 1884 in *The Origins of the Family, Private Property and the State*, trans. from the German by Ernest Untermann (Chicago: Charles Kerr, 1902); this is the edition cited by Kate Millett in *Sexual Politics*.

61. Marie-Alice Waters, "Are Feminism and Socialism Related?" in Jenness, *Feminism and Socialism*, 21.

62. Dianne Feeley, "The Family," in Jenness, *Feminism and Socialism*, chap. 7, 73.

63. Ibid., 78.

64. Fern Winston, "The Family—Is It Obsolete?" *Political Affairs* (August 1971): 62.

65. Angela Davis, "Angela Davis on Black Women," *Ms.* 1, no. 2 (August 1972): 55–59.

66. Vidal, "Chicanas Speak Out," 53–54.

67. Beal, "Double Jeopardy," 51.

68. Betsey Stone, "Women and Political Power," in Jenness, *Feminism and Socialism*, 27.

69. Socialist Workers party, "Towards a Mass Feminist Movement," in Jenness, *Feminism and Socialism*, 153.

70. Lucy Komisar, "Confidential Report to the NOW Governing Board on the Activities of the Socialist Workers Party and the Young Socialist Alliance," undated.

71. Vivian Rothstein and Naomi Weisstein, "Chicago Women's Liberation Union," in Grimstad and Rennie, *The New Women's Survival Catalog,* 203.

CHAPTER 5: A FEMINIST THEORY OF ANDROGYNY

1. Mary Daly, in her third book, *Gyn/Ecology* (1978), declares that she solemnly rejects the term *androgyny*, as a "false word," but she also affirms that she remains faithful to the ideas she expressed in *Beyond God the Father*, ideas that, in her mind at that time (1973), could be covered by the word *androgyny. Gyn/ Ecology*, xi.
2. Heilbrun, *Toward a Recognition of Androgyny.*
3. Ibid., xii.
4. Ibid., 22.
5. J. B. Pontalis, "L'insaisissable entre-deux. Bisexualité et différence des sexes," *Nouvelle revue française de psychanalyse* 7 (Spring 1973): 15.
6. Greer, *The Female Eunuch,* 19.
7. Zella Luria, "Genre et étiquetage: L'effet Pirandello," in collected papers delivered at a colloquium entitled "Le fait féminin" held in Paris in September 1976, published as *Le fait féminin* under the editorial direction of Evelyn Sullerot, 234.
8. Ibid., 234.
9. All are psychology professors. At the time when these works were published, Phyllis Chesler was teaching at Richmond University College, Staten Island, N.Y.; Zella Luria was on the faculty of Tufts University in Massachusetts; Eleanor Maccoby was at Stanford University in California; and Naomi Weisstein was at Loyola University in Chicago.
10. Eleanor Maccoby, paper published in French as "La psychologie des sexes: implications pour les rôles adultes," in Sullerot, *Le fait féminin*, 244, 245.
11. Daly, *Beyond God the Father,* 2.
12. Chesler, *Women and Madness,* 25.
13. Ibid., 15–16.
14. Ibid., 243.
15. Ibid., 29.
16. Thomas Szasz, cited by Chesler, *Women and Madness,* 40.
17. Greer, *The Female Eunuch,* 61.
18. Ti-Grace Atkinson, cited by Greer, *The Female Eunuch,* 166.
19. Marie Bonaparte, *Female Sexuality* (1953); reprint, New York: Grove Press, 1965) cited by Millett, *Sexual Politics,* 204. Millett reminds us that it was in a letter to Marie Bonaparte that Freud made his famous admission, "the great question . . . which I have not been able to answer, despite my thirty years of research into the feminine soul, is 'What does a woman want?' "
20. Chesler, *Women and Madness,* 31.
21. In their descriptions of a "glass ball" or "bell jar," Ellen West and Sylvia Plath used the same image to refer to the same closed world.

22. Daly, *Beyond God the Father*, 6.
23. Greer, *The Female Eunuch*, 5.
24. Among the terms Mary Daly rejected in *Gyn/Ecology* (see chap. 5, n. 1) was the word *God*, because of its "male/masculine imagery" and anthropomorphism. *Gyn/Ecology*, xi.
25. Daly, *Beyond God the Father*, 68.
26. Yates, *What Women Want*, 179.
27. Letty Cottin Pogrebin, "Down with Sexist Upbringing," *Ms.* (Spring 1972): 18.
28. Alix Kates Shulman, a member of the Redstockings, was married according to a contract that stipulated an equal sharing of domestic and parental responsibilities between the spouses.
29. Greer, *The Female Eunuch*, 8.
30. Ibid., 12.

CHAPTER 6: FEMINIST LITERARY CRITICISM

1. Bonnie Zimmerman, "What Has Never Been: An Overview of Lesbian Feminist Literary Criticism," *Feminist Studies* 7, no. 3 (Autumn 1981): 451.
2. Nancy Hoffman, Cynthia Secor, and Adrian Tinsley, eds., *Female Studies VI: Closer to the Ground* (Old Westbury, N.Y.: The Feminist Press, 1972), 100.
3. Ellmann, *Thinking about Women*, 55.
4. Paula Marshall, "The Negro Woman in American Literature," in Exum, *Keeping the Faith*, 33.
5. Ellmann, *Thinking about Women*, 68.
6. Millett, *Sexual Politics*, 16.
7. Ibid., 335.
8. Simone de Beauvoir, *Le deuxième sexe* (1949), 13.
9. Phyllis Franklin, "Traditional Literary Study. In the Subjunctive Mood," in Hoffman, Secor, and Tinsley, *Female Studies VI*, 45.
10. Ellmann, *Thinking about Women*, 29.
11. Cynthia Ozick, "The Demise of the Dancing Dog," in Cooke and Bunch-Weeks, *The New Women*, 12.
12. Kimberley Snow, "Images of Women in the American Novel," *Aphra* 2, no. 1 (Winter 1950): 67.
13. American feminists like to recall the sexist aphorism of Doctor Samuel Johnson, the eighteenth-century English writer, who, in reference to a woman preacher, declared that she reminded him of "a dog trained to dance on its hind legs." The anecdote is reported by Mary Ellmann, Cynthia Ozick, and Cheri Register.
14. Cheri Register, "American Feminist Literary Criticism: A Bibliographical Introduction," in Donovan, *Feminist Literary Criticism*, 19.
15. Firestone, *The Dialectic of Sex*, chap. 6, 158.
16. Josephine Donovan, "Afterword: Critical Revision," in her *Feminist Literary Criticism*, 80.

17. Throughout the late 1970s and the 1980s, feminist literary critics, notably Sandra Gilbert and Susan Gubar, studied and reinterpreted women's literary works. Thus were born what Elaine Showalter has called gynocritics. See Ginette Castro, "La critique littéraire féministe: une nouvelle lecture du roman féminin," *Revue française d'études américaines*, no. 30, November 1986.
18. Anne-Marie Houdebine, "Les femmes et la langue," *Tel Quel* 74 (Winter 1977): 88.
19. Hélène Cixous, " 'La,' ou l'avènement de la femme," proposals collected by Jean-Louis de Rambures, *Le Monde*, 9 April 1976, 20.

CHAPTER 7: A SYNTHESIS OF RECONCILIATION

1. Charlotte Bunch, "Two Feminists Tell How They Work," interviews with Gloria Steinem, *Ms.* 6, no. 1 (July 1977): 92.
2. Friedan, *It Changed My Life*, 115.
3. Freeman, *The Politics of Women's Liberation*, 142.
4. Friedan, *It Changed My Life*, 163.
5. Hite, *The Hite Report*, 303.
6. "Un entretien avec Alain Touraine—'Le moment de l'utopie s'achève'—," an interview with Alain Touraine conducted by Bruno Frappat, the French newspaper *Le Monde*, 19–20 November 1978, 24.
7. Survey cited by Freeman, *The Politics of Women's Liberation*, 92.

CHAPTER 8: THE INSTRUMENT AND PHILOSOPHY OF ACTION

1. At least, "moribund" was the impression I received of the NWP at the time of my visit to Alva Belmont House in July 1977. The library was closed. The secretaries, although pleasant to visitors, knew nothing about the organization. The president was nowhere to be seen.
2. These feminist retreats were inspired by the disappointment that feminists had found in communal living experiments, which reproduced the sexual polarization of the society they were criticizing.
3. We are particularly thinking of the feminist members of the Communications Workers, the Amalgamated Clothing Workers, and the Teamsters' Union.
4. The First Convention of Chicanas had taken place in 1971. It brought together 600 women in Houston, Texas.
5. Lindsy Van Gelder, "Four Days That Changed the World," *Ms.* 6, no. 9 (March 1978): 89.
6. White women represented 64.5 percent of the delegates, whereas they constituted 84.4 percent of the national female population at that time. Middle- and upper-income women (defined as having an annual family income of more than

$20,000) represented 14.1 percent of the delegates, while they constituted 25.7 percent of the national female population. Statistics given by Lindsy Van Gelder in her article "Four Days That Changed the World," 52.

7. Ellie Smeal, quoted in an interview by Susan Dworkin, "Ellie Smeal Brings NOW Up To Date," *Ms.* (February 1978): 64.

8. Lindsy Van Gelder, "Four Days That Changed the World," 52.

9. Starting with Ellie Smeal, the president and national officers of NOW have always received a salary, on the principle that only women who had their own income could afford to give time to the organization.

10. Cassell, *A Group Called Women*, 128.

11. Carol Hanisch, "What Can Be Learned. A Critique of the Miss America Protest," in Leslie B. Tanner, ed., *Voices from Women's Liberation* (New York: New American Library, 1970), 134.

12. A member of the New York Radical Feminists then living underground, whose name is withheld to protect her privacy, personal letter to the author dated 10 March 1979.

13. Grimstad and Rennie, *The New Woman's Survival Sourcebook*, vii.

14. Ibid., 161.

CHAPTER 9: GUERRILLA WARRIORS FOR CONSCIOUSNESS-RAISING

1. The Bridal Fair sold the dream image of marriage, beautiful bridal gowns and wedding gift lists of expensive luxury items. Enthralled by the fair's enticing atmosphere, brides and their mothers bought eagerly, tending to overspend in order to prove their worth in the marriage market.

2. New York Radical Women, "No More Miss America!" leaflet distributed August 1968.

3. According to a Harris poll of 1975, only 17 percent of American women interviewed had a positive view of the Women's movement, whereas 65 percent of them approved, on the whole, of actions "to strengthen and change women's status in society."

4. "The New Feminism," supplement to the *Ladies' Home Journal* of August 1970.

5. Arkansas, California, Colorado, Delaware, Georgia, Kansas, Maryland, New Mexico, North Carolina, Oregon, South Carolina, and Virginia.

6. An independent organization founded in 1968 by the abortion committee of the New York chapter of NOW. This organization used a blank sheet of paper as a symbolic model of the new abortion law.

7. Planned Parenthood, the Board of Managers of Church Women United, the Board of Trustees of the American Medical Association, the Young Women's Christian Association.

8. NOW leaflet entitled "De-sexegrate Wall Street," distributed in New York during the Feminist Days of August 1973.

9. Anne Kainen, "Now—Not Later," unpublished text in the collection of the author, 7 pp.

CHAPTER 10: FEMINISM AND THE LAW

1. "Houston: A Reaffirmation for NWPC," editorial, *Women's Political Times* 2, no. 4 (Winter 1977): 2.
2. Elinor Langer, "Why Big Business Is Trying to Defeat the ERA: The Economic Implications of Equality," *Ms.* 4, no. 1 (May 1976): 106.
3. Jo Freeman, "Women at the 1988 Democratic Convention," *Off Our Backs* (October 1988): 5.
4. "Mr. President, Thank You, But," editorial, *Women's Political Times* 2, no. 1 (Winter 1977): 2.
5. Yet, the requirement for equal division by sex does not apply to superdelegates (members of Congress and governors) whose presence "still tips the balance in favor of males. The 1984 Democratic party convention had 50 more men than women delegates, and in 1988, there were over a hundred more men." *Off Our Backs* (October 1988): 4.
6. Women United to Defend Existing Rights.
7. Langer, "Why Big Business," 102.
8. "ERA Down the Wire," *Women's Political Times*, 2, no. 2 (Spring 1977): 2.
9. Lindsy Van Gelder, "The 400,000 Voter Misunderstanding," *Ms.* 4, no. 9 (March 1976): 67.
10. Diane Fitzgerald, "Liberal Leaders Plan Counter to Right," *Women's Political Times* 3, no. 2 (Summer 1978): 5.
    The participants were Gloria Steinem for *Ms.*; Mildred Jeffrey for the NWPC; Ellie Smeal for NOW; Ben Albert and Victor Kramber for the AFL-CIO; Carl Wagner for the American Federation of State, County, and Municipal Employees; Jim Farner for the Coalition of American Public Employees; the Democratic senator from New Hampshire, Thomas J. McIntyre; Russ Hemenway for the National Committee for an Effective Congress; Joyce Hamlin for the United Methodist church; Carol Costin for Network, and Wes McCuun, a researcher who had specialized for sixteen years in studying right-wing political activities.
11. National Organization for Women, "Declaration of a State of Emergency," March 1978.
12. The NOW boycott was aimed at Alabama, Arizona, Arkansas, Florida, Georgia, Illinois, Louisiana, Mississippi, Missouri, Nevada, North Carolina, Oklahoma, South Carolina, Utah, and Virginia.
13. Berry, *Why ERA Failed,* 106.
14. Cited by Roberta Brandes Gratz in "Never Again! Never Again?" *Ms.* 6, no. 1 (July 1977): 54.
15. Among these were the Alliance against Sexual Coercion, in Cambridge, Massachusetts, and the Working Women United Institute, in New York.

16. U.S. Department of Labor, *Handbook on Women Workers*, Bulletin 297 (Washington, D.C.: U.S. Government Printing Office, 1975), 300.
17. "Femmes, féminisme et recherches," colloquium held in Toulouse, France, 17, 18, and 19 December 1982.
18. These two cases concerned so-called protective legislation, claiming that such laws actually imposed a handicap on women by their provisions forbidding women to lift certain weights and to work overtime.
19. The Women's Work Project, *Women Organizing the Office* (Washington, D.C.: Women in Distribution, 1979).
20. Tepperman, *Not Servants, Not Machines*, 92. Wendy Stevens, "Women Organizing the Office," *Off Our Backs* 9, no. 4 (April 1979): 10.

CHAPTER 11: ALTERNATIVE INSTITUTIONS

1. Peggy Kornegger, "Anarchism: The Feminist Connection," *The Second Wave* 4, no. 1 (Spring 1975): 32.
2. This expression was spread in the movement by Marge Piercy's novel, *Small Changes* (Greenwich, Conn.: Fawcett, 1973).
3. *The Second Wave* offered free subscriptions to women in prison and low-income women on request.
4. *Ms.* 5, no. 1 (July 1976): 5.
5. *Ms.* 4, no. 8 (February 1976): 44.
6. *Ms.* 4, no. 11 (May 1976): 40.
7. Since 1987, following the change of ownership of *Ms.*, this department has been called "The *Ms.* Reporter."
8. Katherine Power and Susan Saxe, "Underground in America," *Off Our Backs* 1, no. 20 (15 April 1971): 3. Also see the supplement to the *San Francisco Women's Art Center Newsletter*, dated March 1975, devoted to the women of the Weather Underground Organization.
9. Kathryn Allen, et al., director, *Self-Health* (San Francisco, The Multi-Media Resource Center, 1974).
10. Denise Bostram and Jane Warrenbrand, directors, *Healthcaring: From Our End of the Speculum* (New York: Women Make Movies Inc., 1976).
11. *Sister* (July 1973).
12. See the "Health" section in *The New Woman's Survival Sourcebook*, 36.
13. CHOICE stood for Concern for Health Options: Information, Care and Education.
14. Records of Santa Cruz Birth Center, as reported by Jackie Christeve in "Midwives Busted in Santa Cruz," *The Second Wave* (Summer 1984): 5.
15. The rate of perineal tearing in the Santa Cruz Center was reported as 6.6 percent in 1973, compared with an episiotomy rate of 73 percent in American hospitals.
16. 1973 U.S. infant mortality rate figures reported by Christeve, "Midwives Busted," from an unnamed source. The U.S. National Center for Health Statistics

reported 16.7 deaths per thousand in 1975 for infants under one year; if infant mortality is examined for the first seven days after birth, the USCHS figures show 39.2 infant deaths per thousand in 1975.

17. *Eurostat: Basic Statistics of the European Community and Comparisons with Canada, the US, Japan and the URSS*, 25th ed. (Luxembourg: Publications Office of the European Economic Community, 1988).

18. "Feminist Karate Union," in Grimstad and Rennie, *The New Woman's Survival Catalog*, 157.

19. Betsy Warrior, "Battered Lives," *The Second Wave* 4, no. 2 (Fall 1975): 8.

20. Work Incentive Program, established by amendments to the Social Security laws in 1967 and 1971.

21. Vicki Breitbart, *Day Care, Who Cares?* (Boston: New England Free Press, n.d.), 1.

22. In French in the English text, Hole and Levine, *Rebirth of Feminism*, 308.

23. "Ventures In Day Care," quoted by Grimstad and Rennie in *The New Woman's Survival Catalog*, 95.

24. *Double-F* referred to the "effeminist" movement and was also the name of its publication. This group felt that the term *effeminist* was more appropriate to them as nonsexist men than the term *feminist*. It also was a witty self-parody on "flaming faggots," men of nonvirile appearance, homosexual or not, who are assumed to be so by the patriarchal society. (Incidentally, did the term *flaming faggots* originate in the burning of homosexuals at the stake, like witches? We wonder.)

25. The titles are: *Martin's Father, Did You Ever, Joshua's Day, The Sheep Book, The Magic Hat,* and *Jo, Flo and Yolanda*.

26. "The Feminist Press," in Grimstad and Rennie, *The New Woman's Survival Catalog*, 11.

27. "Kids' Books: Independence Is Just a Stage," Gazette News, *Ms.* 7, no. 1 (July 1978): 22.

28. The Feminist Press published *Who's Who and Where in Women's Studies* in 1974 and also established the monthly review, *Women's Studies Newsletter* and *Women's Studies Quarterly*. Since 1974, *Women's Studies Quarterly* has provided important coverage of events in women's studies and feminist education; several special issues have been devoted to international conferences on women's studies.

29. Florence Howe, "No Ivory Towers Need Apply: Women's Studies," *Ms.* 2, no. 3 (September 1973): 79.

30. Sally Wagner presented her thesis at the University of California at Sacramento, on "The Social Construction of Female Sexual Experience." Karen Rofkin presented hers at the University of California at Santa Cruz, on "That Word Is Liberty: A Biography of Matilda Joslyn Gage." The degree both women earned is "Doctor of Philosophy in the History of Consciousness, Women's Studies."

31. Hester Eisenstein, "Women's Studies at Barnard College: Alive and Well and Living in New York," *Women's Studies Newsletter* 6, no. 3 (Summer 1978): 5.

32. Howe, "No Ivory Towers," 47.

33. Cited by Howe, "No Ivory Towers," 80.
34. *Women's Studies Newsletter* 6, no. 2 (Spring 1978): 4, 5.
35. Berenice A. Caroll, "Women's Studies and Women in the Community," and Melanie Kaye, "Close-up on Women's Studies Courses: Feminist Theory and Practice," *Women's Studies Newsletter* 6, no. 3 (Summer 1978): 15–23.
36. This course attracted fifty students, including forty-five women and five men, of whom twenty-three were black or Latino minorities and twenty-seven were white. The women included three lesbians. (Information provided by a personal letter from the instructor, dated 10 March 1979.)
37. Vivian Rothstein and Naomi Weisstein, "Chicago Liberation School for Women," *Women: A Journal of Liberation* 2, no. 4 (1972): 5.
38. While waiting to find a location for the school, Breakaway classes met in various women's own homes.
39. Adrienne Rich, quoted by Harriet Lyons in "Woman's Art: It's the Only Goddam Energy Around," *Ms.* 6, no. 6 (December 1977): 41.
40. *Three Lives,* directed by Susan Kleckner, Robin Mide, and Kate Millett (New York: Impact Films, 1971).
41. Cited in an interview by Ellen Freyer, "Nell Cox: Feminist Filmmaker," *The Feminist Art Journal* 6, no. 2 (Summer 1977): 34.
42. Isabel Castellano, director, *El Conflicto de Ruth* (New York: Women Make Movies, Inc., 1975).
43. Artists In Residence, 97 Wooster Street, New York.
44. "Chicago Women's Graphics Collective," in Grimstad and Rennie, *The New Woman's Survival Catalog,* 55.
45. "Health Care Is For People, Not For Profit," Chicago Women's Graphics Collective.
46. "Frustration," Chicago Women's Graphics Collective.
47. Anne Pride, "Getting The Business," in Grimstad and Rennie, *The New Woman's Survival Sourcebook,* 24–26.
48. The First Women's Bank and Trust Company, thought to be the first of its kind, was founded in 1974 in New York with a capital of $4 million. It went through many difficulties, but was still surviving in 1989.

CONCLUSION

1. Cited in Susanne M. Bianchi and Daphne Spain, *American Women: The Decades of Change* (U.S. Department of Commerce, Bureau of the Census, August 1983).
2. Robert H. Haveman, "New Policy for the New Poverty," *Challenge* (September–October 1988): 30.
3. This happened in the long battle for the Nineteenth Amendment when some suffragists used xenophobic arguments, asserting that the votes of women would counterbalance those of immigrants and would guarantee white supremacy in the South. See Flexner, *Century of Struggle,* chap. 22.

Bibliography

Books and Pamphlets

Allen, Pamela. *Free Space*. Washington, D.C.: Times Change Press, 1970.

Atkinson, Ti-Grace. *Amazon Odyssey*. New York: Links Books, 1974.

Ballorain, Rolande. *Le nouveau féminisme américain*. Paris: Denoël-Gonthier, 1972.

Bambara, Toni Cade, ed. *The Black Woman*. New York: New American Library, 1970.

Beard, Mary. *Woman as Force in History*. New York: Macmillan, 1946.

Beauvoir, Simone de. *Le deuxième sexe*. 2 vols. Paris: Gallimard, "Coll. Soleil," 1949.

————. *The Second Sex*. Translated from French (*Le deuxième sexe*) by H. M. Parshley. London: Jonathan Cape, 1969.

Berry, Mary Frances. *Why ERA Failed*. Indianapolis: Indiana University Press, 1986.

Bird, Caroline. *Born Female: The High Cost of Keeping Women Down*. New York: David McKay, 1968, revised ed. 1970.

Boston Women's Health Collective (The). *Our Bodies, Ourselves*. 1970. Reprint. New York: Simon & Schuster, 1973.

Brownmiller, Susan. *Against Our Will: Men, Women and Rape*. New York: Simon & Schuster, 1975.

Cassell, Joan. *A Group Called Women. Sisterhood and Symbolism in the Feminist Movement*. New York: David McKay, 1977.

Chesler, Phyllis. *Women and Madness*. 1972. Reprint. New York: Avon Books, 1973.

Cooke, Joanne, and Bunch-Weeks, Charlotte, eds. *The New Women: A Motive Anthology on Women's Liberation*. Indianapolis, Ind.: Bobbs-Merrill, 1970.

Daly, Mary. *The Church and the Second Sex*. 1968. Reprint. New York: Harper Colophon Books, 1975.

————. *Beyond God the Father: Toward a Philosophy of Women's Liberation*. 1973. Reprint. Boston: Beacon Press Paperbacks, 1974.

————. *Gyn/Ecology*. Boston: Beacon Press, 1978.

Davis, Elizabeth Gould. *The First Sex*. 1971. Reprint. Baltimore: Penguin Books, 1972.

Densmore, Dana. *Sex Roles and Female Oppression*. Boston: New England Free Press, n.d.

Donovan, Josephine, ed. *Feminist Literary Criticism, Explorations in Theory.* Lexington, Ky.: The University Press of Kentucky, 1975.

Ellmann, Mary. *Thinking about Women.* New York: Harcourt, Brace and World, 1968.

Exum, Pat Crutchfield, ed. *Keeping the Faith: Writings by Contemporary Black Women.* Greenwich, Conn.: Fawcett, 1974.

Firestone, Shulamith. *The Dialectic of Sex: The Case for Feminist Revolution.* New York: Morrow, 1970; London: The Woman's Press, 1979.

Flexner, Eleanor. *Century of Struggle.* Cambridge, Mass.: Belknap Press of Harvard University Press, 1959.

Freeman, Jo. *The Politics of Women's Liberation.* New York: David McKay, 1975.

Friedan, Betty. *The Feminine Mystique.* 1963. Reprint. Harmondsworth, England: Penguin Books, 1986.

———. *It Changed My Life.* New York: Random House, 1976.

Greer, Germaine. *The Female Eunuch.* 1970. Reprint. New York: McGraw-Hill, 1971.

Grimstad, Kirsten, and Rennie, Susan, eds. *The New Woman's Survival Catalog.* New York: Coward, McCann and Geoghegan, 1973.

———. *The New Woman's Survival Sourcebook.* New York: Alfred A. Knopf, 1975.

Heilbrun, Carolyn. *Toward a Recognition of Androgyny.* 1973. Reprint. New York: Harper Colophon Books, 1974.

Herschberger, Ruth. *Adam's Rib.* 1948. Reprint. New York: Harper and Row, 1970.

Hite, Shere. *The Hite Report: A Nationwide Survey of Female Sexuality.* New York: Macmillan, 1976.

Hole, Judith, and Levine, Ellen. *Rebirth of Feminism.* 1971. Reprint. New York: Quadrangle Books, 1973.

Jenness, Linda, ed. *Feminism and Socialism.* 1973. Reprint. New York: Pathfinder Press, 1976.

Jones, Beverly, and Brown, Judith. *Toward a Female Liberation Movement.* Boston: New England Free Press, 1968.

Koedt, Anne. *The Myth of the Vaginal Orgasm.* Boston: New England Free Press, 1970.

Komarovsky, Mirra. *Women in the Modern World. Their Education and their Dilemmas.* Boston: Little, Brown, 1953.

Lakoff, Robin. *Language and Woman's Place.* New York: Harper and Row, 1975.

Lerner, Gerda. *The Grimké Sisters from South Carolina: Pioneers for Women's Rights and Abolition.* 1967. Reprint. New York: Schocken Books, 1973.

Lutz, Alma. *Susan B. Anthony, Rebel, Crusader, Humanitarian.* Boston: Beacon Press, 1959.

Masnata-Rubattel, Claire. *La révolte des Américaines.* Paris: Aubier-Montaigne, 1972.

Miller, Casey, and Swift, Kate. *Words and Women.* New York: Anchor Press/Doubleday, 1977.

Millett, Kate. "Prostitution: A Quartet for Female Voices." In Vivian Gornick and

Barbara K. Moran, eds., *Women in Sexist Society: Studies in Power and Powerlessness*. New York: Basic Books, 1971.

———. *Sexual Politics*. 1970. Reprint. London: Virago Press, 1985.

Mitchell, Juliet. *Psychoanalysis and Feminism*. 1974. Reprint. Harmondsworth, England: Penguin Books, 1975.

Morgan, Robin, ed. *Sisterhood Is Powerful*. New York: Vintage Books, 1970.

———. *Going Too Far: The Personal Chronicle of a Feminist*. New York: Random House, 1977.

Myrdal, Alva, and Klein, Viola. *Women's Two Roles, Home and Work*. London: Routledge and Kegan Paul, 1956.

Oakley, Mary Ann. *Elizabeth Cady Stanton*. New York: The Feminist Press, 1972.

Pleck, Elizabeth. *Domestic Tyranny: The Making of American Social Policy against Family Violence from Colonial Times to the Present*. New York: Oxford University Press, 1987.

Redstockings. *Feminist Revolution*. New York: Redstockings, 1975.

Sherfey, Mary Jane. *The Nature and Evolution of Female Sexuality*. New York: Random House, 1972.

Sullerot, Evelyne. *Le fait féminin*. Paris: Fayard, 1978.

Tepperman, Jean. *Not Servants, Not Machines. Office Workers Speak Out*. Boston: Beacon Press, 1976.

Wollstonecraft, Mary. *A Vindication of the Rights of Woman*. 1792. Reprint. New York: Norton, 1967.

Women's Press Collective (The). *Lesbians Speak Out*. Oakland, Calif.: The Women's Press Collective, 1974.

Yates, Gayle Graham. *What Women Want. The Ideas of the Women's Movement*. Cambridge, Mass.: Harvard University Press, 1975.

Periodicals of the New Feminist Movement

Aphra. New York, 1970–1976.

Big Mama Rag. Denver, 6, no. 5, May 1977.

Female State (The), A Journal of Female Liberation. Cambridge, Mass., Cell 16, no. 4, April 1970.

Female Studies VI. Closer to the Ground. Old Westbury, New York, The Feminist Press, 1972.

Ms. New York, 1972–1984.

National NOW Times. Washington, D.C., 1979.

Off Our Backs. Washington, D.C., 7, no. 6, July–August 1977; 9, no. 4, April 1979.

The Second Wave. Cambridge, Mass., 1974–1978.

Women: A Journal of Liberation. Baltimore, 1972–1974.

Women's Political Times. Washington, D.C., 1976–1979.

Women's Review of Books. Wellesley Center for Research on Women, Wellesley, 1, no. 3, December 1983.

Women's Studies Newsletter. Old Westbury, N.Y., 1978–1979.

Federal Government Publications

Bureau of the Census. *American Woman: Three Decades of Change.* U.S. Government Printing Office, 1983.

The President's Commission on the Status of Women. *American Women.* Washington, D.C.: U.S. Government Printing Office, 1963.

The Women's Bureau. 1969 *Handbook on Women Workers.* Washington, D.C.: U.S. Government Printing Office, 1969.

The Women's Bureau. 1975 *Handbook on Women Workers.* Washington, D.C.: U.S. Government Printing Office, 1975.

The Women's Bureau. *Equal Employment Opportunity for Women: U.S. Policies.* Washington, D.C.: U.S. Government Printing Office, 1982.

Index

Abolitionist movement, 10, 28, 29
Abortion rights, 120, 176, 196, 200, 201,
202, 229, 257; and conflict within
NOW, 62; and egalitarian feminism, 47;
evolution of actions for, 264, 266, 268;
and feminist guerrilla action, 191–93;
and feminist health clinics, 230–31; and
"feminization of poverty," 259; and the
law, 205, 212–14, 269, 270; and radical
feminist theory, 77
Abreu, Lucile, 177
Abzug, Bella, 48, 63, 121, 195, 200, 204
Action Committee for Decent Child Care,
236
Action, instrument and philosophy of, 173–
86
Adamnan, 28
Adams, John, 28
Adam's Rib (Herschberger), 13–14, 21
Advertising, 189, 225–26
AFL-CIO, 266, 269
Against Our Will (Brownmiller), 40–41, 194
Ain't I A Woman? (periodical), 265
AIR Gallery, 248–49
Allen, Pam, 22, 187
Altamira, cave paintings of, 27
Alternative institutions, 260; anti-rape
movement, 232–34; communications
network, 223–24; feminist art move-
ment, 246–50; feminist businesses,
250–54; feminist child-care centers and
play groups, 235–37; feminist media,
224–27; nonsexist children's books,
237–40; schools of feminism, 244–46;
"self-health" institutions, 228–32; wom-
en's centers, 227–28
Amazonism, 34
Amazon Odyssey, 102
Amazon Quarterly, 224

"American Feminist Literary Criticism"
(Register), 154
American Indian Women's Leadership Con-
ference, 267
American Law Institute, 192, 193
American Legion, 207
American Library Association, 210
American Revolution, 28
American Woman Suffrage Association, 31
American Women (Presidential Commission
on the Status of Women report), 17–18,
51, 263
Anatolia, 33, 34
"And Ain't I a Woman" (Sojourner Truth),
30–31
Andelin, Helen, 206
Androgyny, feminist theory of, 65, 147,
162, 164, 235, 261; background and ten-
ets of, 125–40; revolution envisaged by,
140–46; and spirit of reconciliation,
163, 166, 167
Anthony, Susan B., 32
Antifeminist backlash, 178, 205–12, 222
Aphra, 224, 253
Arcadia, 35
Aristophanes, 127
Art, 88; feminist movement in, 246–50
Artemis Child Experience Center, 237
Artificial reproduction, 91, 93, 98
Association for the Study of Abortion, 191
Association for Women in Psychology, 174
Association of American Law Schools, 219
Association of Mexican-American Women,
267
Association to Repeal Abortion Laws, 191
Astronauts, 268, 269
Atkinson, Ti-Grace, 64, 67, 68, 70–72, 74,
75, 76, 80, 81, 82, 83–84, 85, 91, 92,
93, 94, 97, 100, 101–2, 103, 105, 108,

289

Chicago Women's Liberation Union (CWLU), 122, 174, 220, 236, 245
Chicana women, 112, 117, 265
Childbirth, 13, 91, 231–32
Child care centers, 58, 59, 91, 200; feminist, 235–37; and feminist radical ideology, 119
Child Care Resource Center at Cambridge, 236
Child rearing, 47, 57, 58, 134, 142–43, 167, 204; and feminist radical ideology, 119; and radical feminist ideology, 91, 98. *See also* Motherhood
Children's books, nonsexist, 237–40
Chisholm, Shirley, 48, 121, 204, 266
CHOICE, 230
Christ, 46, 49, 52, 53
Christianity. *See* Catholic church; Judeo-Christian tradition; Religion, organized; Theological arguments
Church, Frank, 63
Church and the Second Sex, The (Daly), 49, 53, 89, 140
CIA (Central Intelligence Agency), 63, 101, 105
Circumcision, 130
Cité des dames, La (de Pisan), 46
City planning, 60–61, 99
Civil Rights Act of 1964, Title VII of, 18, 19, 215, 216, 263
Cleaver, Eldridge, 41
Clitoral orgasm, 14, 24, 75
Clitoridectomy, 138
Clitoris, 136, 138, 229
Coalition of Labor Union Women (CLUW), 181, 267
Colombo, Joseph, 102
Comisión Feminil Mexicana Nacional, 265
Commissions on the Status of Women, 17–19, 50, 51, 263
Committee on Women in Legal Education, 219
Communications network, 223–24
Communists, 109, 115
Connelly, Laure, 225
Consciousness-raising, 104, 118, 160, 162, 179, 181, 234; and guerrilla action, 187–98; and media, 227; theory and ap-

plication of, 22–25; and women's studies programs, 240, 241
Consensus, 162–69
Contraception, 47, 62, 229. *See also* Reproduction, control of
Copernicus, 11, 12
Cox, Nell, 247
COYOTE (Cut Out Your Old Tired Ethics), 266
Crater, Flora, 200
Credibility, 208
Credit, 204, 210, 252–53, 267
Cultural oppression, 24–25
Cultural revolution, radical feminist view of, 92, 95–98
Culture, radical feminist analysis of, 67, 86–88
Cummings, Anne Flower, 232, 252
Cyrus, Della D., 13

Daly, Mary, 31–32, 45–46, 48–49, 52–53, 56, 60, 81, 89–90, 125, 129–30, 132, 135, 138, 140, 141–42, 143, 162, 164, 166, 223
Darwin, Charles, 33
Daughters, Inc., 251, 266
Daughters of Bilitis, 66, 106
Daughters of the American Revolution, 207
Davis, Angela, 102, 111, 116
Davis, Elizabeth Gould, 26, 27, 32–36, 42
Davis, Rebecca Harding, 241
De Bretteville, Sheila, 248
De Crow, Karen, 201
Dekkers, Onka, 226
Delta Women's Clinic, 230
Demeter and Persephone, myth of, 133–34
Densmore, Dana, 72, 90, 92, 93, 105, 163, 166
Department of Health, Education, and Welfare (HEW), 217
Depression in women, 135
Deutsch, Helene, 128
Dialectical materialism, 36–42, 68
Dialectic of Sex, The (Firestone), 36–38, 86, 98–99
Diana Press, 251, 253, 266
Dick and Jane as Victims, 237–38
Dickinson, Emily, 156
Divorce, 182, 210, 252

Doe v. Bolton, 193
Dole, Elizabeth, 203, 205
Domestic Tyranny: The Making of American Social Policy against Family Violence from Colonial Times to the Present (Pleck), 235
Domestic violence, 234–35
Donovan, Josephine, 145, 160
Double-F Movement, 237
Dworkin, Andrea, 220
Dworkin, Susan, 180

Earhart, Amelia, 239
Eaubonne, Françoise d', 23
Economic revolution, radical feminist view of, 94–95
Edelson, Mary Beth, 248–49
Edhlund, Sandra, 252
Education, 118, 167, 266, 267; and egalitarian feminist ideology, 58, 59, 62; and feminist child care, 235–37; and post-Freudian theory, 11–13, 14, 15; and schools of feminism, 244–46; and women's studies, 223, 240–45, 264, 265, 266
Egalitarian feminism, 122, 123, 146, 162, 163, 183, 205; dissension within, 61–62; and employment issues, 24, 46–48, 50–52, 61, 62, 65, 102; and exorcism of myths, 53–57; and feminist radicalism, 120, 121; and lesbianism, 108; radical feminism compared with, 67, 68, 80–81, 90, 100–101; radical feminists' judgment of, 102–5; and reformism, 48–50; revolution envisaged by, 57–61; and spirit of reconciliation, 164, 165, 166, 167, 168, 256, 257, 258; and women's history, 26; Women's movement judged by, 62–65
Ehrenreich, Barbara, 180, 230
Ehrhardt, Anke, 127
Einstein, Hester, 240
El Conflicto de Ruth, 247
Electra complex, 79, 98
Elitism, accusations of, 62–63, 145, 258
Ellmann, Mary, 145, 150–51, 152, 153, 156–57
Emma Goldman Clinic, 230
Employment issues, 116, 167, 207, 221–22;

and egalitarian feminists, 24, 46–48, 50–52, 61, 62, 65, 102; feminist radical analysis of, 118; and "feminization of poverty," 259; and legal action, 215–22; and myths about working women, 53–54; and postwar feminism, 7–9; and radical feminist ideology, 92, 102; and wage gap, 260
Engels, Friedrich, 37, 38, 79, 113, 115, 119, 120
English, Deirdre, 230
Epic form, 30–31
Episcopalian church, 268
Equal Credit Opportunity Act (1974, amended 1976), 204, 210, 252–53, 267
Equal Employment Opportunity Act, 266
Equal Employment Opportunity Commission (EEOC), 18, 19, 51, 216, 219, 266
Equal Pay Act (1963), 263
Equal Rights, 9, 10
Equal Rights Amendment (ERA), 19, 163, 195, 223, 258; and antifeminist backlash, 205–12; chronology of events related to, 263, 265, 266, 267, 268, 269, 270; and egalitarian feminism, 47–48, 65; and feminist radical program, 119, 121; and "feminization of poverty," 260–61; and labor unions, 61–62, 209, 265, 266; and NOW Proclamation of 1967, 61–62; political factors related to, 200, 201, 202, 205, 215, 217; and postwar feminism, 8–11, 18

ERA. See Equal Rights Amendment (ERA)
ERAmerica, 208–9, 267
Essays on Psychoanalysis (Freud), 153–54
Eternal feminine myth, 53, 60
Ethnic minority women, 196, 258. See also Minority women
Euripides, 126
Evolution, 33, 37, 49

Fair Labor Standards Act (1938), 263
Fall, myth of the, 141, 150
Family, 142–43, 166–67, 259; and egalitarian feminist ideology, 58–59; feminist radical analysis of, 114–15, 118–19; and radical feminist ideology, 67, 78–81; and socialization, 39. See also Child rearing

"Family, The—Is It Obsolete?" (Winston), 115

Farnham, Marynia, 11–12, 13, 16, 128

Fasteau, Brenda Feigen, 196, 228, 265

FBI (Federal Bureau of Investigation), 63, 101

Federal Education Act, Title IX of Amendments to, 217

Federal employment, 216–17

Federally Employed Women (FEW), 174, 181

Feeley, Dianne, 114

Female Eunuch, The (Greer), 145

Female Liberation of Boston, 174

Female Sexuality (Bonaparte), 138

Female Studies, 147, 148

Feminine masochism, theory of, 39

Feminine Mystique, The (Friedan), 14–17, 22, 47, 69, 263

Feminine nature, belief in existence of, 131, 154

Feminine social role, 133–39

Femininity Forum, 206

Feminism. *See* Androgyny, feminist theory of; Egalitarian feminism; Feminist radicalism; Lesbianism, political; Radical feminism

Feminism and Socialism, 67

Feminist Art Journal, 225, 227

Feminist businesses, 250–54

Feminist Economic Network (FEN), 252–53

Feminist Karate Union, 233–34

Feminist law students, 218–20

Feminist literary criticism, 147–61, 162

Feminist Literary Criticism, 147, 160

Feminist media, 224–27

Feminist Press, 238, 239, 240, 242, 266

Feminist radicalism: defined, 21, 66, 67, 68; double or triple allegiance within, 110–12; internal problems in, 122–24; patriarchy as understood in, 112–17; revolution envisaged by, 118–20; Women's movement as judged by, 120–22

Feminist Resources for Schools and Colleges, 242

Feminist socialist radicalism. *See* Feminist radicalism

Feminists, the (group known as), 66, 80,

100, 101, 103, 121, 145, 174,183, 187, 189, 194, 264

Feminists on Children's Media, 175, 237–38

Feminist Studies, 147

Feminist Studio Workshop, 228, 247, 248

Feminist teaching and research, 235–46

"Feminization of poverty," 259–61, 180

Ferraro, Geraldine, 270

FEW. *See* Federally Employed Women (FEW)

Film, 229, 247, 248

Firestone, Shulamith, 20, 36–38, 42, 68, 69, 75, 78, 79–80, 83, 84, 86–88, 89, 91, 92, 95, 96, 97–99, 103, 106, 137, 162, 166, 167, 187

First Sex, The (Davis), 26, 27, 32–36

Fitzgerald, Zelda, 139

Flexner, Eleanor, 31, 32

Flores, Frances, 117

Flying (Millett), 247

Ford, Gerald, 199, 201

Ford Foundation, 239, 259

Franklin, Phyllis, 155

Freeman, Jo, 20, 164, 179, 184, 223

Freeman, Mary Wilkins, 241

Free Space (Allen), 21

Free You, 245

Freud, Sigmund, 12, 13, 15, 52, 74, 137, 138, 152–53

Freudian theory, 39–40, 106, 134, 136; and androgyny theory, 126, 130; and radical feminist ideology, 72, 73, 75, 94

Friedan, Betty, 14–17, 22, 23, 24, 25, 46, 47, 48, 51, 56, 57, 58, 59, 60, 62–65, 100, 145, 162, 163, 164–65, 166, 259, 263

Frigidity, 74–75, 135, 138; and Housewife's Syndrome, 11, 12, 14

Full Employment and Balanced Growth Act, 205

"Functionalist feminists," 14, 15

Fund for the Feminist Majority, 213

Furies, the (group known as), 66, 77–78, 106

Gandhi, Indira, 56–57

Genovese, Kitty, 194

"Getting the Business" (Pride), 250

Kainen, Anne, 197
Kane, Theresa, 269
Kaye, Melanie, 244
Keeping the Faith (Marshall), 151
Kennedy, Florynce, 64
Kennedy, John F., 17, 259, 263
Keys, Martha, 204
Kinsey survey, 12
Kirkpatrick, Jeanne, 203
Kitty Genovese Women's Project, 194, 268
Klein, Viola, 14
Know, Inc., 251
Koedt, Anne, 21, 109
Komarovsky, Mirra, 14, 243
Komisar, Lucy, 122
Koontz, Elizabeth, 54
Kornegger, Peggy, 187, 223
Kreps, Juanita, 205

Labor Law Reform Bill, 209
Labor unions, 10, 32; and ERA, 61–62, 209, 265, 266; and women office workers, 221–22
Ladies' Home Journal, 175, 189–90, 191, 226, 265
Laing, Ronald, 139
Langer, Elinor, 201, 207
Law, 8–9, 41; and abortion rights, 192–93, 212–14; and antifeminist backlash, 205–12; and employment issues, 214–22; and feminist reform platform, 199–200; and political activism, 200–205
Law firms, 252
Lawrence, D. H., 152, 153
Law students, 218–20
Law Women's Caucus (University of Chicago Law School), 219
League of Women Voters, 48, 173, 266
Left. See Political Left
Lerner, Gerda, 28, 242
Lesbian Feminist Liberation, 196–97
Lesbianism, 77, 122, 148, 164, 179, 267; and dissensions in Women's movement, 63, 64; forms of, 123; political, 66–67, 105–10, 122–24
Letters on the Equality of the Sexes and the Condition of Women, The (Grimké), 30
Levine, Ellen, 173, 218, 224, 236
Lewis, Augusta, 32

Liberal feminism. See Egalitarian feminism
"Liberal Takeover of Women's Liberation, The" (Hanisch), 99
Life insurance pensions, 55
Lilith, 225, 226
Lindsay, John, 174
Literary criticism, 147–61, 243
Literature for children, nonsexist, 237–40
Little Miss Muffet Fights Back, 238
Liza's Pioneer Diary (Cox), 247
Lollipop Power, 238–39
Los Angeles Woman's Building, 228, 250, 266
Los Angeles Women's Health Center, 175
Los Angeles Women's Union, 174
Love, 47, 65, 106, 108, 110, 166; in androgynous feminist utopia, 143–44; perversion of, 136, 137–38; radical feminist analysis of, 67, 83–88
Lowell, Massachusetts, women workers of, 32
Lund, Caroline, 111
Lundberg, Ferdinand, 11–12, 13, 16
Luria, Zella, 127–28, 129
Lutz, Alma, 32
Lyndon, Susan, 75
Lyon, Phyllis, 106
Lysistrata, 93

McCarthy, Eugene, 121
McCarthy, Mary, 13, 157
McCarthy era, 11, 109
Maccoby, Eleanor, 54, 128, 134–35
MacKinnon, Catharine A., 220
Maginnis, Patricia, 191
Mailer, Norman, 87, 152, 153, 157
Mainardi, Patricia, 85, 103–4
Manhattan Women's Political Caucus, 194
Mann, Judith, 205
Marriage, 135, 166–67; and androgyny theory, 142, 143; and egalitarian feminist ideology, 58–59; homosexual, 72, 143, 208, 209, 210; and post-Freudian theory of Housewife's Syndrome, 11–13, 15; and radical feminist ideology, 67, 73, 78–81, 92
Marshall, Paula, 151
Martial-arts training, 233–34, 246
Martin, Del, 106, 235

dissension within, 61–62, 66, 176; and ERA, 206, 207, 210–11, 268, 269; founding of, 19, 21, 25, 264; ideology of, 46–47, 48; and media, 189, 190; and political power structure, 200, 201, 203; radical feminist criticism of, 102–3; speaker's service bureau of, 227; and synthesis, 257; and women's studies programs, 242

National Organization of Religious Women, 210

National Research Council, 259

National Right-to-life Committee, 212

National Stop ERA Movement, 206, 208

National strike by women (26 August 1970), 25, 62, 63, 163, 265

National Woman's party (NWP), 8, 9–11, 173, 205

National Women's Agenda, 199

National Women's Conference in Houston (1977), 65, 169, 178, 179, 180, 199–200, 268

National Women's Education Fund, 203

National Women's Political Caucus (NWPC), 120, 173, 174, 178, 181, 195, 200, 201, 203–5, 206, 209, 227, 228, 256–57, 265

National Women's Studies Association (NWSA), 174, 243, 268

Nazi Germany, 39

NBC, 268

Neurosis, 11–12, 14, 16, 139

"Never Again! Never Again?" (Gratz), 212

"New" criticism, 155

New Feminist Talent Agency, 227

"New masculinism," 52

New Right, 201, 211

Newsweek, suit against, 216, 264

New Woman's Survival Catalog, The, 184, 229, 230

New Woman's Survival Sourcebook, The, 184, 185–86, 234, 246

New York Commission on Human Rights, 51

New Yorkers for Abortion Law Repeal, 192

New York Radical Feminists (NYRF), 66, 174, 181, 185, 187, 193–94, 227, 244, 264, 265

New York Radical Women (NYRW), 66, 68, 100, 175, 228, 264

New York Stock Exchange, shock action against, 196

New York Womanschool, 246

New York Women Against Rape, 194

New York Women's Center, 265

Nikulsi, Barbara, 203

1969 Handbook on Women Workers, The, 265

9 to 5, 174, 221, 267

Nixon, Richard, 195, 235

Nonsexist children's books, 237–40

Nonsexist Curricular Materials for Elementary Schools, 242

North American Indian Women's Association, 265

Norton, Eleanor Holmes, 205

Notes from the First Year, 264

Not Servants, Not Machines: Office Workers Speak Out (Tepperman), 221

NOW. *See* National Organization for Women (NOW)

NOW Bill of Rights, 47, 192

NOW Statement of Purpose, 46–47, 48, 58, 59

Nymphomania, 138

NYRF Newsletter, 66

Oakland Feminist Women's Health Center, 253

O'Bannon, Helen, 177

O'Brien, Joyce, 85

O'Connor, Sandra Day, 203, 205, 269

October 17th Movement, 103

Oedipus complex, 79, 98

Office workers, 52, 220–22, 267, 268

Off Our Backs, 224, 225, 226, 265

Older women, 197, 266

Older Women's Liberation (OWL), 266

O'Leary, Jean, 196

Olivarez, Grace, 205

Olivia Records, 253

Operation Wake Up, 206

Orgasm, 12, 14, 15, 17, 22, 24, 75

Osgel, Sandy, 250

Otis, James, 48

Our Bodies, Ourselves, 23, 229

Our Bodies, Ourselves collective, 267

Religion, organized, 129–30; and abortion rights, 212; and ERA, 207, 209; and socialization, 129–30. *See also* Catholic church

Representativeness, issue of, 258–59

Reproduction, control of, 38, 117, 118; and conflict within NOW, 62; contraception, 47, 62, 229; and egalitarian feminist ideology, 59; and radical feminist theory, 76–77, 78, 79, 91, 92. *See also* Abortion rights

Research, 235–46

Restaurants, 252

Retirement plans, 218, 269

Revisionism, 104–5

Rich, Adrienne, 246

Richardson, Dorothy, 160

Ride, Sally, 269

Riesman, David, 52

Rituals, 195–98

Roberts, Barbara, 132

Robinson, Ruby Doris Smith, 263

Rockefeller Commission, 63

Rockefeller Foundation, 259

Roe v. Wade, 193, 212–14, 266, 270

Rofkin, Karen, 240

Rogers, Katharine, 147, 150, 152, 153, 154

Roman Catholic church. *See* Catholic church

Romance of Tristan and Iseult, The, 155

Romantic sentimentalism, 86

Room of One's Own, A (Woolf), 157

Roper, Elmo, 7

Rossi, Alice, 244

Rural feminism, 178

Santa Cruz Women Against Rape (Santa Cruz WAR), 195, 233

Sarachild, Kathie Atmaniek, 21, 103–4

Schapiro, Miriam, 246, 249

Schizophrenia, 139

Schlafly, Phyllis, 206, 208, 209

Schools of feminism, 244–46

Schroeder, Patricia, 204

Schulder, Diane, 219

Science, 88, 91

Scott, Artie, 210

SCUM, 164

SCUM Manifesto, 72–73, 85, 91, 92, 101, 165, 264

Sears, 207

Seattle Radical Women, 122

Seattle Women's Divorce Cooperative, 182

Second Sex, The (de Beauvoir), 36, 155, 256, 269

Second Stage, The (Friedan), 60

Second Wave, The, 224, 225, 226, 253

Secretaries. *See* Office workers

Secret Power of Femininity, The (Andelin), 206

Seese, Linda, 95

Self-criticism, by radical feminists, 99–102, 121

Self-defense, 41, 194, 233–34, 246

Self-hatred, 135, 138

Self-Health, 229

"Self-health" institutions, 228–32

Self-sacrifice, 133–35, 137

Seneca Falls Declaration of Sentiments and Resolution, 29–30, 36, 45

Separatism, 57, 110, 123–24, 164, 257; and notion of sisterhood, 89–90

Sexion, 126–27

Sexism, creation and meaning of term, 23

Sexism in Children's Books, 237–38

Sexual class, 75–78, 112

Sexuality, 12, 14, 164–66, 229; and feminine castration, 136–39; and feminist concept of androgyny, 126, 144, 145; and feminist literary criticism, 152–53; need for feminist position on, 24; as 1960s feminist theme, 21–22, 24; and post-Freudian theory of Housewife's Syndrome, 11–12, 14, 15, 17; radical feminist theory of, 67, 72, 73, 74–83, 86–87, 89–94; and subculture of romantic sentimentalism, 86–87; and women's studies programs, 242

Sexual Politics (Millett), 246, 265

Sexual revolution, 47, 72; radical feminist vision of, 89–94, 95

Shelley, Martha, 108, 233, 252–53

Shelters for battered women, 234–35

Sherfey, Mary Jane, 74–75, 94, 165

Shock actions, 21, 184–85, 187–98, 255

Shulman, Alix Kates, 143

Signs, 147, 224, 225, 243, 267